CONQUERING
PANIC *and* ANXIETY
DISORDERS

DEDICATION

This book is dedicated to Patty Miranda (the artist formerly known as Anna Rae) for being the sunflower that somehow popped up in my garden of weeds. She was the original success story—the one that inspired this book.

It is also dedicated to Sir Anthony Policastro, for giving me a reason to get up, fight back, and remember I still had a lot of living and loving to do.

It is dedicated to my family, because even though they didn't understand what was happening to me, they didn't give up on me. For my mother, Lori Glatzer, who carried me out of malls, yelled at security guards when I needed to sit near exits at concerts, and accompanied me on late-night walks. For my dad, Mark Glatzer, who held me through one of my toughest attacks. For my brother, Paul Glatzer, who never forgot to tell me how proud he was and how happy he was to be with me whenever I made it out of the house. For my sister, Lisa Glatzer, who is a great listener and friend.

And to everyone in the world who has ever known what it's like to fight tooth and nail to hold on to hope when it feels like there is no hope left.

ORDERING

Trade bookstores in the U.S. and Canada please contact:

Publishers Group West
1700 Fourth Street, Berkeley CA 94710
Phone: (800) 788-3123   Fax: (510) 528-3444

Hunter House books are available at bulk discounts for textbook course adoptions; to qualifying community, health-care, and government organizations; and for special promotions and fund-raising. For details please contact:

Special Sales Department
Hunter House Inc., PO Box 2914, Alameda CA 94501-0914
Phone: (510) 865-5282   Fax: (510) 865-4295
E-mail: ordering@hunterhouse.com

Individuals can order our books from most bookstores, by calling
(800) 266-5592, or from our website at www.hunterhouse.com

CONQUERING
PANIC *and* ANXIETY
DISORDERS

Success Stories,
Strategies,
and Other Good News

Edited by Jenna Glatzer,
with commentary by Dr. Paul Foxman

Hunter House
PUBLISHERS

Hunter House Inc., Publishers
PO Box 2914
Alameda CA 94501-0914

Library of Congress Cataloging-in-Publication Data

Conquering panic and anxiety disorders : success stories, strategies, and other good news / edited by Jenna Glatzer ; with commentary by Paul Foxman
p. cm.
Includes bibliographical references and index.
ISBN 0-89793-382-6 (cl) -- ISBN 0-89793-381-8 (pb)
1. Panic attacks--Treatment--Popular works. 2. Anxiety--Treatment--Popular works.
I. Glatzer, Jenna. II. Foxman, Paul.

RC535 .C665 2002
616.85'223--dc21   2002068578

Project Credits

Cover Design: Brian Dittmar
   Graphic Design
Book Production: Jil Weil, Hunter House
Developmental & Copy Editor:
   Kelley Blewster
Proofreader: John David Marion
Indexer: Nancy D. Peterson
Acquisitions Editor: Jeanne Brondino
Editor: Alexandra Mummery
Editorial & Production Intern:
   Claire Reilly-Shapiro

Publicity Coordinator:
   Earlita K. Chenault
Sales & Marketing Coordinator:
   JoAnne Retzlaff
Customer Service Manager:
   Christina Sverdrup
Order Fulfillment: Lakdhon Lama
Administrator: Theresa Nelson
Computer Support: Peter Eichelberger
Publisher: Kiran S. Rana

Printed and Bound by Bang Printing, Brainerd, Minnesota

Manufactured in the United States of America

9 8 7 6 5 4 3 2 1   First Edition   02 03 04 05 06

CONTENTS

Topics Addressed in Stories

For a discussion of:	See:†
Abusive relationships	Chapters 3, 11, and 25
Agoraphobia	Chapters 1, 4, 9, and 12
Alcohol dependence	Chapter 21
Anxiety due to a medical condition	Chapter 23
Attention deficit disorder (ADD)	Chapter 28
Body dysmorphic disorder (BDD)	Chapter 28
Breathing techniques	Chapter 30
Cognitive-behavioral therapy (CBT)	Chapters 2, 7, and 9
Depersonalization (out-of-body experiences)	Chapter 7
Desensitization (gradual exposure to feared situations)	Chapters 15, 16, and 20
Emetophobia (fear of vomiting)	Chapter 3
Hypoglycemia, overweight, and diet	Chapter 29
Journal writing	Chapter 14
Low self-esteem	Chapters 5 and 13
Meditation	Chapter 23
Obsessive-compulsive disorder (OCD)	Chapters 5, 19, 24, and 28
Post-traumatic stress disorder	Chapters 2, 8, and 16

Relaxation techniques	Chapter 2
Role of family members, caregivers, and support persons	Chapters 25 and 31
Sexual abuse	Chapters 13 and 22
Social-anxiety disorder	Chapters 13, 18, and 21
Spiritual perspectives in recovery	Chapter 22
Stress management	Chapter 17
Suicidal feelings	Chapters 1, 12, 21, 28, and 29

†Be sure to read both the applicable chapter and the commentary following it.

IMPORTANT NOTE

The material in this book is intended to provide a review of information regarding panic and anxiety disorders. Every effort has been made to provide accurate and dependable information. The contents of this book have been compiled through professional research and in consultation with medical professionals. However, health-care professionals have differing opinions, and advances in medical and scientific research are made very quickly, so some of the information may become outdated.

Therefore, the publisher, authors, editors, and the professionals quoted in the book cannot be held responsible for any error, omission, or dated material. The authors and publisher assume no responsibility for any outcome of applying the information in this book in a program of self-care or under the care of a licensed practitioner. If you have questions concerning the application of the information described in this book, consult a qualified health-care professional.

FOREWORD

Early in my career, which now spans over thirty-five years, I received a telephone call from the adult daughter of an elderly woman we will call Mrs. S. Mrs. S.'s daughter was responding to a newspaper article characterizing some of our work with people with agoraphobia at a time when articles on this subject were still very rare. "This sounds a lot like my mother," she said, and asked if it was at all possible that I could evaluate her. "The problem is," the daughter went on, "my mother hasn't been out of her apartment for twenty years. Is there any possibility you could go see her in her apartment?"

Several days later, I found myself in a lower-middle-class section of the city in front of a multifamily house. I rang the bell and entered a narrow hallway. Mrs. S. was nowhere in sight, but knowing that she lived on the second floor, I walked up the stairs and knocked on the door at the top. I knew she was expecting me and I heard a meek voice asking me to come in. I opened the door. Mrs. S. was sitting in her living room and from the threshold I could quickly see the layout of her apartment. The living room was in front, the kitchen in the back adjoining a porch, and to the right of the stairs was one bedroom with an adjoining bath.

Mrs. S. was very friendly and obviously glad to see me, offering me homemade cookies and coffee. In fact, she had been looking forward to my visit all day, since I was to be the first person she had seen in several weeks.

Over the next hour her story unfolded, conveying vivid images of a wasted life. And yet, she continued to struggle against her fate and make the best she could of her limited existence. I learned that she had not left the apartment in twenty years and had suffered from excruciatingly terrifying panic attacks for well over thirty years. She was not even safe in her apartment and had not answered the door by herself for the past fifteen years since she was afraid to look into the hallway. She could go to the front of her kitchen and access her stove and refrigerator, but for the past ten years she had not been to the back area of her kitchen, which overlooks the backyard.

Thus, for the past decade, she had been confined to her bedroom, her living room, and the front half of her kitchen. Her adult daughter, who lived some distance away, was able to bring her groceries approximately once a week, but had been out of town during the previous two weeks. Her only other visitor was her parish priest, who came to deliver communion every two to three weeks, when he could. Her husband, who had abused both alcohol and Mrs. S., had died ten years earlier of alcohol-related causes. She told me that as long as she stayed in her apartment she was relatively free of panic and, since she was near the end of her life, there was no longer any reason to venture out. She declined treatment.

The tragic case of Mrs. S. has stayed with me my whole life and has launched me on a long career of studying the mysteries of anxiety and panic. And while we have miles to go, we have come an incredibly long way in our understanding of the causes and treatment of anxiety disorders over the past thirty years. We know that panic disorder with agoraphobia is a very common disorder, with between 3 and 5 percent of the population experiencing its ravages at some point. We know that it usually begins in early adult life, from the midteens through about forty years of age. We know that it is principally reported by women, with the percentage of women sufferers increasing in direct proportion to the severity of the agoraphobic avoidance. We also know that it occurs all over the world, although it may take different forms in different cultures. For example, among the Inuit (Eskimo) populations in Greenland, the condition is sometimes referred to as "Kayak Angst." And finally, we now have effective treatments for anxiety disorders, including new drugs with proven effectiveness and powerful new brief psychological treatments. Since this disorder is chronic and tends to last a lifetime unless concerted action is taken, the existence of these treatments becomes all the more important. We've also come a long way in the treatment of other anxiety disorders, such as social anxiety disorder, obsessive-compulsive disorder, post-traumatic stress disorder, and phobias. All of these disorders and their treatments are covered in this book.

Not everyone benefits from the same treatment. Among those who do benefit from one or another treatment, not everyone is "cured." That is why the book you are about to read is so important. It is increasingly easy to find descriptions of one treatment or another in a magazine or on a website. However, we seldom learn how individuals— real people—incorporate these treatments into their lives along with the many other techniques, remedies, and suggestions that have enabled each of the thirty-two individuals portrayed in this book to fight the good fight and overcome, for the most part, their anxiety disorders. The editor, Jenna Glatzer, has done a beautiful job of editing these life stories so that they come across in the most powerful and useful way. And the expert commentary by Dr. Paul Foxman enhances the value of each of these triumphs over adversity for those who are fighting their own demons. This book is guaranteed to give you hope. And, as Jenna Glatzer perceptively points out, "Hope and determination are the most powerful weapons you can have against this dragon."

— David H. Barlow, Ph.D.

Professor of Psychology & Psychiatry
Director, Center for Anxiety and Related Disorders
Boston University

PROLOGUE

On top of my desk is a little origami dragon, made by a woman who overcame panic disorder. I've never met her, but that little dragon has been a very important symbol for me.

A therapist gave it to me when I was just starting to make steps toward my recovery. He explained that a former client of his had made the dragon to remind herself that the enemy—anxiety—was a fierce adversary, but it had a weak spot. It's a paper dragon, something that looks awfully scary and unbeatable, but something that can be torn up, set on fire, and thrown away. It's something that's not as tough as it wants to be. Today, I am a dragon slayer. However, I didn't always believe I had that kind of strength.

When I was about twenty-two and trying to convince myself to get out of bed every morning, I didn't have any faith that I would ever walk out my front door again. I was agoraphobic. Even though doctors assured me that most people can recover from anxiety disorders, I didn't believe them. I figured they *had* to say that. Besides, I thought no one in the world had ever endured such a bad case of anxiety as I had. Maybe other people got better because they were never so "messed up" in the first place.

"Even if I get a little better," I thought, "I'll never lead a normal life. I'll always have these stupid attacks and these stupid fears." I'd never heard from anyone who had been through what I had. Lots of times, people would tell me they understood—well-meaning friends would say, "I know just what you're going through! I've had panic attacks, too!" After a few sentences, they'd tell me that they'd endured two or three attacks while driving on the freeway, or something along those lines. To me, that was nothing. They didn't understand what it was like to be too scared to check their mail or to have friends over for dinner.

I was aching to hear real success stories from people like me. I didn't want to hear it from a doctor or a self-help guru. I wanted someone in the world to say, "Hey, I couldn't leave my front door either, and now I have a full-time job, and I'm happily married, and I travel."

I got very lucky. That message came one day, via e-mail, from a stranger who subsequently opened up her life to me. That person was Patty Miranda, whose story appears in Chapter 30 of this book. She was the first person I'd "met" who really did understand, and who had really recovered. Her correspondence with me was all I had to look forward to; her words gave me hope, and she taught me to appreciate every small success on the road to recovery.

I promised myself that if I ever did recover, I would share that message. I would shout it from the rooftops. I would tell everyone who ever had a really difficult anxiety disorder that the doctors weren't lying, that people really could get better and lead happy lives.

That day has come, and *Conquering Panic and Anxiety Disorders: Success Stories, Strategies, and Other Good News* is my fulfillment of that promise. To collect the stories in this book, I posted messages on bulletin boards all over the Internet asking for contributions, and I asked friends if they knew of any good "success stories." I got responses from all over the world, from women and men of all ages and all walks of life. Each of the stories is in the contributor's own words. Many of the essays you're about to read brought tears to my eyes as I empathized with the authors' struggles. More tears came when I read about their triumphs and celebrated their victories—happy tears, because I know how hard it is to get there, and I know what a fantastic relief it must have been for each of them to find out that they could beat this awful thing.

The people in this book are some of the bravest, toughest, strongest-spirited, and most remarkable people I've encountered. What binds us together? We've been to hell and back. We've all seen how dark the world can get, and we've all fought with every ounce of our strength to regain our lives and our passions.

While editing this book, I also got a few notes from people who wrote to tell me that this was a futile effort, because no one really "recovers" from an anxiety disorder; sufferers just learn to deal with them better. I didn't come this far in my life to learn how to "deal." I came here to conquer. I told these naysayers, with all due respect, that the entire purpose of my book was to prove them wrong. I also told them they should feel free to tell any of the more than one hundred people who submitted their wonderful stories that they weren't "really" recovered. Harrumph!

Every story I read reminded me why I wanted to put this book together in the first place: to give hope to the hopeless, proof to the doubters, inspiration to the struggling, a hand to the faltering, understanding to the lonely, and a big mental hug to every one of us who has seen the anxiety dragon and wondered if we would ever learn how to conquer him.

The overriding theme in all of these essays is this: YOU ARE NOT ALONE. If you don't believe me now, you will by the end of the book. Probably the most difficult part of anxiety disorder is the bottomless feeling of loneliness and isolation that seems to come with the territory. We believe we're "going crazy" and that no one else feels these irrational fears, strange compulsions, intrusive thoughts, or odd physical sensations. We secretly worry that we belong in mental institutions, or that people will find out that we're really nutcases.

What you are about to read isn't always politically correct, but it's real. We've cut out the stuff that wouldn't look good on our "permanent records" and talk about the real causes, the real struggles, and the real cures for our problems. We address drugs, abuse, "loony bins," sexual compulsions, anger, and lots of other things that might make your second-grade teacher wince.

People have shared what worked for them, and Dr. Paul Foxman (author of *Dancing with Fear*) has contributed the Introduction and added his comments to the end of each story. In his commentaries, you'll find information about why certain techniques work and on the benefits and pitfalls of different "remedies," as well as suggestions for how you can benefit from each contributor's methods for recovery. As the director of the Center for Anxiety Disorders in Vermont and as a former anxiety sufferer himself, Paul Foxman has decades of experience in helping people overcome anxiety disorders. He is also of the firm belief that there is hope for everyone to make a total recovery.

Although we've kept "advice" to a minimum, some contributors will encourage you to try their solution, whether it is prescription drugs, therapy, diet, meditation, or anything else. Obviously, no one is offering medical advice, and you should always consult with your doctor or therapist and follow your own gut instincts to determine which courses of action you'd like to try.

No matter what anyone tells you, there is no single cause of anxiety disorders, and there is no single cure. The simple truth is that different things work for different people, but there *is* a solution for you. Most of the time solutions don't come easily. You may feel exhausted from trying; I know I did! But you've got to keep knocking on doors and keep experimenting with different methods until you find something that works for you. Your life is worth it, and you are worth it. Don't give up on yourself because you're tired of trying. Find little glimmers of hope wherever you can, and hang on to them for dear life. Hope and determination are the most powerful weapons you can wield against this dragon.

I hope you will relate to the stories in this book, and I hope that as you read these pages you'll feel as encouraged as I did. And, most of all, I hope you conquer the anxiety dragon, too. Scratch that—I *know* you will.

Keep fighting, keep reaching out, and keep remembering: You are not alone.

Love,
Jenna Glatzer

INTRODUCTION

by PAUL FOXMAN, PH.D.

As a psychologist specializing in anxiety disorders, I am honored to introduce these uplifting anxiety-recovery stories and my role as commentator. The honesty, determination, and success of these anxiety conquerors touch me deeply, and I expect that readers will also be inspired by their recovery journeys. I speak for all the contributors in hoping that this book will help increase the number of people who receive a proper diagnosis and treatment for anxiety.

Anxiety is now recognized as the most common, chronic, and costly of all emotional disorders in our country, and perhaps in the world. Anxiety disorders outrank depression, alcohol abuse, and other mental-health issues. Based on major demographic studies, the National Institute of Mental Health indicates that some thirty million Americans suffer from anxiety that is severe enough that these people would probably benefit from professional help. This does not include another three million children who are also affected by severe anxiety. It is also estimated that 25 percent of all American adults (sixty-five million) will suffer from severe anxiety at some point in their lifetime. Preliminary research is available on the situation worldwide, and all indications suggest that we are witnessing a soaring global trend.

We also know that about 80 percent of all medical visits are for symptoms that, although quite real, have no physical cause. Many of these visits are related to anxiety, but proper diagnosis and treatment is provided for only about half of those who need help, a theme that resounds throughout the stories in this book. The fact is that many physicians are not attuned to the anxiety underlying many physical symptoms, and even when they can identify an anxiety disorder, they may lack knowledge about treatment resources.

1

On the positive side, anxiety has been coming out of the closet in recent years and gaining recognition by health-care professionals as well as the public. Before 1980, panic disorder was not even listed in the *Diagnostic and Statistical Manual of Mental Disorders*, the bible of psychiatric diagnoses. In 1994, the American Psychiatric Association recognized children as vulnerable to the same anxiety disorders as adults. The recent development of new medications for anxiety, along in the continuing education of health-care professionals, has helped in the recognition of anxiety disorders. In addition, I have witnessed a tremendous growth in literature on anxiety in the few years since my own book, *Dancing with Fear: Overcoming Anxiety in a World of Stress and Uncertainty*, was first published in 1996.

In my early years of training, treatment for anxiety disorders was limited to psychoanalytic therapy, addictive tranquilizers with troublesome side effects, and hospitalization for severe cases. However, during the 1970s a wave of new treatment approaches emerged for anxiety and depression, such as cognitive-behavioral therapy (CBT). The period also saw the emergence of the human-potential movement, health consciousness, and an interest in Eastern religions, all of which brought new interventions—such as diet/nutrition, exercise, self-help programs, systematic desensitization, meditation, and yoga—to bear on the treatment of anxiety. More recently, new medications, notably the selective serotonin-reuptake inhibitors (SSRIs), have been developed, and new therapy techniques for anxiety, such as eye-movement desensitization and reprocessing (EMDR), have been researched. All of these interventions are discussed at various points in my commentaries that accompany each of the stories in this book.

The stories break new ground by making a convincing case for the assertion that anxiety recovery is absolutely attainable, no matter how severe the condition. Such an optimistic and hopeful premise may contradict the experience of some anxiety sufferers who have not yet found the key to recovery or the opinion of some doctors and psychotherapists who lack training and expertise in anxiety treatment. Nevertheless, anyone who reads these stories will appreciate the success of those who have conquered even the most disabling anxiety.

The National Institute of Mental Health reports that the success rate for anxiety treatment is about 80 percent *with appropriate help*, and I can attest to this statistic based on my own years of clinical experience. Anxiety recovery does not necessarily require intensive professional help, as some of these stories demonstrate; however, a correct diagnosis and proper recovery steps, such as understanding the disorder, acquiring new skills, changing thought patterns, and in some cases medication, are necessary. The stories and my commentaries illustrate how anxiety recovery is possible by taking these steps.

My personal experience with anxiety recovery adds to my conviction that recovery is possible. Beginning in childhood, I developed several anxiety conditions, including post-traumatic stress disorder (PTSD), generalized anxiety disorder (GAD), and panic disorder with agoraphobia. A number of childhood experiences set the stage for these conditions. These included my parents' divorce, sexual abuse, a near-death experience requiring an emergency tracheotomy, and growing up in a violent and racially tense community in New York City known at the time as Hell's Kitchen.

For many years I was unable to relax, and I often distracted myself through work and relationships. I was anxious most of the time, and my stress level was high due to my perfectionism, need for control, high achievement drive, and other personality traits. Like many contributors to this book, I concealed my anxiety and presented myself as outgoing and self-confident. Yet the more success I had in the outer world—high school track star and team captain, academic honors at Yale University, a Ph.D. in clinical psychology, publications in prestigious journals, leadership positions in my profession—the more the discrepancy between my hidden anxiety and my visible accomplishments grew.

Many of the strategies that were helpful in overcoming my own anxiety are reflected in the contributors' stories. Such strategies include learning how to relax, the use of daily meditation, journal writing, exercise and outdoor recreation, maintaining a healthy diet, using yoga, expressing feelings more directly, increasing self-education through research and reading, addressing anxiety-producing personality traits, and changing cognitive patterns such as worry and negative thinking. While I did not use prescription medication, I tried other drugs in an effort to relax and gain control of anxiety. My recovery was an eclectic process of trial and error, as it has been for many contributors to this book.

In addition to my personal anxiety background, my nearly thirty years in practice as a psychologist has been devoted primarily to anxiety. My treatment philosophy is based on the belief that anxiety is largely a learned reaction to stress, and that with practice it can be replaced by more productive responses. In my view, there are three ingredients in the development of an anxiety disorder, which I discuss in some of my commentaries and more fully in *Dancing with Fear*: biological sensitivity, anxiety personality traits, and stress. If you have the first two ingredients, you are an anxiety disorder waiting to happen. The onset of symptoms usually occurs after a period of stress overload.

Feelings of anxiety and vulnerability are a normal reaction to threatening or stressful circumstances, such as a job interview, an exam, and world events, including terrorism. However, an anxiety *disorder* is a fear reaction (the fight-or-flight response) in situations where no actual or imminent danger exists. In other words, anxiety is usually an *irrational* response, typically triggered by stress overload and misinterpreted by the survival center of the brain as a threat.

As a brief technical orientation, think of anxiety disorders as predictable and organized symptom patterns. For example, *panic disorder* is characterized by sudden and intense episodes of anxiety that may seem to appear "out of the blue," and *agoraphobia* is the associated pattern of avoiding situations in which panic attacks are anticipated. *Generalized anxiety disorder* (GAD) is a pattern of worry and negative thinking, often accompanied by sleep difficulty and fatigue. *Social anxiety* is associated with being around other people, and those suffering from this disorder cope by avoiding social interaction or by simply enduring it when escape is not possible. *Post-traumatic stress disorder* (PTSD) is the combination of anxiety symptoms—such as nightmares, flashbacks, difficulty relaxing, and emotional distress when reminded of the trauma—that develops in response to an intensely negative event. *Obsessive-compulsive disorder* (OCD) is anxiety associated with un-wanted thoughts (obsessions) or pressure to engage in repetitive be-havior patterns (compulsions). Examples of all these anxiety disorders will be found in the contributors' stories.

Readers will note that all but a few of the contributors are women, a fact that might suggest a gender difference in the incidence of anxi-ety. However, while four times as many women as men seek therapy for anxiety (roughly the gender ratio for all psychotherapy clients regard-less of presenting problems), this does *not* mean that anxiety is more prevalent in women. In my opinion, anxiety afflicts men and women equally, but men are more reluctant to seek professional help for emo-tional problems—especially anxiety. For many men, anxiety equates with weakness or powerlessness, feelings that go against the grain of male socialization and emotional style. The myth of "real men"— strong, independent, always in control—as portrayed by role models in movies, sports, and politics is a barrier for men going public or seeking help.

Some of my commentaries may appear to contradict the recovery paths taken by the writers. In those cases, my intent is to provide alter-native considerations or additional suggestions for readers who may have similar forms of anxiety. Anxiety treatment is not an exact science, and it is often necessary to experiment with a variety of approaches to find the key to recovery.

These stories are full of hope and promise for anxiety recovery. May they fulfill their mission to spread the word and inspire many others to conquer their anxieties.

CHAPTER 1

GROWLING BACK AT THE BIG BAD WOLF

by JENNA GLATZER

When I was a kid, my mother read me stories every night. My favorite parts were always her "bad guy" impressions—she'd animate the voices of the Big Bad Wolf, or the Evil Queen, or Cruella De Vil, and I'd imagine these sinister creatures. By the end of every story, though, I could count on the hero to defeat the villain with a grand flourish. Hooray for the good guy! That's the way life is supposed to be...right?

When I was twenty-one, fresh out of college, my world turned upside down. Nothing could have prepared me for my real-life battle with the ugliest scoundrel of all: panic disorder. I had my first panic attacks while out with friends in crowds, and they were absolutely terrifying. For no good reason, my heart would race, I'd get terribly disoriented, feel sure I was about to faint, my hands would sweat, my legs would give out under me, and I'd feel nauseated. Sounds were amplified, and everything around me seemed giant and out of proportion. My feet hovered over the ground, and I felt drugged, like I'd overdosed on cold medicine and caffeine at once.

What in the world was causing this? Panic disorder never even entered my mind. Why would it? I was a very social person. I lived in a house with twelve friends, threw big parties almost every weekend, acted and sang in front of thousands of people in community theatres, and traveled the country to meet people on road trips. I loved people. How could I possibly be afraid of them?

I muscled my way through the attacks for a while, beating myself up for these weak transgressions. Nothing was going to stop me from attaining my goal of becoming a professional actress, not even these weird "attacks." I joined a children's-theatre troupe in Albany, praying the attacks wouldn't hit me onstage. What a nightmare that would be! I'd always had a healthy dose of stage fright, even though I had basically popped out of the womb singing "There's No Business Like Show Business." But that energy fueled me; these attacks were different. They were debilitating.

Luckily, I never did have an attack onstage...but I had them constantly on my way to the theatre and backstage. Gradually, the work I adored was becoming a chore; the stress of dreading an onstage attack wore away at me.

It must have been something physical, I decided. Low blood sugar, maybe. Or...or maybe I was just going crazy. Maybe I had finally snapped, and this was an early sign that I was going to wind up homeless and babbling to myself. It wasn't until a friend of mine approached me with the textbook from his abnormal psychology course that I had an inkling of what was really happening. As I read the description of the symptoms of panic disorder, I broke down in tears. There it was! An actual disorder, with a name, and a possible cure.

Now that I had a name for it, I thought for sure I would just go to the doctor, and he'd tell me how to fix it. However, it wasn't that simple. At all.

I went through three medications and four therapists. Instead of getting better, I progressively got worse, until I was completely housebound. The turning point was the last day I lived in Albany. There was no food in the apartment aside from peanut butter and jelly. All I had to do was drive one block to the convenience store for bread. One block. I could have walked or driven. But I was unable to do either.

I stood at the door, hand on the knob, fighting with myself. "Come on!" I yelled at myself. It was futile; I was frozen with fear and couldn't coax myself outside. I didn't eat at all that day, because I couldn't walk outside to get the food I needed.

It was humiliating to have to move back in with my parents, give up my job, and admit that panic had taken control of my life. I lost touch with all my friends as they got sick of my habit of turning down invitations or breaking plans at the last minute.

No one outside of my family knew how bad it had gotten, because I was too embarrassed to tell anyone. I didn't want anyone to see that SuperJenna had turned into a weak, scared little girl. I wanted my friends to remember the strong, dynamic, fun woman I'd been. After a while, I stopped answering my phone. I had nothing new to say. Every time someone would call, I'd only have depressing news to share, and no one wants to be called by the "bummer friend."

Every day, my world shrank a little smaller, until I felt like a pathetic shadow of the person I'd been before. What started as a problem only in big crowds had advanced like a tidal wave, rendering me incapable of normal social interaction. I couldn't even invite someone over to watch television with me.

I began sleeping days and staying up all night, in order to avoid people altogether. I had to really search to find reasons to keep on living. I had a diabetic cat, and often I talked myself out of suicide only because I convinced myself that she needed me. If I died, who would take care of her insulin shots? She'd nuzzle up alongside me, and I'd hang on for one more day, knowing how implicitly she trusted me and how she wouldn't let anyone else come near her with a needle. For me, she purred and took her medicine well; she knew I would only do right by her. That was all I had left some days.

My life revolved around the computer—my sole source of contact with the outside world. I began writing for magazines and websites, and I met another writer online who'd also suffered from agoraphobia.

She sent me e-mails every day, encouraging me and reminding me that there was a light at the end of the tunnel. After all, she had beaten it. She'd seen the worst of it and had gone on to get married, raise kids, go on vacations, and attend all sorts of parties and weddings. I devoured her stories. I always looked forward to her e-mail, and I'd ask her to tell me more about her life after panic. I was that little kid eagerly begging Mom to read the bedtime story again: "Tell me the one about the woman who beats the Big Bad Panic Monster and runs away with the prince."

At some point, though, I just grew weary of getting my hopes up. Maybe there was no light at the end of my tunnel. Maybe only other people got better, and I was doomed to a life of confinement forever. What kind of life was it, anyway? No one knows "lonely" until they've spent years with hardly a visitor.

That was it for me. I was going to be that crazy old lady with sixteen cats whom the mailman finds stinking and rotten in her home. I gave up trying. No more medications, no more therapists, no more new-age stuff. Just me and my messed-up head.

It's funny how the miracles always seem to happen just when you've given up. Mine came in the form of a sort-of blind date.

When I was in high school, I'd worked as a secretary for a band that played at weddings. Sean, my boss (and friend), kept up with me through the years. He called me around this time, insisting that I should meet the band's new saxophonist. I explained that it was impossible. Of course I couldn't date—I couldn't even leave the house.

Sean was persistent. "He's perfect for you," he said. "He's cute, shy, a great musician...." I didn't even want to hear the words. What a tease! There was no sense in getting my hopes up. No man would ever want me in my condition. Why would anyone in his right mind knowingly enter a relationship with a woman who would never be able to go out, meet his family, or even see him perform?

"No," I insisted. "Don't do this to me. Even if we met, and he thought I was great, eventually he'd get really bored of the fact that I'm a hermit. And then he'd break my heart, and I just don't need one more thing to push me into the depths of depression."

Of course, that made sense. I was protecting my heart and his. But something inside Sean's suggestion brought that old fantasy back to life. You know: meeting the prince, getting swept off my feet, and running off to live in a castle somewhere. I'd been single for so long, and I was aching for love, but I knew I couldn't make myself that vulnerable again.

That's why it shocked me when I got a mysterious late-night e-mail from a certain stranger who wrote, "Sean suggested you might be awake." Gasp! I closed it and didn't respond. How could Sean have given this guy my e-mail address after all I had said to discourage him?

The next day, a haiku landed in my inbox. Okay, fine, I would respond, I thought. I mean, how could I ignore a man who would send me a haiku? But I would be very clear with him and tell him I was not looking for romance, and I would not ever meet him. In fact, I wouldn't even give him my phone number. This was strictly an e-mail exchange. I explained to him that I knew if I gave him my phone number, eventually he'd say, "So, what are you doing Friday night?" Then I'd have to turn him down. I didn't want to put either of us in that position.

Over the next few weeks, I looked forward to Anthony's notes more than anything. This guy was funny, charming, smart, and very sweet. He was everything I didn't want him to be, because it was only feeding my fantasy—the fantasy that would never come true.

Knowing my stance about phone calls, he finally dropped a clever "P. S." into one of his e-mails: "If you happen to dial a wrong number tonight, let it be 555-2727." I wrote back to assure him that my dialing fingers were quite accurate, and I wouldn't be dialing any wrong numbers.

Don't ask how he wore me down, but I did wind up calling him after more than a month of daily e-mails. We spoke for eight hours. Yes, eight. We didn't even break for meals. The following day was more of the same. Soon, we were having "phone dates"; we'd spend the whole day on the phone together, eating at the same time, watching television "together," talking about the sunset we saw out of our respective windows....

And then I did something really crazy. At midnight, after weeks of this phone dating, someone very brave possessed my vocal cords and said, "Come over."

"Really?" he asked.

"Yes. Quickly, before I come to my senses."

First, though, I set up a few rules. He could only come with the understanding that I wasn't going to go anywhere. We could sit and watch a video together, but there would be no driving, no eating, no long walks—just my living room. He agreed, as thrilled as if he'd just won an Olympic medal, and rushed over.

My life came into focus the moment he walked in the door. Here was a man who knew all about my dirty little secret and who had already grown to love me, knowing full well that I was agoraphobic. We hugged at the door, and I felt profoundly comfortable in his presence. There were no facades—I didn't have to put on a brave face while I panicked inside. Instead, I just plum forgot to panic.

I broke all my rules that night. I was on such a high from the feeling of accomplishment that I decided to push my limits even further. "Let's go to the diner and get some take-out food," I suggested.

After we both recovered from the shock of that suggestion coming out of my mouth, I got into his car, and we did it. We went to the diner. Then we came back to the living room and had an indoor picnic. Finally, we wound up at the local park for our first kiss.

In three years, I hadn't been to a diner or a park. In three years, I hadn't been able to eat in front of anyone outside my immediate family. I'd never expected to do those things again, much less in the course of one night with a man I'd never met.

Lest you think this was a magic cure, I have to admit I did have panic attacks after we met. The difference was that I was no longer embarrassed by them, and that fact erased all of the "pre-panic." I wasn't afraid to panic in front of him, so I didn't have all the anticipatory anxiety before going out with him. As soon as that lifted, my whole outlook improved. As you probably already know, the anticipation is almost always worse than the panic itself. I used to get myself so worked up when I knew I had to do something (like go to a doctor) that I would paralyze myself with terror for hours, or even days, before the event.

We took small steps together—we'd sit in a parking lot or agree to just stay in the mall for ten minutes. Whenever I would start to panic, he'd do something funny to divert my attention. He'd sing to me, loudly, in German, in the middle of the diner. He'd pull me in close for a slow dance in the middle of the grocery store. It's very tough to continue panicking when you're laughing and dancing.

I was lovable again. I stopped feeling boring and unsexy and crazy and weak and pathetic and started seeing myself the way he saw me. I wasn't just a walking panic disorder. That was only one part of who I was. Actually, I was a heck of a gal. I deserved love like this. And I deserved to have a life.

Instead of beating myself up every time I panicked, I gave myself permission to be imperfect. If I had to leave somewhere, so what? If I felt like hiding in my room for a day or two, so what? If people saw me having a panic attack, so what? It dawned on me that if this great guy wasn't humiliated to be seen with me, then I shouldn't be humiliated to be seen with me.

He made me want to fight again. I wanted so badly to surprise him one day by driving to his apartment by myself. I wanted him to be proud of me, so I worked harder to do things that were tough for me. He gave me the perfect reason to beat this demon. I was going to have to knock out this panic disorder so I could live that lifelong fantasy and marry the prince.

The day I knew I had triumphed came when we stood in front of a casino. I turned to him and realized what I'd already done, before I even walked in the door. We had just driven four hours to another state. I had made plans to go to a crowded casino, and I hadn't backed out. Even if I got inside and had to walk right back out, I'd already won. I didn't let the panic stop me from getting there. I didn't let the panic tell me I couldn't do it.

I'd spent so long trying to figure out just what had caused this disorder in me; there was no dearth of possible explanations. Maybe it was because I was raped as a little girl, or because of an abusive relationship in my early teens, or from my fear of losing the first "home" I'd ever had (college), or the drug-laden environment I'd forced myself into. Then again, maybe it was because I was an overachiever who felt compelled to work two and three jobs at a time, get straight A's, manage a household, and live life to extremes, never leaving any leeway for downtime or stress management. Or maybe it was physically based. Or genetic. Or....

In the end, I realized that it didn't really matter what had gotten me there. Now it was time to figure out what lessons I was supposed to learn after this forced "vacation" from life. Among other things, I learned to stop snowplowing over my emotions; to pay attention when my brain was begging for a reprise. I learned to strive for excellence instead of perfection, and not to be devastated if I didn't achieve either in all areas of my life. I learned how to be by myself and how to validate my own existence, regardless of how I appeared to others. I learned to give over just a little bit of control to others I trusted.

One year later, I'm proud to say that my prince and I just bought our first home, and it's an absolutely ideal den of serenity. I can now run my own errands, and I can be in the house alone when he's at work. I can even go out to parties and restaurants. There's absolutely nothing off-limits to me anymore, and that feels wonderful! Every accomplishment I make now means so much more than it ever would have before the panic. I take nothing for granted. I still congratulate myself every time I have a successful trip to the post office or the bank, even though I've done it many times now. I still feel proud whenever I walk out my front door, because I know how hard it was to get to that point. What a light all of this turned out to be at the end of my tunnel!

You know, sometimes it takes the hero the whole book to figure out how to defeat the villain. This Little Red Riding Hood just needed to remember that she was bigger and tougher than the Big Bad Wolf after all. And so are you.

I am a full-time writer, the editor in chief of www.absolutewrite.com (a big website for writers), a produced playwright, and an optioned screenwriter. I've written everything from books to articles to greeting cards to slogans for doormats, buttons, magnets, and bumper stickers. Anthony and I live in New York. We appeared on Lifetime TV's "Love Letters of a Lifetime" last Valentine's Day, which fed right into my quest for fifteen minutes of fame. I'm eager to get back to the stage soon, and I'm still working on my lifetime goal to write a screenplay, direct it, star in it, and sing on the soundtrack—but I'll generously let someone else operate the lights! Maybe.

Commentary by Paul Foxman

What stands out about Jenna's story is how a love relationship served as her therapy. In fact, her romantic recovery from panic disorder and agoraphobia involved the same steps that would be advised in professional therapy: graduated exposure to feared and avoided situations. This approach, known as *desensitization*, will be discussed more fully in my commentaries on other stories.

Panic disorder involves sudden episodes or "attacks" of physical arousal symptoms that are often mistaken for a heart attack or another serious medical condition. Jenna's particular disorder, agoraphobia—from the Greek words for fear (*phobia*) of the marketplace (*agora*)—refers to a pattern of avoiding any situations in which anxiety attacks are anticipated. The avoidance pattern does relieve anxiety, but usually at the price of life restriction. In Jenna's case, the pattern progressed to a housebound state, which illustrates just how extreme the condition can become. Since her anxiety was associated with being in public, she was unable to shop, socialize, travel, or participate in other activities. A related fear was that she would lose control in public and embarrass herself.

To complicate matters, Jenna experienced another symptom known as *depersonalization.* This troubling symptom is reported as a feeling of disorientation or unreality with altered perceptions, and it is often accompanied by fears of "going crazy" or "losing my mind." In my opinion, this numbing sensation is the mind's attempt to cope with anxiety, similar to shock as the body's response to extreme physical pain. While this is one of the most frightening symptoms of anxiety, I can assure readers that it is not a permanent feeling, and it usually subsides with appropriate help.

Jenna's anxiety illustrates how an anxiety disorder usually develops. She was vulnerable to anxiety due to a high-achieving, perfectionist personality coupled with a creative imagination and strong need for control. She also had a trauma history—including rape as a young girl and an abusive relationship in adolescence—that added to her potential for anxiety. What put her over the edge was a period of high stress she experienced while living in a house with twelve people, throwing "big parties almost every weekend," acting and singing before thousands of people, and taking road trips around the country. It is important to note that Jenna did not view this lifestyle as stressful, because it was enjoyable and positive. Let's call it "good stress," while recognizing that too much of a good thing still qualifies as stress overload.

Anxiety disorders often involve depression, which can make diagnosis difficult and confusing. In most cases, the depression is secondary to or associated with the anxiety disorder, and it develops as a result of difficulty sleeping, fatigue, life restriction, and discouragement about lack of control. Jenna's depression reached suicidal proportions, but this is atypical. Depression usually subsides when the anxiety disorder is addressed, as was the case with Jenna.

Jenna sought help from several doctors and therapists, but these efforts failed to yield results. Unfortunately, this is all too common with health-care providers who have not received special training in anxiety treatment, and we will find this theme repeated throughout many of the stories in this book.

Several medications were tried, but they were ineffective in Jenna's case. While medications can be helpful in controlling anxiety symptoms, they do not teach the skills required for long-term recovery. Furthermore, many anxiety patients are sensitive to the side effects of medication and are easily frustrated by the process involved in establishing the right drug and the right dosage. Even when pharmaceuticals are effective, patients may still experience a strong reaction to discontinuing them. In several other commentaries, I will address the pros and cons of medications for anxiety.

There are many effective alternatives to medication for panic disorder with agoraphobia, and I will discuss them throughout the book. They include cognitive-behavioral psychotherapy, self-help programs, guidebooks, online support groups (caution: a knowledgeable leader should be present to prevent symptom-swapping), and telephone consultations with trained therapists. One program for housebound agoraphobia sufferers is CHAANGE, a structured, self-help, sixteen-week audiocassette program with a success rate higher than 80 percent. (Refer to the Resources section at the end of the book to learn how to obtain a free information packet about CHAANGE, including a list of trained therapists. Readings about other techniques discussed in my commentaries will also be found in the Resources section.)

Like many others in this book, Jenna's recovery story inspires hope. She progressed from a housebound agoraphobic woman to a successful writer for whom "there is absolutely nothing off-limits ... anymore." As a psychologist, I enjoy specializing in anxiety treatment, because stories like this are everyday occurrences in my practice.

CHAPTER 2

HOLDING MY HEAD HIGH

by LORI DOWNS

Panic disorder took hold of my life when I was fifteen years old. I was a happy, outgoing child and had no major self-esteem issues, except for a wee bit of angst over my entirely normal teenage acne. Then, one day, while riding my bike home from a friend's house, I had a dreadful attack of diarrhea, and I didn't make it home on time. I felt utterly ashamed. Utterly, utterly shaken to the core. I don't know why I took this incident so much to heart. I snuck into my house, rinsed my clothes, showered, and did the cleanup and laundry in secret. I never told anyone what happened.

I began to dread times when I needed to bike anywhere; in fact, I avoided biking or walking at all. I lived in El Paso, Texas, where the desert landscape offered no convenient bushes to duck behind, and I worried constantly that my bowels would revolt, that I would have no warning, and that I'd be humiliated in front of someone. Yikes! Coo blimey! I thought I'd flat *die* if that were to happen.

Soon, the anticipatory anxiety began to rule me. I could go places only if I knew there was a bathroom nearby. I experienced head tingling, hand sweating, faintness, and nausea if I was trapped in a bathroomless place. I felt my guts roil anytime I didn't have a quick way out. I couldn't sit in a classroom if the door was closed. I couldn't wait in a drive-through line if there were cars hemming me in. I couldn't take long drives unless I was the one driving. Traveling became a misery of dread before, panic during, and shame following. And I had been such a fun-loving girl; now I was a lonely girl trapped in her room. I kept journals, listened to the Beatles, and read everything I could get my hands on. I functioned well at school, and only a few girlfriends were aware that I was struggling.

I had no name for my problem. I couldn't explain it to my parents, who thought I was strangely capricious because I wouldn't go shopping or out to dinner unless outright forced to do so. I was living in hell. Really suffering intensely.

I remember climbing up the tree in my backyard and crying so loudly that the neighbors called the next day to ask my parents what was going on. My mother chastised me for embarrassing her. I felt like a freak.

Then, in my sophomore year of high school, I was taken with a lad I'd seen in a school play. I wanted to win his heart, so I stepped out of my shell a bit until I did. He was sweet, and he made himself available to me in "safe" places. We ditched school and broke into my locked house for a place to hang out. The phobias eased, but never abated completely. I fainted in the high school registration line at the beginning of my junior year. I said it was the flu.

I had an incident of loss of bowel control probably once or twice a year—just often enough to keep me terrified. My parents finally had an upper and lower GI series done (highly traumatic for a young virgin: think anal probe), only to find no physical cause for the symptoms. My dad offered counseling at that point, and I said no. I was desperate for the help, but I couldn't face the ten-minute drive to the doctor's office.

There were no Oprah Winfrey–type shows to help me name my problem, but finally I heard the word *agoraphobia* somewhere, and I began reading up on the topic. I can't tell you how profound my relief was upon learning that other people were suffering like me, that I wasn't totally alone, and that there was hope I could conquer it. I felt it was a dreadful character flaw, a weakness, an indulgence of my psyche somehow. I felt guilty and ashamed, but I was helped by the fact that typical sufferers were described as highly intelligent and creative people for the most part. At least I felt kind of smart!

Life went on, and I met my second boyfriend. I pulled myself together enough to go out and about with him a bit, always with difficulty, always taking baby steps. He was understanding and sweet, just like my first guy. He bedded me at seventeen and wedded me at eighteen. I wanted out of my parents' house desperately, and he was my ticket. The idea of college terrified me, even though I was a straight-A student and was expected to go, as the people in my family were all educators.

So I married to escape college, and we moved to Louisiana. My mom had to choose my wedding dress, and she basically planned my whole wedding with me on the sidelines nodding "yes" or "no." I had to be dragged out of bed on my wedding day, but I coped. I worked and went to college for a year as an art major. The panic attacks abated when I was in my normal daily routine, but came back full-tilt boogie when I had to travel home for visits. They completely disappeared during my first pregnancy, and it was a joyful release. I shopped!

Four days after my daughter's birth, I went hobbling through the mall close to my house—my first postbirth outing. Thank God the babe was at home with my mom. I felt the old familiar rumble, ran for the bathroom, and didn't make it. As I was crying and cleaning myself up in the mall restroom, a kind woman said, "Honey, you just hold your head up and walk outta here. There's no reason for you to be ashamed." I think she'll never know what that kindness meant to me.

Years passed, and I explored medications with my doctor. I tried Xanax, but needed too much of it and feared addiction. I tried BuSpar, which didn't seem to help; Paxil, which destroyed my libido (and I *like* my libido, thank you!); and finally got a respite from it all with Tranxene.

I was marginally functional while home tending babies. I moved back to my hometown and stayed home until my second child was three. I braved college again, but had a brush with a near-divorce in the midst of my last year. I was seeing a counselor during the marriage crisis, and she told me that I was amazingly functional, considering my history of panic attacks, and that she found my spirit inspirational. She was a godsend.

I think I finally knew I could overcome my panic disorder when I began to trust my medication. I could control the scariest symptom, the diarrhea attacks, with Kaopectate or Lomotil. But I couldn't live while constantly taking Kaopectate every day, so I'd step out on normal days and only medicate if I knew I had to shop or travel or whatnot. The respites I enjoyed during pregnancy and nursing made me fundamentally believe, in a visceral way, that the problem was not a character flaw or an unconscious choice, but rather physical. At the time, I thought it was hormone related, and now I know more about issues related to serotonin reuptake. (Many people with anxiety disorders don't have enough of the neurotransmitter serotonin. In an attempt to correct this problem, medications for these disorders often block the reabsorption of serotonin into the brain's neurons. Such drugs are called *selective serotonin-reuptake inhibitors* (SSRIs), and they keep the serotonin in use for as long as possible to make up for the fact that there's not enough of it circulating in the body.) But those respites gave me a glimpse of how fun "normalcy" can be, and I wanted more of it. Life is so good.

I take nothing for granted. I still struggle now and again, and I've had minirelapses, but nothing long term. Even when I relapse for a while, I know I can "come back." I know I'm okay.

My real release happened when I broke out of the anticipatory "thinking-dreading" cycle. I think that happened to some extent when I moved away from home and had the freedom to decide for myself what I was comfortable or uncomfortable attempting to do. I no longer had the extreme pressure from my family to truckle to what others wanted or needed me to do.

That was step one. The medications were step two. And finally forgiving myself and releasing myself from the blame and guilt set me free. Now if I fail, oh well, I can try again. I don't experience these things as cataclysmic anymore.

So it was medication that helped me, but even more it was a release of guilt and an allowance for failure. I knew I could be happy, and I knew it was worth the discomfort of pushing my own envelope to get there. I now am quite a spirited public speaker. But writing is a skill I developed in my solitude, and I wouldn't trade my years alone, in retrospect. Okay, I lied. Maybe I would, but I can't, so I just want to enjoy the rest of this life!

To make a long story short, I have worked in education ever since college, finally got divorced after twenty-one years, have two happy, cool kids, and at forty, I'm a happy and functional human. I take 25 milligrams of Celexa daily, and I keep a stash of Xanax in my purse, but rarely need it. I can do just about anything. I travel, I love, I socialize, I work, and I exercise. I still avoid bus trips, but I am going to work on that. I prefer to be the driver on long trips, but I can deal with someone else driving. I no longer experience paralyzing, cyclical anticipatory anxiety. That was the torture that held my mind, and being free of it is my biggest joy.

I love being alive on the planet. I love who I am. I take the joy and sorrow as it is vouchsafed me, and I know it all stems from the same source.

I am forty years old and have two teenage kids. I grew up in El Paso, Texas, married at eighteen, moved to Louisiana, and then moved back to El Paso. I was an art major during my first stint in college and took my degree in elementary education on my second go-round. I taught in the public schools in El Paso for five years, and after moving to Trinidad, Colorado, in 1997, I worked at the local junior college as a staff developer, curriculum specialist, and tutor coordinator.

I am a voracious reader, and I love to travel, dance, sing, and paint. I am newly single and my kids are about to be up and out, so I am thinking about what that means. I love people and life and am looking forward to the second half of mine.

Commentary by Paul Foxman

Lori's anxiety developed as a result of a traumatic experience, and therefore her condition could be considered a form of post-traumatic stress disorder (PTSD). The trauma—an attack of diarrhea—resulted in a messy bowel accident at the self-conscious age of fifteen. Lori's shame, secrecy, and fear of a recurrence resulted in a pattern of anticipatory anxiety and agoraphobia. As is often the case with avoidance, this coping style led to severe life restriction.

An effective treatment approach for this combination of agoraphobia and PTSD involves three components: education, changes in thinking, and desensitization to the dreaded situations. The educational goal is to understand the link between the traumatic event and anxiety symptoms, including attempts to prevent it from happening again. For example, Lori would learn that her worrying and avoiding were actually attempts to protect herself from anxiety, but it came at the price of life restriction and chronic anxiety.

The cognitive aspect of treatment consists of replacing "what if" worries with new, rational thinking. For example, while Lori behaved as if she would die if she had another attack, in reality her worst scenario would be inconvenient, but not life-threatening. Diarrhea is usually a private experience, not a public display, and Lori's fears of its happening "in front of someone" were disproportionate.

Finally, it is essential to face feared situations in order to master them. For this component of treatment, a technique called *floating through*, pioneered by Dr. Claire Weekes in her books on agoraphobia (see the Bibliography), is helpful. The floating-through technique consists of four steps:

- *Facing*—not avoiding or running away from feared situations
- *Accepting*—having an attitude of acceptance towards anxiety rather than one of rejecting or fighting against it
- *Floating*—relaxed breathing through/during the anxious feelings
- *Letting time pass*—trusting that the anxiety episode will subside

The effectiveness of this approach rests on developing skill at relaxing, which you can master with practice. The best way to do this is to practice relaxing in a safe and comfortable environment, when you are not feeling anxious. Use recorded relaxation instructions, or simply take a few minutes several times a day to experience deep relaxation. With practice, you will be able simply to think *relax*, take a deep breath or two, and feel yourself physically relax. Your breathing will become fuller and slower, your muscles will relax, and your mind will calm down. Once you have practiced the relaxation skill, you will find it to be more effective for use in the middle of an anxiety episode.

Professional help from an experienced anxiety specialist using these steps could accelerate the anxiety recovery process. Medication can also be helpful in controlling anxiety symptoms and providing a sense of "normalcy," as Lori puts it. However, medication alone is usually insufficient for agoraphobia and PTSD because it does not educate the sufferer or address the thinking patterns that underlie these conditions. Besides its treatment limitations, an additional problem with medication includes the frustration that is often encountered in the process of finding the right drug and the right dosage. For many anxiety sufferers, this process can be discouraging and can result in giving up on medication. Furthermore, unpleasant side effects, such as the loss of sexual drive that Lori found unacceptable, can be a barrier to using medication. Generally speaking, medication makes sense for controlling anxiety symptoms while the person learns and practices the steps outlined above.

Learning to relax is an especially important step when gastrointestinal (GI) symptoms are involved. Proper functioning of the GI system requires relaxation, because digestion and elimination are disrupted by tension, stress, and worry. Think of relaxation as a skill that you can practice daily through meditation, quiet reflection, relaxing stretches or yoga, use of a relaxation audiotape, listening to soothing music, enjoyable reading, and other methods. Experiment with relaxation approaches and discover what works for you. As with any new skill, practice is necessary for mastery.

CHAPTER 3

EMETO-WHAT?

by SUSAN BLAKESTON

Hi, my name's Susan and I'm emetophobic!

Emetophobia is a fear of vomiting. There are a number of variations on this fear, ranging from the fear of others throwing up to the fear of oneself throwing up. Because it is a phobia that you cannot run away from, it's very debilitating and runs the lives of most sufferers. A lot of emetophobes also suffer associated phobias, such as OCD (obsessive-compulsive disorder), GAD (general anxiety disorder), and agoraphobia.

Here's my story.

I grew up in England and had what you might call "troubled" childhood and teenage years; I endured several traumatic incidents, including abandonment by my father, abuse by my stepfather, and rape. Looking back, I wonder if the reasons behind my emetophobia stem from these traumas.

As a child I rarely vomited, and so it is something I never got used to, never perceived as being "normal." I remember being sixteen years old and counting how many years it had been since I had thrown up: five years. I didn't realize until I was twenty-four that I was scared of vomit.

At the age of eighteen I underwent surgery on my knees, and four weeks later I was hospitalized with acute tonsillitis. I was in the middle of changing jobs, and my boyfriend had just broken up with me, so I was really unhappy. The stress affected my stomach. For two weeks I didn't eat or drink anything because I felt so nauseated, but at the time

I didn't realize I was scared to throw up. I finally went to the doctors, who promptly hospitalized me for severe dehydration.

While I was in the hospital the nurses gave me some little white pills. They made me feel much better, and I was able to eat after taking them. They were an antiemetic called metoclopramide.

When I was released from the hospital a week later, I had put on five pounds and was ready to face the world again.

That night I made cheese sandwiches, but after eating them I felt sick. Really sick. So I stopped eating and drank only water for a week, by which time I'd lost ten pounds. I went to the doctors and asked for the little white pills, which, amazingly, they gave me. They also put me on Prozac, which had the most wonderful effect on my libido!

For six months, I continued getting pills. Then one night I ate fish and chips for dinner. At 2:20 in the morning of 18 September 1993, I vomited for the first time since I was eleven years old. Needless to say, I felt much better after that, and within two weeks I had thrown away the little white pills and was living happily ever after.

But wait....

In 1998, I had to have emergency surgery on my breast. At the same time, I had just started an incredibly high-pressure job, my twin brother got married, and my husband and I tried to buy a house.

Again, the stress affected my stomach. This time I knew what was going on, so I went to the doctors for metoclopramide and antidepressants. I stopped eating again and lost forty-five pounds within four weeks. The doctor was extremely concerned and signed me off work due to stress. I didn't go back to that job.

My husband and I moved into a delightful cottage in the country, and I tried hard to get better, but I still felt nauseated all the time and didn't realize I was scared. My husband had taken to hitting me whenever I had an "episode." I stopped going out and couldn't sleep. I cleaned obsessively and overcooked food, which I then didn't eat.

My husband and I moved into a townhouse in the city center, and I found a new doctor who was incredibly supportive. By this time my husband was so annoyed with me that he called my doctor and asked for a referral to a psychiatrist. I was so afraid of everything that I readily agreed to go see the nice man in the white coat.

He recognized that I had a phobia and sent me to an organization called Triumph Over Phobia (TOP). My first night there, the leader of the group gave my condition a name: *emetophobia*. I cried and cried on her shoulder. I was bouncing off the walls because I was so happy that I wasn't a nutcase or a freak, and that what I was afraid of had a name!

TOP gave me much support and helped me set goals. I had to write down every name I could think of for *vomit* so the word itself wouldn't bother me. They worked with me on eating foods I'd classified as "unsafe" and on setting goals such as riding the bus for two whole stops. At the same time, my shrink diagnosed me with OCD and sent me to the local loony bin for a week! The only reason I managed to secure outpatient status was because I lived across the road from the facility. With all the help I was getting, I finally realized I could beat this thing.

One night my husband and I decided to emigrate from England to America (land of the free and all that), and we booked our tickets for eight weeks later. I finally had a major goal to work toward; I did not want to be afraid of the flight, of "unsafe" food, and the like.

The people at the mental hospital worked with me on turning my obsessive thoughts into good thoughts; the only thing that worked every time I thought of "vomit" was to turn the thought into a jelly donut (how could I be scared of that?).

Finally, it was moving day. I said my good-byes and with trepidation stepped on the plane.

I felt so happy when I landed on American soil. I vowed never again to let my phobias rule me. I developed sheer determination of the sort that makes me push myself to do things that would cause most people to throw up: go on fairground rides, drink copious quantities of alcoholic beverages, eat sushi. I even watch "vomit movies": films that are notorious for their vomit scenes (*Angela's Ashes*, *Drop Dead Gorgeous*, *Stand by Me*). I left the husband who beat me and have since hooked up with the most amazing, wonderful man.

I still feel nauseated from time to time, but I know I'm not going to barf, and I know I don't need to panic. It works. The big test will come when I really do get sick, but for now I don't need to worry. I know it will happen sooner or later, and I can accept that, so I don't dwell on it and just take each day as it comes.

And I really am living happily ever after.

> *I'm twenty-six years old. Originally from England, I moved to the United States in 1999 (trust me, sunny California is much better than the UK!). I love to read; it was of my saving graces when I went through emetophobic episodes. I also love to sing and dance (unfortunately, I'm not much good at either). Since the time I wrote this essay I have been doing great at my wonderful job, and all of my fear and panic about vomiting is OVER! It's amazing.*

Commentary by Paul Foxman

Susan's story illustrates the role of stress in the development of an anxiety disorder. Her condition began at age eighteen, following a period of stress overload that included knee surgery, a hospitalization for tonsillitis, a job change, and a relationship breakup. This period of high stress affected her stomach, and her primary symptom was nausea. She lost interest in food and drink due to the nausea, which resulted in hospitalization for dehydration. The same pattern occurred again at a time of high stress, when Susan had emergency breast surgery, started a new high-pressure job, tried to buy a house, and her twin brother married.

Like many sensitive people, Susan experienced a strong reaction to her symptoms. Her reaction to nausea involved fears of vomiting and avoidance of certain foods. A restricted lifestyle developed as Susan attempted to control her symptoms.

In my view, stress is one of three ingredients in the development of an anxiety disorder. The other two are a genetic factor, which I call "biological sensitivity," and a particular personality type common among people who develop anxiety. Biological sensitivity includes stronger-than-average reactions to outside stimuli (lights, sounds, weather, etc.) and to internal bodily reactions and sensations. The personality traits include perfectionism, difficulty relaxing, high standards and unrealistic expectations, a strong need to please others, frequent worrying, and other traits I describe in my book *Dancing with Fear*. If you have the biological sensitivity and these personality traits, you are an anxiety disorder waiting to happen. As it did with Susan, stress overload usually determines *when* anxiety symptoms appear. In addition to the stressors she experienced as an adult, Susan was aware of a stressful and traumatic childhood, and she rightfully notes that her early background contributed to anxiety.

To overcome an anxiety pattern, follow a step-by-step process to reverse the fear. Begin by understanding the relationship between stress and bodily reactions. Learn to manage stress through a variety of methods, including relaxation practice and other forms of stress reduction (meditation, gentle stretching, listening to soothing music, setting reasonable limits and expectations, exercise, and so on). Rule out a medical basis for the physical symptoms, and take comfort in obtaining a proper diagnosis (emetophobia in Susan's case). Identify and take small steps towards reversing the anxiety; in Susan's case, this involved expanding her list of "safe" foods and setting small goals such as short bus rides. It is also helpful to replace the thought patterns that create anxiety, such as changing worry into positive thoughts ("I can get over this condition"), and choosing alternative words to describe the anxiety ("I have an unreasonable fear of my physical reactions to stress").

Susan's health deteriorated due to her anxiety. It was appropriate to hospitalize her for dehydration, significant weight loss, and probable malnutrition. In addition, she benefited from a structured group program in England. The American equivalent is the intensive outpatient program (IOP), available in many communities for the treatment of severe anxiety and other disorders. These structured programs are an intermediate step between outpatient psychotherapy and hospitalization, and they consist of group therapy, skills training, individualized progress plans, nutritional counseling, expressive art therapy, medication, and other components in a closely supervised environment. Participants typically spend several hours per day, several days per week in the program. To locate an IOP in your community, contact your local mental-health center, hospital department of psychiatry, or one of the mental-health professional associations (psychologists, clinical social workers, mental-health counselors) in your state.

Anxiety recovery means that you no longer fear your symptoms or reactions. When you reach this point your symptoms are likely to diminish. You will worry less and live each day more fully. Susan did it, and so can you.

CHAPTER 4

CONQUERING *IT*

by BRIGET MURPHY

Born and reared in southwestern Pennsylvania, I was the eldest (and, my sisters emphasize, the brattiest) of three daughters. My parents were warm, caring, educated, artistic, and possessed a great love of life and laughter.

Always surrounded by books, music, paintings, and creative projects in various stages of completion, I developed an avid and enthusiastic interest for a wide array of ideas and subjects, most of which became lively topics of discussion over the family dinner table. These discussions were a handy tool for me, as they provided a distraction while I was hiding lima beans and other yucky vegetables in my napkin. I would then promptly excuse myself to flush them down the toilet.

In school I was involved in extracurricular activities as diverse as the Spanish club, student government, and the school newspaper. I set many athletic records at school and belonged to summer softball teams, where I was one of those annoying players who constantly shouted, "No fair, no fair!" I played tennis (badly) and rode horseback (English style). The summer of my junior year I lived in a Youth Conservation Camp in Allegheny National Forest, where I worked with other teenagers to protect the environment.

Naively believing the ads and wanting to be more than I could be, I joined the Army after high school. Soon I was duckwalking in the rain, shooting M16s, throwing hand grenades, being teargassed, camping out in the snow, and generally being legally tortured in all sorts of creative ways. When the boot-camp instructors ran out of ideas, they packed me off to Ft. Leonard Wood, where I learned to drive tractor-trailers. When, for the fourth time, I narrowly missed backing into an instructor, the Army truck-driving people said, "Aha! Let's send her to those scoundrels in Washington, D.C."

And so I became chauffeur for the post commander and post command sergeant major at Ft. Myer, Virginia, part of the Military District of Washington. There, I saluted the officers, looked cute in my Class As, and used my terrible sense of direction to get lost at every turn. (Query from the back seat: "Private, are you *sure* you know where you are going?" Briget: "Yes, sir! This is just a shortcut I know about, sir!")

I was visiting Memphis on the country's bicentennial when my daughter, Jennifer, was conceived. Jennifer's father and I were married two months later by a justice of the peace.

I had caught a few fuzzy glimpses of the dragon called *panic disorder* before the birth of my daughter, but he'd always been a fairly benign dragon—more of an occasional annoyance than anything. His behavior changed drastically after Jennifer was born. She was born at Walter Reed Army Hospital, where new mothers were forced to watch Army training films with titles such as *Germ Warfare: Lysol and Your Baby!* and *Your Six-Week Checkup: What the Soviets Don't Know.*

About this time, the dragon became my constant companion, never leaving me in peace for even one moment. If he wasn't actually attacking, he was lurking, taunting me before delivering the next wave of terror. I lived in a constant state of dread, under black, ominous clouds that were so heavy they weighed me down and almost smothered me. This feeling of doom was a physical, nearly tangible substance. I lived in blackness and terror.

At my worst, which was before I was diagnosed, I endured a continuous heavy feeling that something horrifying was about to happen. Occasionally this feeling was so strong I would curl into a fetal position in bed for several hours, thinking the end of the world must be near. My stomach was in a constant knot, my throat felt closed up tight, and many times I could not swallow food. My chest felt tight also; it seemed

I couldn't take a deep breath. I was dizzy and lightheaded almost constantly. I felt shaky inside, and sometimes my hands would tremble. Many times a day, a wave of panic would wash over me, although early on, before I was diagnosed, I wouldn't have called it *panic*—the symptoms were so physical that I never recognized them as anything else: A flash of heat would engulf me and my heart would race. My legs would shake and feel like jelly. I'd become so dizzy that it felt like the earth was moving violently under my feet. I'd be nauseated.

The dragon was so overwhelmingly awful and frightful that at first I ran away blindly. Gradually, I began fighting back, but to no avail. The dragon was impervious to any counterattack I conceived. Nothing could stop him. I began to hide in my cave, and I became almost housebound for several years. Just going to the neighbor's house to sit and chat on the porch was a major excursion for me. Even at home I wasn't safe from the dragon, but what else could I do?

Of course, there was no literal dragon. At the time, I referred to what was happening to me as *it*. I was certain that it was going to either drive me insane or kill me. I went to doctor after doctor trying to find out what was wrong with me, and time after time I was given a clean bill of health. Doctors would tell me that I was just under a bit of stress; that's all. I told them that this was much more than a reaction to a bit of stress! No doctors understood. No doctors knew what was wrong with me. Panic disorder was relatively unknown in the late 1970s.

Meanwhile, I hid it as well as I could. After all, it sounded crazy, even to me, and I didn't want anyone else to know that I was "nuts." As best I could, I went through the motions of life. No matter how I felt, I had to go to work. After all, I couldn't just phone the command sergeant major and say, "I have this problem. I feel like I'm either going insane or going to die, and I can't come to work today!" I lost a lot of weight, but aside from that, nobody would have known anything was wrong with me. I became quite a good little actress.

A year later my enlistment was up and I was given an honorable discharge. The panic attacks were no better at all. My husband, daughter, and I moved to Memphis, my husband's hometown. We rented an apartment and I became a stay-at-home mom. I didn't know anyone in Memphis. Agoraphobia kicked in big-time. Before long I had to force myself to go to the grocery store, which was right next door. Any place I went was a horrific ordeal. Terror was with me every moment of the day. I even awoke from sound sleep in a panic. I lost more weight; at one point I was down to eighty-eight pounds (I'm five-feet-five-inches tall). During these years, my average weight was ninety-five pounds. I tried to explain to my husband that *something* was wrong with me. He didn't want to hear it. I stopped trying to talk about it.

Another year passed and we moved again—this time, across town to an old Victorian house we'd bought. The next three years were a mixed bag. I had wonderful neighbors and a beautiful, smart daughter whom I loved like mad. I didn't tell anyone about my problem, and my daughter, new friends, and neighbors made life somewhat enjoyable, regardless of the fact that the panic attacks had not lessened. I kept busy renovating the house, working in my yard, and taking care of my daughter. I forced myself to go places, but in all honesty it was hardly any fun. I was much too anxious and panicky to enjoy myself, although I put up a good front. Every night I prayed that *it* would go away, and every morning it was still with me. However, one day at the end of this three-year period—after I had suffered alone and in silence for five years—I learned that it had a name and that other people knew exactly how I felt.

I discovered that I had panic disorder while watching a local TV talk show. There were people on the show describing exactly how I felt! I was relieved and absolutely elated. I could hardly wait for my husband to come home from work so that I could tell him. His reaction: "That's a bunch of bull****. It's all in your mind. There's nothing wrong with you."

I stared at him blankly, shocked and unbelieving at first, then growing angry, frustrated, and hurt. How could he stand in front of me and say this? In several seconds, he had dismissed it all and walked away. He refused to give credence to something that had horribly affected every moment of every day of my life for the past five years.

The next morning I called the television station and got information about the people who had been on the talk show. They were participating in an intensive two-week self-help group. I called the director of the group and asked to be admitted into the next session. How fantastic it was to be with a group of other people who knew exactly what I had been going through! The approach this group used to wage battle against agoraphobia did not work well for me, although I learned a lot of other useful information: relaxation techniques, what panic disorder is, how agoraphobia develops, how diet and exercise affect the disorder.

A person in the self-help group referred me to Claire Weekes's books, which I still believe to be the most practical of any books on the subject, and of great comfort. I practiced what she preached: not to fight the panic attacks, but to relax and "float" through them. Using this approach, I gradually grew more relaxed in what were, to me, panic-inducing situations. My "comfort zone," where I could feel relatively relaxed, began to expand. I now had about a two-mile radius around my house where I could go grocery shopping, to the post office, to restaurants, etc. I knew that if I felt the panic come on, I could return home quickly. I had given up trying to get any support from my husband. He ridiculed me if he saw me reading any books on panic disorder, so I learned to read them in private. To me, knowledge is empowering.

Although I was doing better, I still experienced many panic attacks and setbacks. During one particularly bad setback, I read a magazine article about Xanax. I asked my doctor for a prescription and with it got immediate relief from panic symptoms. Xanax really takes the edge off. However, as the drug is very addictive, it should only be used for short-term relief.

I seemed to hit a plateau in my recovery. I stayed about the same for many years. I still had panic attacks, and I still had a certain comfort zone, but the panic disorder wasn't top priority in my life. I was busy, I worked, and I was involved in my daughter's school, with friends, and in my neighborhood. I gained weight. The agoraphobia was limiting, but not extremely so. The panic was almost reduced to being merely an annoyance at times. But even a not-so-limited lifestyle was too limited for me, and the panic attacks were exhausting. I believed, however, that this was as good as it was ever going to get for me. I was wrong!

In 1996, I logged on to Compuserve's Panic Disorder Support Group. Again, I was in touch with people who knew what it felt like! Every Wednesday I logged on at 8:00 P.M. Central Standard Time to chat with a bunch of fun, zany women who suffered from panic disorder. We laughed so hard we cried, we gave each other support, we shared tips and research, and we e-mailed each other during the week. (Unfortunately, Compuserve has discontinued the Panic Disorder Support Group, but some of the original group members still chat online at the website Araneum Nostrum: http://araneum.mudservices.com.)

One woman, Robin, was not a regular in the group, but she'd pop in every once in a while to "push" Prozac. She claimed it had stopped her panic attacks cold. Another woman, Diane, decided to go for it. Her doctor put her on Paxil, a close nephew of Prozac. After several months, Diane wasn't having any more panic attacks. I asked my doctor for a prescription for Prozac. It sat on a shelf for months until Diane finally convinced me that it wasn't going to make me feel weird, that I was going to feel absolutely normal, but with no panic attacks.

That was five years ago. I haven't had a panic attack since the Prozac kicked in. I never thought I'd be able to say that! I can now drive anywhere without a second thought and fly all over the country, alone. I hope to travel overseas soon. I should emphasize that becoming "unagoraphobic" was *not* just a matter of the Prozac, as more than twenty years of panic-disorder habits also had to be broken. I went about it methodically, pushing myself further and further, strewing my "crutches" along the way.

I sometimes have anxiety now, but it's normal anxiety. It's in proportion to the stimuli and never comes out of nowhere like the panic attacks did. My comfort zone is now the entire world. I have no limitations! With the help of "Vitamin P" (as Diane calls it), I slew the dragon!

I still make my home in midtown Memphis and enjoy it thoroughly. I am now divorced. I work for Christian Brothers University, where I am pursuing a bachelor's degree in marketing. You may contact me through my website, www.cbu.edu/~bmurphy.

Commentary   by Paul Foxman

Briget had many of the "anxiety personality traits" before she developed panic disorder. She was high achieving, hardworking, and aimed to please others. She was, in effect, an anxiety disorder waiting to happen, and her symptoms appeared in full force following periods of high stress (e.g., unplanned pregnancy and childbirth, marriage under pressure, and frequent relocations during and after military service). After her symptoms appeared, Briget developed some secondary fears, otherwise known as "fear of fear." She worried about losing her mind, and she became preoccupied with hiding her symptoms from others, including her husband.

Briget was able to diagnose her anxiety disorder after learning about it from a television program. This is an important first step in anxiety recovery, achieved in Briget's case without the help of her doctors, who failed to identify the anxiety condition or refer her to an appropriate therapist. In addition, she participated in a self-help group that proved helpful to a limited degree. I think Briget would have benefited much more from a professionally led therapy group, with greater structure and guidance. On the other hand, Briget did benefit from the educational phase of recovery as a result of reading and learning from others.

Fortunately, Briget discovered the "floating through" technique first published by Dr. Claire Weekes and discussed in the commentary following Chapter 2 (also see the Bibliography for more information about books by Dr. Weekes). This approach is similar to methods taught in childbirth-preparation classes, where the goal is to relax through the contractions rather than intensifying the pain with fear and tension. Contrary to our fight-or-flight instinct, which compels us to brace for battle or run from it, the relaxation skills that are fundamental to the floating technique require repeated practice. You can view each anxiety episode as an "opportunity" to practice these skills, but remember that practicing them even when you're not feeling anxious is essential to mastering them. Once you have practiced and refined the techniques in a way that works best for you, you will find them more effective in the middle of an anxiety episode.

In addition to relaxation, don't forget the other steps in the floating technique: facing, accepting, and letting time pass. Your goal should be to develop the skills and confidence to handle anxiety. As a result, you will have less anxiety.

The issue of medication is highlighted in this story. Readers are reminded that medication confers both benefits and pitfalls. For example, Xanax is a quick-acting and effective drug for anxiety ("Xanax really takes the edge off"), but it has high addictive potential.

I wonder whether Briget would need to rely on medication if she had received help from a therapist specializing in anxiety. Nonetheless, I am glad to hear that Briget has benefited from Prozac, which is not habit-forming and which has been approved by the Food and Drug Administration for panic disorder.

CHAPTER 5

FINDING PEACE

by NIKI TAYLOR

My own story of conquering anxiety disorder might not have been possible if it weren't for the therapy I underwent at the hands of two compassionate psychiatric professionals skilled in treating this awful malady.

In childhood, I had a hearing problem, which made it difficult for me to socialize. My shyness didn't help either. I had a few friends, and even though I was an easy target for taunts from boys, I threw myself into my schoolwork and made As and Bs. I loved to read (I started reading when I was four), and I loved to make up stories using my huge imagination. As an only child, I engaged in many solitary activities, such as watching television. When I was in eighth grade, I was number one in the class. I was a nervous child, but my success at schoolwork helped my self-esteem.

After I got a hearing aid at age twelve, my academic work really took off! I participated in science fairs, history fairs, and math contests. I had learned about the reproductive system in health class, and I was waiting for my period to come. My stomach started hurting on a regular basis when I was fourteen, and I thought I was starting my period. But by the time I was sixteen, I still hadn't had a period.

My mother took me to her OB-GYN (the doctor who delivered me), and after he gave me a brief pelvic exam I knew something was wrong. The nurse smiled at me and patted my leg. The doctor explained to my mother and me that he would have to do exploratory surgery to find out what was going on "down there." After the surgery, he said that my ovaries were fine, but the uterus was incomplete, and he was going to have to remove it. I was in denial. I thought instead of removing it he could fix it and cause me to have my period. The truth finally dawned on me when my mother called his office after the surgery to ask about a bladder infection I had, and she identified me to the secretary as the one who'd had the partial hysterectomy. Something snapped in me then, and I haven't been the same since.

I graduated from high school fourth in my class; the one who graduated above me, third in the class, had had a baby a couple of years earlier. How ironic! I went to a local university and majored in English with a concentration in writing. Academically I was going strong, but my everyday life was unsettling. I couldn't drive; my mother had to take me to school. I had panic attacks; I remember lying awake at night and feeling like I was having a heart attack.

I was obsessive-compulsive. I constantly pushed the refrigerator door shut or the cushion to the back of the couch. I would take a shower and repeatedly wash my private area. After using the bathroom, I would rub my private area with toilet paper until it was raw. I couldn't even read in peace. I would get stuck on a certain word in the newspaper (it didn't have to relate to my problems) and be compelled to read it over and over again.

Not only was I anxious, but I also became depressed. Thoughts of people having children and women having periods made me angry and tearful. After I graduated from college with a B.A. degree in English, I went into a slump for a couple of years. Supposedly I was looking for a job, but I was really trying to live in a body that I hated. (While I was in college, I had reconstructive surgery to correct misaligned jawbones, which didn't help my body image.)

Finally, I tired of the obsessive-compulsive rituals, so I told my father I needed help. His insurance allowed me to go to a psychiatric nurse, and a consulting psychiatrist prescribed Prozac. Hallelujah! A light at the end of the tunnel! If anybody needed help, I did. Not only was I anxious and depressed, but I didn't like how I looked. I constantly imagined that I had somebody else's face—usually that of some attractive female celebrity.

The psychiatric nurse was a big help to me. She introduced me to small-step therapy. Instead of worrying about driving a car in heavy traffic, I should break down the driving into steps, no matter how small. On the first day, I would just sit in the driver's seat in the car. The next time, I would start the car and simply sit there. Then, another time, I would back the car out of the driveway and then come back. Another day, I would drive the car around the neighborhood. Gradually I increased how far I drove.

As for the Prozac, it took a couple of months to take effect. The results were wonderful. I didn't experience any side effects except drowsiness. The Prozac increased my confidence and virtually erased the OCD and made me more confident. Due to insurance reasons, I had to stop seeing the psychiatric nurse and psychiatrist. Now I'm seeing another psychiatrist. I was still plagued by social nervousness, so she prescribed BuSpar, which has been helpful in making me more comfortable socially.

My body-image concerns are not as bad as they once were. Even though I still fret from time to time over my physical problems, I'm much more comfortable in my own skin. I never expect to be the most outgoing person, but I'm more competent socially. I even work with children at my church.

Three years after beginning treatment for anxiety disorder, I don't get depressed anymore. Although I worry a little too much sometimes, the major anxiety and obsessive-compulsiveness are gone.

Best of all, I can drive. The woman who couldn't drive out of her own front yard now drives at night and in the pouring rain! I'm a freelance writer, and I'm at peace with myself. What I've learned from all this is that whether you have a perfect body or an imperfect one, if you can just find peace within yourself you're way ahead of the game and can conquer anything!

Niki Taylor is a writer/book reviewer/website-content manager from North Carolina. She has degrees in English and library science from East Carolina University. She also participated in the university's master of arts program in creative writing. After library work, she began her freelance career. Her work has appeared in Lambda Book Report, Aaj Magazine, Pediatrics for Parents, *and* The Writer. *Her website is www.nikianntaylor.com. Those with questions and/or comments may reach her at nat0607@yahoo.com.*

Commentary by Paul Foxman

Niki's story illustrates the three ingredients in the development of an anxiety disorder. The *biological factor* included her shy, nervous, and sensitive disposition as well as some medical problems. She also had the *personality traits* common in people who develop anxiety, such as perfectionism and a high achievement drive that resulted in her being at the top of her class in school. The *stress factor* included her medical problems, notably a hearing problem in childhood, a partial hysterectomy in adolescence, and reconstructive surgery in college.

Several forms of anxiety developed in Niki's case. These included social anxiety, panic attacks, agoraphobia (inability to drive and social avoidance), and an obsessive-compulsive component. Some of her symptoms resulted from an attempt to control her anxiety. For example, her social isolation was an effort to avoid situations that made her uncomfortable.

Niki also reported that she became depressed. It is not unusual for anxiety sufferers to become depressed due to social isolation, frequent worry, sleep disturbance in some cases, and an overall feeling of discouragement about their lack of control over their environment. I refer to this as *secondary depression*, a reaction to the anxiety condition, and I find it interesting that many of the medications used to treat anxiety are actually antidepressants. These include selective serotonin-reuptake inhibitors (SSRIs), such as the Prozac that helped Niki. Other antidepressants used to treat anxiety include (by brand name) Paxil, Zoloft, Tofranil, Norpramin, Pamelor, Anafranil, and Desyrel. Fortunately, the depression usually subsides when the primary anxiety disorder is successfully resolved.

The small-step therapy described by Niki is appropriate and effective for agoraphobia. This process involves gradual exposure to feared or avoided situations. You can practice it mentally by imagining yourself doing an anxiety-arousing task while relaxing. This will improve your success with those small steps in real life.

For the obsessive-compulsive component, I recommend the "three Rs": *relabel* the obsessive thoughts or compulsive rituals in an attempt to control anxiety; *refocus* your attention on more productive activities; and *relax*. It has been demonstrated that this cognitive technique can actually alter brain chemistry in people with obsessive-compulsive disorder (OCD). For further insight into this approach, I recommend reading *Brain Lock: Free Yourself from Obsessive-Compulsive Behavior*, by Jeffrey Schwartz, M.D. (see Bibliography).

It is also necessary to learn to tolerate the anxiety you are likely to feel when you discontinue the obsessive thinking or ritual behavior. This requires a set of anxiety-control skills, such as the "floating" technique discussed in my commentary following Chapters 2 and 4.

CHAPTER 6

SEVENTY-TWO THOUSAND THOUGHTS

by KIM PHELAN

Anxiety is one of the scariest disorders one can have. Hell is an easy comparison because strong feelings of anxiety are so overwhelmingly frightening. After your first panic attack, your world is never the same, and you are scared every day because you do not know when the next one will hit you. You feel like you are going to die, and you are afraid that others will see you freak out, and this causes more fear and embarrassment. Losing control—isn't that one of the biggest fears of any human?

My anxiety started when my grandmother died. I left the cemetery and had my first panic attack. After that, panic attacks became frequent visitors in my life. I came from a dysfunctional family. My mother was depressed and my father drank. My grandmother was my rock, and when she passed on, I felt alone and vulnerable. Who was going to handle my dysfunctional family? Would this now be my responsibility since I was the eldest of four children? I did not want to take on that role, and I was scared. I was also in a marriage I no longer wanted to be in, and my two best friends had just moved far away. As most people with anxiety know, when our support system changes we become more prone to attacks.

Despite the dysfunction in my family, before my problems with anxiety began I was quite happy-go-lucky and outgoing. Once anxiety hit, however, I took to hiding in my home on the weekends. I could no longer go shopping or get on a bus because I was afraid of having a panic attack. I called the APA (American Psychological Association) and got the name of a good cognitive therapist, who helped me for two years. I also took an antianxiety drug for a period of time. I had a wonderful spiritual teacher, and with all the support I grew and blossomed.

Anxiety exists to tell or teach us something. Perhaps our way of life is not working and we need to change, or we need to resolve deep issues from the past. Anxiety is a gift in that it forces us to change if we can face the challenge of dealing with it. I know how easy it is to give in to the disorder and become agoraphobic, but I urge everyone to not give up and to seek the help they need.

We have about seventy-two thousand thoughts a day. Most are the same as the ones we had yesterday, and if they are mostly negative, this destroys our inner peace. Monitoring your thoughts is so important, and changing them to more loving, kind thoughts is key. When you have anxiety, you need to learn new ways of living, and you need to be patient throughout the process. Compare it to a child learning to walk. He gets up, falls down, and gets up again. We do not yell at the child or put him down; we encourage him and we are patient. This is what you need to do with yourself.

I wasn't brought up to think I should go to college or that I should nurture any dreams. I was told to just get a job. My anxiety made me rethink my life and to allow myself to dream. I started going to college at night. I took an art class, which I loved, and I went to Italy with a girl-friend to see all the beautiful art. I got a divorce from a man who was unsupportive of my growth.

My family disliked the changes in me because they could not rely on me anymore; I was starting to live my own life. They grew angry and said I'd changed and had become selfish. But I was no longer a bird with clipped wings; I was allowing myself to spread my wings and fly. I was no longer afraid of life. I took planes and traveled. Soon I quit my job, and eventually I sold my home and moved to Manhattan. I started to do work I loved and became vice president of an organization that helps those with bleeding disorders. I educated people to help them find a better quality of life. I left my small, isolated, limiting world, and it was so well worth it.

I no longer had to be secure and safe. I was able to take chances and be okay with not always knowing where I was going in life. My therapist used to say to me, "It's okay if you do not know all the answers right now—it will come to you," and my spiritual teacher would say, "When you live in a way that is uplifting on all levels, all will fall into place."

My panic attacks were caused by a lot of negative thinking and beliefs that I was not good enough, I was not smart enough, and I did not deserve to be truly happy because my mother was not happy. I had to slowly change my belief system and learn that I was allowed to have happiness and that I was smart and could do whatever I put my mind to doing. And the most important thing I had to learn was that it was okay to fail. I'd never before believed that, but I had to change from a safe mode to a new way of looking at the world. I had to say to myself, "Just try and see—if you do not try, how will you know? Look how many people fail before they reach success." With this in mind, I allowed myself to take chances.

When I had panic attacks, my head would get light and my palms sweaty. I felt like I could not breathe and thought I was going to lose consciousness or freak out. When I started reading books on anxiety, many of them said that I would never really get over it—that it would be a part of my life always. I refused to believe that; I knew if I worked really hard I could live a life free from anxiety. It is possible. I am an example of this truth. Now when I feel a little nervous about something or I feel my inner peace being disturbed, I sit with myself right away, and I can turn those scary thoughts around in two minutes and calm myself down.

I am so in touch with myself and my world. I knew my anxiety was gone when I was walking one day and realized that I had not felt anxious for a long time. I thought, "How funny this thing is. It comes with no warning and it leaves the same way, without even a good-bye—it's just gone."

My life is peaceful now. I can set my own hours at work. I love what I do. I get to travel. My daily routine consists of walking for forty minutes, stretching, meditation, healthy eating, writing in my journal, and listening to meditation tapes every night. I will always work on myself to maintain a peace within. I remember asking my spiritual teacher when I would stop having to work on myself. He said, "You never stop. You always work on yourself and learn many things."

This is something I do for me, and I love it. In life, we run so fast and we never take the time to sit quietly and get in touch with our feelings. I believe this is why many people catch diseases; they're in a state of dis-ease with their bodies. I believe it is important to take time each day to sit with yourself and get in touch with your thoughts.

I used to take care of everyone except myself. Anxiety taught me to take care of myself first, because if you do not take care of yourself, you really cannot take care of others. It taught me to set healthy boundaries and to say "no" when I really mean it. Anxiety helped me to become the person I was meant to be—to stop and smell the flowers, to look up at the sky and see the beautiful sun, clouds, and stars. Anxiety taught me to dream and believe that all things are possible. Anxiety taught me to be grateful.

We are all unique individuals and are wired differently. Each of us needs to find out what works best for us. The best way to do this is to first look at all aspects of your life. Some people need to look at their diet and rule out hypoglycemia, which fosters the same symptoms as anxiety. It is important to get a good physical checkup and not merely diagnose yourself with anxiety disorder, because the symptoms could actually indicate a physical condition. Some people have allergies and think their symptoms indicate anxiety. I've read many nutrition books and tried vitamins and the like. I learned that calcium and magnesium are essential for the nervous system, and a lack of them can cause various problems. I highly recommend that people with anxiety look into supplementing their diets with these minerals.

Second, people need to really dig deep within and see what is causing their anxiety. Some need to work on anger, some on forgiveness, and some were abused and need to work on those issues. The most important thing is to not give up, to keep working until you discover what it is. It's a lot of hard work. People need to take the time and patience to discover their uniquely wired way to proper healing.

My life has changed dramatically, and I am so glad. The road was not easy. It was bumpy and scary, but once you get through the bumpy and scary parts, you come to a place of peaceful acceptance. You change what you can and you love all parts of yourself. You no longer try to fix everyone else, but, instead, you learn to take care of *you.*

Love, Kim

I am from New York City. I am vice president of a nonprofit organization called the Coalition for Hemophilia B, I am on the consumer advisory board of the Genetics Institute, and I am executive director of the Anxiety and Phobia Peer Support Network. I do volunteer work at the Mary Manning Walsh Home for the Elderly with Alzheimer's, where I sing and help out with charity functions. I enjoy reading, music, and art. I can be contacted through my website at Anxietytofreedom.com or via e-mail at Kim@anxietytofreedom.com.

Commentary by Paul Foxman

Kim's uplifting story illustrates a number of important issues in how anxiety develops, as well as the steps for successful recovery.

Before she developed panic disorder, Kim had many of the personality traits that I find common in people who develop anxiety. She was a perfectionist with a strong need for control, and she focused on pleasing others while thinking poorly of herself. Like many people with low self-esteem, Kim felt she had to *earn* love, respect, and appreciation from others. These traits have both a negative and a positive side. For example, many ambitious and successful people have similar "driven" personality styles. However, this personality style made Kim very susceptible to an anxiety disorder. All she needed was an overload of stress to trigger her anxiety symptoms.

Kim's family background was another risk factor for anxiety. She lived with an alcoholic father and a depressed mother; her family was a "dysfunctional" one in need of organization and leadership. It can be safely assumed that in her childhood Kim received little positive attention, as her parents were wrapped up in their own problems. Fortunately, Kim found strength and a positive role model in a grandmother who was, as she put it, "my rock." In fact, Kim's anxiety symptoms emerged when her grandmother died. The loss of her grandmother was the stress that triggered her first panic attack.

Panic attacks—those sudden and scary episodes of intense anxiety—involve physical symptoms such as rapid heart rate or pounding chest, lightheadedness, sweaty palms, difficulty breathing, and fear of losing consciousness or "freaking out." Kim experienced all of these "overwhelmingly frightening" reactions. Furthermore, she describes a pattern of anticipatory fear of anxiety symptoms, which created more symptoms and anxiety. When such a pattern continues, the panic/anxiety sufferer begins to avoid situations in which the attacks might occur, and her world shrinks as she develops the additional problem of agoraphobia.

Fortunately, Kim called the American Psychological Association and was directed to an appropriately trained therapist. A cognitive approach—proven to be effective for anxiety—helped Kim change her negative thinking habits. She learned that we each have approximately seventy-two thousand thoughts per day (about one every second), thoughts which can disturb our inner peace if they are predominantly negative. She monitored her negative thoughts and patiently changed them to "more loving, kind thoughts." She also learned how to be more reasonable in her standards and expectations, and how to take chances in order to succeed. In other words, Kim modified those personality traits that create stress and anxiety.

Kim also understands the vital importance of physical health in anxiety recovery. Her daily routine consists of walking, stretching, meditation, eating healthily, and journal writing. I would encourage everyone to experiment with different "self-health" activities and develop a regular routine. Your daily program should include at least one form of relaxation, such as yoga, meditation, relaxing music, or quiet activity, as well as a choice of aerobic exercise. A healthy diet—low in refined sugars, hot spices, caffeine, and alcohol—can also go a long way toward anxiety control. For most people, a healthier diet means more grains, fruits, and vegetables. Also, to keep your blood sugar steady, try eating smaller quantities of food four to five times a day—rather than two or three large meals.

In the process of recovery, Kim had a spiritual awakening that contributed to her new sense of peace and gratitude. I would encourage you to develop a spiritual dimension to help with anxiety recovery. It is easier to give up control when you can trust a higher power, whether you call that entity God, Spirit, the universe, Source, the All That Is, or whatever. Also, viewing yourself as a worthy and lovable person—as God does—can improve your self-esteem. Try my suggestion of treating yourself as you would treat a friend: with kindness, understanding, patience, and compassion. Refrain from saying anything to yourself that you wouldn't say to a friend. For example, if a friend made a mistake, you wouldn't say, "What an idiotic thing to do. You're such a loser." Yet many people regularly use negative language like this against themselves. Pay attention to how you talk to yourself, and train yourself to stop abusive self-talk.

Other methods for developing your spirituality include quiet reflection or meditation, spending time in nature, daily prayer, spiritual reading and study, and practicing a loving attitude towards yourself and others.

PANIC

by JO L.

I remember it like it was yesterday. The year was 1962 and I was ten years old, standing in the kitchen of my house. My mother was standing in front of the refrigerator, and suddenly I felt funny. At the time I had no name for it, but I looked at her and said, "How do I know you're my mother?" She said, "What do you mean? I am your mother." Although baffled, she thought nothing of the question, and reality returned. That was my first panic attack.

I don't remember having another one until I was sixteen years old, smoking pot one night with friends. I remember "waking up," though I hadn't been asleep, and screaming, "I want my mother." I felt as if I had been gone; my mind had stopped working for what could only have been seconds. My friends saw no change in me during the time I was "gone." I knew exactly what was going on around me, although I didn't feel "there." My friends were scared; they knew they had to do something. I heard them ask each other if the pot could have been laced with LSD, but no one else was having the reaction I was having.

They drove around town with me for hours, letting me see familiar things, familiar people. I talked to them, but it didn't feel like my voice speaking. I told them about a character on a soap opera who'd gone through the same thing I was experiencing. But she had to go to the hospital. They assured me I wouldn't, and kept driving.

I call what happened an "out-of-body experience." My mind left my body and was looking down on what was going on around me. I believe it is one of the scariest events that can happen to a person. You're afraid you're never going to come down or return to normal, and it's so frightening. How could one live like this, I wondered. In fact, I doubt anyone could without ending up in a psychiatric hospital.

Eventually I did come down. The next morning I did not feel totally myself, but I did feel better. However, the anxiety, panic, and out-of-body feeling began happening frequently; just the thought of the previous episode could trigger another one. Pot brought out feelings of panic and paranoia in me, and ultimately I stopped smoking.

Unfortunately the panic didn't stop. It would happen at various times. One of the worst episodes happened when I was a college student. There appeared to be no trigger; my mind just left my body. When I spoke, it sounded like an echo to me. I knew I was in my apartment talking with friends; I just didn't feel as if I was doing the talking. That lasted for three days. I told only one person about it, one of my roommates, who helped me as well as she could. She attempted to "talk me down," which is what people do when their friends get too high on drugs. But I was not on drugs.

I lived for the next twenty years with panic attacks, fearing them, knowing the feeling right before the onset, attempting to stop them, and feeling unsure what to do about it all. I didn't have a name for it. I once saw a psychiatrist who told me I was fine. An internist told me I was having hypoglycemic episodes and to eat yogurt to treat the hypoglycemia. A therapist told me the same thing. For some reason, I could not convince people, the very people who should have heard me, that there was something very wrong.

In 1985, I had a nervous breakdown. Did I see it coming? Absolutely not. Was I having more panic attacks than usual? No. At the age of thirty-two, a single parent with two very small children, I'd decided to go back to school. I had met the man of my dreams in 1983, and a little over a year later we got married. Getting along with my stepson was very difficult for both me and my children. Stepfamilies are an entity in themselves and deserve the multitude of books written about them and the therapists who specialize in them. Going to graduate school full-time, getting remarried, and finding the marriage and household stressful put me over the edge. I am not sure which event took the lead.

It happened one night. I woke up in the middle of the night, numb from the top of the right side of my head to my right toe. I was terrified and woke my husband, thinking I was dying or having a stroke. As I look back, I know the breakdown was affecting my physical being as well. At the time, I was in an HMO (health-maintenance organization). I saw my doctor, who said, "I see a lot of numb women; it's stress." She ordered some tests—a spinal tap and CAT scan to name two—but when I asked her to refer me to a psychiatrist, she said no, but she also said to call her anytime I felt like I was losing it.

I felt like I was losing it all the time; in fact, I had lost it. I went to school part-time instead of full-time, and I only managed that by sheer determination. I had fantasies of jumping in front of a city bus. I remember calling my doctor from a hall outside my classroom for help. She was useless. The neurologist she sent me to tried to rule out multiple sclerosis. Eventually, I paid for an outside neurologist to do some further testing, including an MRI, and after several years MS was ruled out. In the meantime, following the same pattern as fifteen years earlier, no one was listening to me.

I was in a graduate program for social work, and, frankly, I believe the professors would have listened and taken me seriously. Upon reflection, I am sure I didn't confide in them because being a social worker was what I had wanted since I was a child. I desperately didn't want to fail. If I revealed to my professors what was happening, I feared my dream would die, along with whatever sanity I still had left.

My brain felt cold; I was having visual as well as audio hallucinations. There were times I thought I should be in a hospital, but I didn't want to leave my children. My kids were what kept me at home, though much of the time I saw them through a fog—a fog that made my world look and feel unreal.

My husband helped me by talking me through the very rough times. Some periods were worse than others. For months, though, there was never a time when I felt sane or normal. There was never a time when I felt like me. That is what my nervous breakdown felt like to me—as though I were someone else and somewhere else, not in this world, but aware enough to know that. It was incredibly scary, and in retrospect, I should have gotten help. This isn't an indictment of HMOs; however, had I had the health care I have today, I would never have had to suffer to the extent that I did.

I stopped being able to eat. Food wouldn't go down. I wasn't anorexic. I wanted to eat, but couldn't. I attempted milkshakes as often as I could, because they were liquid and I didn't have to chew them. I lost fifteen pounds. I have one recollection of a classroom discussion. For a few minutes I felt almost normal, then I looked down at my hands and they didn't look like my hands. I again left this world. No one noticed, although I could hardly breathe.

Taking fewer classes and having some of my neurological symptoms subside made me feel better. Eventually I got better. I can't even say how long it was, but I can guess that it was six to nine months before I felt like myself. The cloud and fog lifted, and I wasn't as numb as I had been. I was left with some residual neurological sensations, such as pulsing in my face and tingling in my foot. Still, I finished graduate school and started working. I thought I would be fine, but I never knew when the next panic attack would strike or if I would go back into the tunnel and perhaps not return. My fear of having another nervous breakdown could trigger a panic attack, so I worked hard not to think about it.

More than twenty years of suffering could have been avoided had I had good medical care. We had insurance and money, yet there was no help for me until 1991.

I remember the night I decided to try again to get psychiatric help. I was driving alone on a dark road and had a panic attack. The attacks were happening on a regular basis. They happened in the usual places: supermarkets, traffic, and waiting in line. They had reached a point where they were disrupting my life because I wouldn't go for long car rides. I wouldn't get on a bus because I couldn't get off if I felt the need.

I could only go to a movie theatre or a show if I sat at the end of a row so I could leave.

This particular panic attack was no worse than the others, but because I was alone and it was dark, I was very scared. I did what I had taught myself to do. I opened the window, turned up the radio, took deep breaths, and talked myself down from wherever I had gone. I talked myself back to being me.

The next day I went to my primary care physician. At this point we had left the HMO. I told him my history, and he prescribed Xanax. It helped the acute panic attacks subside, but not totally. After a year, my doctor told me he wanted me to see a psychiatrist who would be better able to prescribe the right medication. I am so thankful for that moment because it changed my life.

I went to see Dr. M., who believed me. He believed I had suffered a nervous breakdown. My husband, although he was there every step of the way, never believed me. He didn't want to think about how badly I really felt. I think my condition scared him terribly. Even to this day he just sort of nods his head when I mention it.

Dr. M. told me he believed I had a chemical imbalance—an organic problem, not something that would ever be treatable with talk therapy. I was so relieved because talking about my panic brought on the panic, so what good would that have done? Some sufferers say talk therapy does some good. As a social worker, I understand behavior modification and other therapies for various disorders. However, I never thought my panic was psychological. It just didn't feel that way to me. He told me that like a diabetic who needs insulin, I would most likely need medication for the rest of my life to keep me stable. He never used the word *sane*.

We began the process of finding the right medication. I never stopped working or driving, although some of the medication made me very tired. That was a difficult period, because my husband was critical of my need for a nap when I came home from work, and I found myself nodding off in the middle of a conversation with my children. Prozac turned me into a zombie. Next, we tried a combination of Zoloft and

Klonopin for a couple of years. For about five years now, I have been on a combination of Wellbutrin, Klonopin, and BuSpar, and I haven't once had a panic attack. Oh yes, one time I did; my stepson gave my husband a joint, we smoked it, and it brought on the same old feelings of panic!

I am now as normal as anyone else. I go on long car rides; I can wait in traffic and take the bus. I must admit I don't like to wait in traffic and will avoid it if I can, and I'd rather not take the bus, but I don't panic at those times. Those are residual fears that may never go away, but thanks to a wonderful psychiatrist, new medication, and my family (although not everyone in my family knows the whole story, at least now everyone knows I am on medication), I can wake up without fear of panic. I will always have tingling in my foot, I think, most likely the result of nerve damage. But I can live with that. I am in this world, I am in my body, I am integrated, and that's what counts.

> *I am a baby boomer born and reared in Massachusetts. Finding myself empty nested, I am fulfilling my dream of living on the ocean with my husband of eighteen years and two dogs. Professionally, I am a social worker, certified personal trainer, and substitute teacher. I nurture my soul by writing; I nurture my body by working out. At this point in my life, I owe all I am to my two incredible adult daughters, and I dedicate all my writing to them. I can be reached by e-mail at jobythebay@aol.com or via my homepage at http://hometown.aol.com/ jobythebay/myhomepageindex1.html.*

Commentary by Paul Foxman

Some panic/anxiety sufferers endure "out-of-body experiences," also known as *depersonalization*. This altered state of consciousness involves a sense of detachment, numbness, or unreality. The experience can be frightening and bring on additional fears about losing one's mind or going crazy. My view is that the out-of-body experience is an involuntary effort to cope with intense anxiety by mentally shutting down, similar to shock as the body's attempt to cope with pain. On the other hand, the same out-of-body experience can be positive and desirable, as reported by some people while meditating or under the influence of mind-altering drugs.

Fortunately, the out-of-body experience is temporary and usually subsides when anxiety is brought under control. Reassure yourself about this and remember that you are not going crazy. Refocus on the steps that will reduce anxiety.

The most successful approach to panic disorder is a cognitive-behavioral sequence involving several components. Education, relaxation practice, change in thinking patterns, and desensitization (gradual exposure to dreaded or avoided situations) are the key ingredients. The success rate of this approach is high—approximately 80 percent. In addition, the "floating" technique (relaxing through anxiety while trusting that it will pass, as detailed in my commentary following Chapters 2 and 4) is the right strategy for coping with panic episodes. A structured self-help program, such as the sixteen-week CHAANGE process (see Resources), would accelerate these anxiety-recovery skills. Additionally, in some cases medication is needed to control anxiety symptoms.

The educational phase of recovery includes learning about the role of stress in anxiety. Jo certainly had a high level of stress in the form of full-time graduate school and a remarriage involving stepchildren. It is also important to understand how fear of symptoms leads to more symptoms and a spiral into severe anxiety.

The relaxation component requires daily practice of at least one method for achieving deep relaxation. (See my commentary following Chapter 2 for some ideas about relaxation techniques.) This practice should start immediately and should continue as a regular form of stress management. Relaxation practice can also help prevent future anxiety relapses, once the panic disorder is brought under control.

The cognitive component of treatment involves changing the way you think so that you do not *create* anxiety. Worrying, negative thinking, perfectionism, fear of criticism or failure, all-or-nothing thinking, and other thought patterns need to be replaced with more productive thoughts if anxiety is to be brought under control. To change negative thought patterns, follow these steps:

- Pay attention to your thinking, and identify specific patterns to be changed
- Work on only one or two patterns at a time (you can add others in the future)
- If it is helpful to do so, write down the thoughts you wish to change
- Construct a positive alternative for each thought you wish to change
- Use positive alternatives that are reasonable and possible
- Use the present tense when constructing positive thought patterns: "I have faith in myself and trust that I can handle whatever may happen" or "I live in the present and take things as they come"
- Each time you notice yourself thinking a negative thought, replace it with the positive alternative. For example, replace "It's no use having any dreams; they all get crushed" with "Just for today, I can take one small step towards making a dream come true" or with "Some of my dreams have come true in the past, so it's possible to have more dreams come true." Another example would be to replace the fearful thought "What if the medical tests show a serious illness?" with "I live in the moment and deal with things as they come"
- Continue making positive substitutions until they become your default thinking pattern

The desensitization phase of anxiety recovery is necessary for those who have begun to avoid specific situations in an effort to control anxiety. This process involves gradual exposure to the feared or avoided situation, in small steps that can be mentally rehearsed before attempted in real life.

Finally, Jo's story illustrates the potential for even trained professionals to misdiagnose anxiety. The HMO system of health care can also contribute to the problem if your insurance does not cover specialists out-side the system. Jo's doctors apparently failed to understand her condi-tion, particularly the out-of-body experience. She suffered unnecessarily, and her condition deteriorated into a "nervous breakdown." My sugges-tion is to trust your intuition. If you are not benefiting from professional help after a reasonable effort, seek alternatives and keep searching until you find satisfaction.

CHAPTER 8

CROSSROADS

by DONNA VAN LEUSDEN

The dreams were the first hint that something was wrong. Violent, graphic images held me hostage at night. I used to dream about horrible tortures and loved ones' cries of pain. Eventually the nightmares drove me away from sleeping, and I would find other things to do at night. I would walk around my house, chat online, or watch late-night television—anything to keep me from the grasp of those dreams.

I hadn't always lived with such fear. In my not-so-distant memory, I had been a normal, active, nineteen-year-old girl. I had a boyfriend, a family who loved me, and a dream of pursuing an acting career. That all changed the night a group of friends and I went out to a local nightclub. "Take care of each other," my mother called as we drove away giggling. How prophetic those words would soon to prove to be.

After a night of dancing and having fun, it was time to go. The bar was closing, and we decided to walk the few blocks to an all-night restaurant. At the last minute, I remembered some items I wanted from my friend Janelle's apartment. She decided to walk back with me; we would meet up later with the group. I would come to regret every moment that followed that choice.

We had to cross a local roadway that was known for being busy during peak time, but at 2:10 in the morning it was practically deserted. Not wanting to walk the extra fifty feet to the crosswalk, we carefully checked both ways and crossed to the median. Again, we looked for oncoming traffic. Headlights were a ways off, but we should have easily made it across. We jogged, laughing because Janelle had a crush on one of the cooks at the restaurant, and she would soon see him.

We were only a few feet from the curb when I realized we were not going to make it. I thought about my family and my boyfriend, and my last thought was "How much will it hurt?" Would it break both my legs or just one? I was relieved when I stepped onto the sidewalk. I turned to Janelle to comment on how close we had come to really getting hurt.

The words died in my throat. Janelle, somewhat shorter than I, was unable to cover as much ground as I did. I heard a scream a split second before the car hit her. I will never know if it was she or I who screamed. She flew through the air, and after turning two complete cartwheels, her head bounced off the curb. She lay on the grass, still.

I ran up to her, wanting to tell her to lie still, that help would arrive. Of course, she was unconscious. I first fixed her top, knowing how embarrassed she'd be that everyone could see her breasts, and then began to check her heartbeat and breathing. I called to her, "Janelle, Janelle, don't worry, honey. I know it hurts, but I'm here and I'm going to take care of you. Don't be afraid; I won't let anything happen to you. I love you." At that moment, my friend's heartbeat stopped.

A witness and I began CPR and mouth-to-mouth resuscitation. A huge crowd was standing around, talking. I had told some guy in a red shirt to call an ambulance; I'd done everything I was supposed to. I was so calm. Friends would tell me later how impressed they were that I didn't break down. The breakdown came later.

I rode in the ambulance to the hospital, but I didn't stay. I called my mom, who came to get me. While waiting, I washed Janelle's blood from my hands and from under my nails. I had tried so hard to bring her back. I remembered the unnatural softness of the back of her head, the sharp bone protruding from her leg, the loud gurgling I heard after I exhaled into her lungs. I tried to cry at that moment. Tried to let all of the emotion out, but it didn't come. I tried again when my mother got there. She put her arms around me and I sobbed, then it stopped. I couldn't release the feelings from where they were now bottled. I went home, exhausted, hopeful, guilt ridden.

Early the next day, I got the phone call that she had died. Died? How could she? I did everything I was supposed to. I promised her she would be fine. She wasn't allowed to die, not while I lived.

I didn't realize the effect Janelle's death had on me. It took almost four months for it to really come out. I stopped eating, couldn't cry, and drank a lot. When I stopped sleeping at night and stopped enjoying sex, I went to my family doctor. I am forever grateful that my doctor was able to diagnose what I was really suffering from. He prescribed Prozac and temazepam to help me sleep and sent me to a wonderful psychologist named Dr. Rowan.

Dr. Rowan recognized not only the symptoms of the depression I was exhibiting, but also the cause for them: post-traumatic stress disorder. I was stunned. I had always thought of PTSD as something that affected war veterans, not regular young women. I began the slow, sometimes unbearable voyage back.

My despair was often overwhelming. For a long time I had a plan to kill myself, not because I wanted to die but because the pain seemed almost insurmountable. I hated being out of my "safe place," my home. I would get anxious when I was out and demand to be taken home. I was convinced that I would die in a car accident. The passage of time caused me distress because I felt I was wasting my life and that soon the other shoe would drop. I hated needing help because I'd always believed myself to be strong. I could "handle" it. Except I couldn't. I refused to be physically intimate with my boyfriend. It finally got to the point where he waited until I had taken my sleeping pill and had sex with me while I was unaware. After our breakup, I continued my treatment, and every day I grow a little bit stronger.

Eventually, I stopped wincing whenever I heard a car's tires screech. The smell of burning rubber didn't make me nauseated anymore. I felt I was getting better. It was important to notice that my recognition of my behavior as abnormal was my hope. If it were normal to feel this bad all the time, why would I hate it so much? I knew there had to be something else because I wanted that something so badly. During therapy, we discussed everything, but especially the accident and how it made me feel. The survivor guilt I felt was a normal thing. It might not make it easier, but at least I knew other people had gotten through this experience before me.

It took a long time. Almost two years later I finished school and was planning my future. I had a new man in my life who understood what I was going through and helped push me through it. Only one obstacle remained: getting my driver's license. The feeling of dread that came over me whenever I considered getting into a driver's seat was palpable. I was terrified. I went back into therapy just to help me through it. After a few months I was ready, and on my first try I passed.

I am not completely the girl I was before this experience, but neither am I the lost soul I was during my struggle. I have grown into some strange hybrid: stronger, wiser, and more compassionate. I have a better understanding of myself and what I am capable of, which after my long journey back is anything I set my mind to.

"Everybody has to leave the darkness sometime"—from Sting's "I'm So Happy That I Can't Stop Crying"

Since the experiences outlined in this essay, I have rejoined life as a normal twenty-four-year-old woman. I am planning my wedding in October and have been working in marketing and communications for an international aerospace company. I enjoy traveling, reading, and writing. Although almost no evidence of my PTSD symptoms remain, I still remember the terrible pain, and my thoughts are with anyone going through something like it. You will get through this! Think of your life as a novel. With such an interesting character as yourself starring, who knows what might happen next? Work towards finding that out.

Here is a poem I wrote:

I step from the darkness

arms out, blinking

at the brightness of the sun.

Frightened and exhilarated by the power of life

> *that courses through my veins,*
>
> *and my awareness of it.*
>
> *My path before me I walk, ready to lead,*
>
> *ready to follow,*
>
> *ready to stumble,*
>
> *ready to fall,*
>
> *ready not to fall.*

Commentary by Paul Foxman

In one of this book's most gripping stories, Donna witnessed the death of her best friend. Her story offers hope for recovery from even the most devastating loss.

As a result of the sudden and unexpected death of her friend, Donna developed the anxiety condition known as post-traumatic stress disorder (PTSD). This condition can occur following a tragic, traumatic, or unusual event, such as a rape, an automobile accident, a house fire, a serious injury, witnessing violence or death, or—in Lori's case as related in Chapter 2—a bout of diarrhea in which she did not make it to the bathroom on time. Like many people, Donna was under the impression that PTSD affected only war veterans (the diagnosis was coined in relation to war trauma). She was surprised to learn of her diagnosis from a knowledgeable psychologist, whose diagnosis and therapy helped her recover.

A period of shock following a traumatic loss is typical, and in Donna's case it lasted about four months. During this period she emotionally and physically shut down. She stopped eating, sleeping, and enjoying intimacy with her boyfriend, and she used alcohol to dull her emotional pain. Although she does not mention it specifically, Donna probably experienced feelings of detachment.

In the next stage of PTSD, Donna began to experience anxiety about driving, dying in a car accident, and being out of her "safe place." This is common among PTSD sufferers, who experience anxiety on exposure to any situation that resembles the original trauma. In Donna's case, this included the smell of burning rubber and the sound of car tires screeching. In addition, she experienced "survivor guilt," which can strike survivors of a trauma that killed or caused injury to others, as well as graphic nightmares. Other PTSD victims might report flashbacks, difficulty relaxing or sleeping, memory loss, a sense of reliving the experience, and avoidance of activities, places, or people that arouse recollections of the trauma. These symptoms can last for many months or even years.

Donna recovered from PTSD with the help of sleep medication combined with psychotherapy by a psychologist who understood the condition. The medication helped control Donna's symptoms and enabled her to benefit from psychotherapy. Her case illustrates the findings of the National Institute of Mental Health that the combination of these two forms of treatment is more effective than the use of either one alone.

Among other things, Donna learned that her feelings were normal for the circumstances. If I were her therapist, I would follow the educational phase of treatment with relaxation techniques to counteract her chronic arousal, and I would encourage daily practice of the techniques. I would then address her survivor guilt and other cognitive aspects of the condition. For example, I might ask, "How would your best friend want you to live without her? Would she want you to continue suffering?" In order for PTSD victims to improve, they must give themselves permission to recover.

Finally, I would use a gradual desensitization and exposure process to help Donna and other trauma victims reintroduce themselves to the activities associated with painful memories. The goal would be to replace the anxiety response with natural and positive feelings that allow for pleasure in life again.

CHAPTER 9

MY STORY OF RECOVERY

by JAN BURNETT

I had a wonderful life before anxiety hit me.

I have lived in Oklahoma all my life, and I have been married to the same terrific man for most of my life. We were married very young, and we have three adult children and six beautiful granddaughters. Before the anxiety hit, I was very active in my church, in my children's activities, and with my full-time job as a bookkeeper. I loved people and adventure. My all-time goals were to be a good mother and raise three productive adults and to do well at a job I loved while studying to become a CPA.

The first panic attack occurred while I was driving down the interstate, coming home from my mother's house. I pulled off the road and thought I was going to die right there. My chest was pounding, I couldn't see where I was going, I was sweating, and my legs felt like rubber. Although it was only about fifteen minutes, it felt like hours until I was able to get back on the highway and drive the thirty miles home. I still don't remember how I got there.

After this, it was all downhill. I started having panic attacks at work. My boss was so kind that he allowed me to take the books home and work on them when I felt like it. However, the guilt of not being able to go into work got to me, so I quit, and I became housebound.

There was a period of almost six months during which my husband had to take me to the emergency room about three times a week, but the visits never helped. I learned how to manipulate the staff to take me in quickly by telling them about my chest pains. I really hated myself for doing this to people, but I had to be in control and get what I thought I needed.

My adult kids would come and sit with me when I was having what we called one of my "spells." Because I had previously been so active, everyone knew there had to be something very wrong when I couldn't even go out to dinner. I stopped eating, and in three months' time I lost forty pounds.

Four years and six doctors later, I found out I had agoraphobia. By this time I was phobic about everything. I couldn't go to grocery stores, the post office, or Wal-Mart. My husband even had to take the checkbook, as I could no longer think clearly enough to pay the bills. Since I had been a bookkeeper, this was really hard on my pride.

In 1983 I found a support group. It was the first time I'd ever met anyone who felt like I did. By the end of my first meeting I was on cloud nine. I had found hope. That was eighteen years ago.

My family was very supportive during the hard days. That wonderful husband wouldn't give up until we found help. There were so many days when I would just cry, day and night. By the time I found help, I was having at least twelve panic attacks a day, and I only got a few hours of sleep a night before waking up with another attack. I paced the floor many nights. I did lose a few friends during those years, but now I know they were part of the problem. Some people just have black clouds over them.

Through the support group I finally found a doctor who specialized in treating this disorder. He convinced me that medications wouldn't kill me and talked me into trying them. That's when I started my recovery. I also did a self-help tape program using cognitive-behavioral therapy (CBT). I practiced getting out every day, even if it was just walking a block; the next day I'd try two blocks. Then I practiced driving the car for a block or two at a time. It was a very long process of recovery, but I learned so much about myself during that time.

I now spend my life helping others. I am the moderator of the support group I started attending eighteen years ago. I help others practice overcoming their phobias. I also moderate two support lists online, and I have given speeches to second-year medical students at the Oklahoma University Medical School for the past nine years. I became president of the State Mental Health Consumer Council, and I'm active in the National Alliance for the Mentally Ill. I'm also proud that most of the mental-health clinics in Oklahoma refer people with this disorder to me. It seems I'm getting a reputation for knowing a lot about the disorder!

My life is wonderful again. I get such pleasure out of every day. I love playing with my granddaughters. I love helping fellow anxiety sufferers find their way, but most of all I have learned that I need to take care of myself. That is the most important point I try to share with people: If you don't take care of yourself, you will not be any good for others.

My future goal is to keep on keeping on. I love what I'm doing. Now that my husband works less, he and I are traveling more, and we enjoy it greatly. In fact, as soon as I finish writing this essay, we're going to leave on a weekend trip.

I wish all of you the same kind of recovery and joy that I've found, and I encourage you to reach out and get the help you need.

> *I am a member of the ADAA (Anxiety Disorders Association of America), and I attend all conferences on this disorder. I'm also a big Oklahoma University football fan. You can reach me at cburnett@mmcable.com.*

Commentary by Paul Foxman

Jan's story illustrates the progressive nature of panic disorder, and it provides an opportunity for me to describe an effective self-help program designed specifically for panic disorder with agoraphobia.

Beginning with her first panic attack in an automobile, Jan developed a pattern of avoiding situations in which she anticipated anxious feelings.

The pattern progressed to include a wide range of situations, such as work, shopping, and errands. As a result, Jan eventually became home-bound, but she continued to have panic attacks even there. Her downward spiral was reinforced by repeated treatment failures by medical doctors and emergency-room staff who did not recognize the anxiety disorder underlying her symptoms. In order to recover, Jan needed to understand that she feared not the many outside situations but rather the internal anxiety she anticipated in those situations.

Most people with severe anxiety prefer structure, and therefore they benefit most from step-by-step treatment programs. While Jan does not specifically identify the self-help tape program that helped her recover, it sounds similar to the CHAANGE program.

The CHAANGE program—developed by two women who recovered from agoraphobia with help from their therapist—is a sixteen-week, structured, step-by-step homework course. Participants may take the course either on their own or under the direction of a CHAANGE-trained therapist. The program includes most of the treatment components required for a lasting recovery, including education about anxiety, relaxation training, stress management, cognitive and behavior change, self-esteem work, and desensitization. Emphasis is on repetition and daily practice of new skills in order to replace old habits, such as worry, negative thinking, situational avoidance, fear of anxiety, problems with conflict and assertiveness, and a host of other issues associated with panic attacks and agoraphobia.

CHAANGE views anxiety as a learned behavior pattern that can be "unlearned," rather than as a mental illness or chemical imbalance. Medication is compatible with CHAANGE because it can help control distracting symptoms, but the goal is long-term recovery without reliance on medication. The broad range of new skills taught in the program makes it helpful for all anxiety disorders.

I have used the CHAANGE program with several hundred patients and find that I am repeatedly pleased with the results. Several research studies have verified a success rate over 80 percent. One study reported that CHAANGE graduates reduced their health-care expenses by 54 percent, suggesting that once people recover from anxiety they no longer waste time and money seeking unnecessary medical treatment. The program has benefited over sixteen thousand people worldwide, and it is now available in a Spanish-language version.

Learn how to obtain a free information kit about this self-help program in the Resources section at the back of the book.

CHAPTER 10

FINDING "NORMAL"

by TARA BLAZER, as told to Jenna Glatzer

Until I was thirty years old, I never knew what it was like not to have panic attacks. I was born with it, and that's what I knew.

I grew up just outside Washington, D.C. I remember a time in the second grade when I really wanted to go to an area of the playground that was farther away from the school building and covered by woods. No matter what I wanted, though, I would think to myself, "I can't go there. I'm scared to go there." Why? I wasn't afraid that the boogeyman was going to jump out of the woods. I was just scared.

Even as a little girl I analyzed myself and wondered what was wrong with me. Many years later I realized that the school building had been a "safe place" for me, and the farther away from it I went, the more the attacks came on. Whenever I walked home from school, as I got closer to home, I thought I was going to die. I couldn't breathe, and I felt like all of the oxygen was being sucked out of the air. It was terrifying. I would get home and have to lie down until it passed.

As a Girl Scout, I couldn't go out and sell Girl Scout cookies. I'd get to the nearby apartment buildings, make it to the stairwell, and have to stop. I couldn't use elevators or stairwells. Things always got worse when the seasons changed. I especially dreaded spring and summer, because I knew I would be sick during those months.

I spent a lot of energy trying to make sure other people didn't find out what was happening to me. When commercials about mental illnesses would come on television in the 1950s and 1960s, I thought,

"That's what I have. I'm mentally ill." I never had a name for what plagued me, and I thought I was the only one in the world with these strange behaviors, so I tried my best to keep them hidden. It worked, too, for a very long time.

In 1980 and 1981, when I was twenty-nine, there came a time when I couldn't hide my attacks anymore. My worst attacks happened during that period. I was working as the public relations director for the Cleveland Museum of Natural History, and we had an international press conference coming up. I wasn't nervous about it, but I knew we were short a few press kits, so I went to a bookstore to buy some extra folders. I picked them up off a lower shelf, and as I stood up, it hit. I thought, "Oh, no, here we go again." But this time, it wouldn't go away.

The attack happened on 30 June 1980, and it never let up until about 24 May 1981. A turning point came when I had to go downtown to meet with a reporter to discuss the museum. The reporter was a good friend of mine, but by the time I got there I was freaking out. He looked into my eyes and said, "Tara, what's wrong with you?" It was the most horrifying thing that I could imagine—it meant that the outside world could see what was happening to me. After twenty-five years of keeping it hidden, now it was obvious.

Prior to that, I could go into my office and close the door. People would assume I was inside working on a public relations masterpiece, but really I was having a panic attack. As terrifying as it was, the only thing that kept me going was an even greater fear of becoming a vegetable. I was afraid that would happen if I didn't keep going out and doing things.

I was going to therapists and hoping someone would figure out what was going on. One doctor told me, "I think you have a stressful job. Just relax, and stop wearing pantyhose to work." As if sandals and bare legs were going to cure me. Maybe I was crazy, but I wasn't that crazy, and that wasn't the answer! I don't blame him now, though; that was the best they could do back then. Doctors just didn't understand anxiety disorders.

I had a prescription of Valium, and I would look at that bottle some days, thinking, "I should just swallow it all, go to sleep, and let that be the end of it." But something made me say, "Don't do it. Tomorrow may be the day they finally figure out what's wrong." My tomorrow finally came.

A therapist said to me, "I honestly don't know what's wrong with you, but you're not crazy and you're never going to be crazy. I want you to go see a former student of mine. He's a cardiologist, and he's interested in learning about the mind/body interaction in disease." The time came for my appointment, and I couldn't go. I couldn't even get out my front door. I called the office to cancel, and the nurse said, "Fine," and I thought that was the end of it. I figured I could reschedule when I was feeling better.

Instead, this doctor, who had never met me, called and said, "Tara, I understand you can't come. But you have two choices: either you get in your car, come see me, and I'll help you, or you stay in your house for the rest of your life." Looking back now, I realize the doctor had a lot of experience with phobic patients!

So I got into the car and drove the four and a half scariest miles of my life. By the time I got to the office, I was really in bad shape. I thought I was going hysterically blind. As I filled out the paperwork, I couldn't even remember the year. I remembered we were celebrating the museum's sixtieth anniversary, so I counted back to figure out what year it was.

They took me into an examining room, and this bearded man in a white lab coat appeared with a hypodermic needle that looked about a foot long. I stared at it and thought, "Great. Here comes the lobotomy." He said, "You're going to have to trust me. Stick out your arm." I did, and he gave me the injection. Instantly, for the first time in my entire life, I knew what it felt like to be normal. This was what I always dreamed "normal" would feel like.

My life started on that day. All the therapy, the delving into my past, into the anger and depression—none of it had worked. And here it was—my cure, with no effort. The cardiologist told me I would have to take medication every day, probably for the rest of my life: The medication would include something to keep my heart rate even and a tricyclic antidepressant.

I said, "Oh, no. Crazy people take 'mind' drugs. If I take them, it means I'm admitting I'm crazy."

He said, "Go with me on this. Would you agree that your brain is a physical organ in your body?"

Yes.

"Insulin is produced in the pancreas, which I believe you'll agree is another physical organ. If you were a diabetic, and your pancreas was not producing enough insulin, wouldn't you put it there synthetically, any way you could?"

Yes.

"Well, your brain isn't producing enough serotonin, and we're going to fix that, and you're going to be fine."

This made sense to me. It was as if a doctor had said to me, "The bad news is you have cancer, but the good news is that we found the cure for cancer last night. There's a name for this, and we can fix it." It meant no more visits to the emergency room, no more misdiagnoses. The cardiologist was a god to me.

The injection he had given me was a superdose of Inderal, a medication to keep my heartbeat even. It combats mitral valve prolapse, a condition that is very closely associated with panic disorder. More than 50 percent of people with mitral valve prolapse will develop panic and anxiety disorders within their lifetime.

I now take nine pills a day (Inderal and imipramine), and I haven't had a panic attack in twenty years. I'm on the board at a local hospital, and I was just appointed to the American Association of Physician Specialists as the national consumer advocate in neuropsychiatry. I help to give panic and anxiety seminars at hospitals in Illinois, and now I've met hundreds of people who've gone through this. All of them, like the rest of us, didn't have a name for it and thought they were crazy. There are zillions of us, completely isolated and thinking we're the only ones.

When I speak to people, I advise them to always ask for an echocardiogram (a test of the sound of the heartbeat). Check to see if there's a physiological basis for your anxiety. Then go to your doctor, armed with information and documentation, and ask for the right medications. This disorder can be controlled. After twenty panic-free years, I'm proof of it. And you will be, too!

Tara Busser Blazer is the executive director at the Rockford Museum of Art in Illinois. She is married and has a nine-year-old son.

Commentary by Paul Foxman

Since many symptoms of anxiety are physical, it is tempting to believe that they are caused by a biological or genetic abnormality, such as a chemical imbalance or problem with hormone production (e.g., serotonin deficiency). In fact, anyone with high or chronic anxiety will exhibit an alteration in biochemistry, at least during anxiety episodes. When we are frightened, our glands produce activating hormones such as adrenaline, serotonin, norepinephrine, and a host of other chemicals that help us to "fight" or "flee" from danger. This is part of our survival mechanism—our automatic response to both actual danger and the perception of danger.

Biochemistry, therefore, is the *mechanism* of anxiety rather than its cause. Yet our biochemistry can become faulty. Why?

Alterations in bodily chemistry, such as irregular hormone production, are usually caused by chronic stress. During chronic stress, our bodies are expected to produce the "survival" chemicals on a frequent or even constant basis. This can damage the glands that produce those chemicals, similar to the breakdown of our liver when taxed by drugs or alcohol or of our pancreas due to frequent insulin production in cases of chronically high blood sugar. Thus, in a person who has been highly anxious for a long time, the body's normal biochemical responses break down. In this case, the breakdown in bodily chemistry is actually the *result* of anxiety rather than the cause of it.

What do I mean by chronic stress in a person with a long-standing anxiety disorder, such as Tara? Chronic stress consists of repeated false alarms in which the worried mind tells the body that danger is present, causing the body to go into survival mode. If this stress persists, the body's ability to regulate itself breaks down and disrupts normal hormone regulation of organ functions.

The cardiologist who saw Tara used the tools of his trade to diagnose and treat her symptoms. He treated Tara's "serotonin deficiency" with a drug designed to regulate her heart function. In other words, the medication was used to correct the body's inability to regulate itself. This helped Tara by controlling a symptom (irregular heartbeat) that produced a conditioned response: her fear of bodily symptoms.

An alternative approach would have been to help Tara understand how her perceptions of danger, beginning early in her life, were triggering her body to react in a life-or-death mode. She would learn that her thinking patterns were producing a constant danger signal to her survival center and that her natural defense mechanisms were being over-stressed. Caught early enough, she could have learned to alter her perceptions and thinking patterns, as well as calm her body down through relaxation practice. Medication could have helped her to experience what "normal" feels like, but it might not have been necessary as a long-term solution.

It is very encouraging to note that Tara is now panic-free, and it shows that even people who have suffered for most of their lives are capable of complete recoveries.

CHAPTER 11

YESTERDAY, TODAY, AND TOMORROW

by TWYLA CHOATE

My story of panic disorder began many years ago. I remember even as a child feeling very anxious. Not all the time—mostly at school, when I had to speak in front of others or when someone said something hurtful to me. My mother would say, "Twyla, you are just a nervous child." I was always fidgeting or had a stomachache. During those days, panic attacks were less widely understood than they are now.

During my teens, the doctor prescribed something my mother called "nerve medicine" to keep my anxiety under control. I was having these strange attacks, but they weren't very intrusive, so I didn't worry about them much. When I hit my twenties, things got worse. I was in an abusive relationship, and doctors blamed the anxiety on my living situation.

Instead of getting better after I got out of the relationship, my attacks peaked when I was about thirty years old. I had just been diagnosed with trigeminal neuralgia (damage to the trigeminal nerve in the face). I had suffered from it for about six months before the doctors could find a reason for my pain. After getting it under control with medication, I believed that my life was going to be better. Boy, was I ever wrong.

One evening as my husband and I sat watching TV, just having a normal night at home, I started to feel like tons of bricks were being laid on my chest. The feeling grew worse and worse as the minutes ticked by. I began to hyperventilate. I couldn't breathe. My husband rushed me to the hospital emergency room, where they treated me as if I were having a heart attack. I was finally given a shot and sent home; they didn't know what my problem was.

These attacks came more frequently as time passed. It didn't seem to matter where I was or what I was doing. It never took long for a small attack to turn into an enormous need for breath. For the life of me I didn't feel as if I could breathe deeply enough to get sufficient oxygen into my system. I spent many hours at doctors' offices, in emergency rooms, and even in my bed, praying that this terrible feeling would go away. My life got to the point where I could not work a full day without having one of my "not being able to breathe" episodes (that is what I called them before being diagnosed). I just knew that life as I had known it was on a downhill slide. Not knowing when or if this was going to happen again made me afraid to go shopping by myself, to be at home by myself, or even to be at home alone with my young son.

I began to ask myself each day if I was going crazy or if I was dying from some unknown disease. I was one of those people who loved life and enjoyed my friends, my family, and most of all my children. But it was becoming increasingly difficult for me to do any of the things I liked for fear of being unable to breathe. The worst part of the entire thing was the fact that I was a thirty-year-old mother of two boys who felt I couldn't be alone with them for fear of having one of my "not being able to breathe" attacks.

My husband and my mother never gave up on the fact that somewhere, somehow, someone would be able to tell me what was wrong. My mother had walked this same road with me while learning about my trigeminal neuralgia, and now she found herself searching for another doctor to tell her what was wrong with her daughter.

Finally, after about six months, we found a doctor who took time and listened to my complaints and fears. He asked if I had ever been told about panic disorder or panic attacks. Of course my answer was no. He described the attacks and how they made people feel. When he mentioned the fear and hyperventilation I knew instantly that he'd hit the nail on the head. I had to be the happiest woman in the world at that moment; simply knowing that my condition had a name was wonderful news.

He first put me on Xanax. I couldn't believe the difference it made. For the first two weeks I took 1.5 milligrams three times a day, to get the attacks under control. I was eventually weaned down to 1 milligram three times a day. This worked great for almost two years. Then I began having problems again. The doctor decreased my Xanax to 1.5 milligrams once per day and added Paxil at bedtime. Since I've begun to take Paxil, my life has been so different. I take these drugs every day to control my attacks, but I also am learning to control them on my own.

I have a life again. I can talk to people. I can go to the grocery store and be with my children and their friends without worry of being unable to breathe. I can't say that the attacks no longer exist; I do suffer small ones every now and again. But I now live my life to the fullest that I can, and my husband and mother are so happy for me. But no one can be as happy as I am. I turned forty-one this year and feel as if I have a whole new lease on life. My panic attacks have been under control for almost ten years, and I am blessed.

Life is looking bright. When you're feeling low, I hope you'll remember this: Yesterday may have been a terrible time, but it's gone forever. Today is looking really good, because it's the day you begin to live again. Tomorrow is looking even better, because it is your future without panic attacks.

I grew up in Forney, Texas, and now live in Elysian Fields, Texas. I am married with two sons, and I am the administrative secretary at the Cumberland Presbyterian Church in Marshall. I enjoy computers, reading, writing, and my family. My goals include raising my sons and continuing to write online for the pure enjoyment of writing.

Commentary by Paul Foxman

Twyla's story illustrates two of the key ingredients in the development of an anxiety disorder. As a "nervous child" who was "always fidgeting," she already had a biological disposition towards anxiety. She also experienced high stress, and as a young adult her anxiety symptoms peaked during an abusive relationship and when she suffered a medical problem involving chronic pain.

Twyla endured the typical downward spiral of anxiety. Like many anxiety sufferers, she sought help from doctors and even a hospital emergency service, but failed to receive a correct diagnosis for her symptoms. This added to her anxiety, and she began to fear that she was "going crazy" or "dying from some unknown disease." Although her difficulty in breathing was due to muscle tension in her chest, which put pressure against her lungs, she feared she would suffocate or die. This is why tightness or pain in the chest is often mistaken for a heart attack. These fears intensified Twyla's anxiety condition.

In my experience there are three fears associated with anxiety: going crazy, dying from a life-threatening illness, or losing control in public. None of these fears are reality-based, but they are common among anxiety sufferers until they receive a correct diagnosis and proper help. Treatment is usually unsuccessful without a correct diagnosis, as was the case with Twyla, who received "nerve medicine" as a child and a "shot" in the emergency room. Even after receiving the diagnosis of panic disorder, medication was helpful for only a limited period of time before her symptoms reappeared.

Medication is most effective when it is used in combination with psychotherapy or an anxiety self-help program, such as CHAANGE, E. Bourne's *The Anxiety and Phobia Workbook*, Lucinda Bassett's Attacking Anxiety and Depression, and others (see Bibliography and Resources for information on these resources). Based on research conducted by the National Institute of Mental Health and other organizations, the effectiveness of medication is significantly improved when combined with cognitive-behavioral therapy. It is important to understand the cause of an anxiety disorder, as well as to learn skills for reducing stress and anxiety symptoms. In addition, it is important to alter the thought patterns that trigger anxiety, such as worry and misinterpretation of bodily reactions. These self-regulation skills can continue to be effective without medication.

More physicians today are expecting their anxiety patients to participate in counseling as part of their treatment plan. They know that medication compliance and effectiveness is likely to be greater in combination with psychotherapy. I would add that the best practice would be to work with an anxiety specialist during the counseling part of treatment. This approach makes it possible to discontinue medication in many cases, once new stress- and anxiety-control skills are acquired.

CHAPTER 1 2

FINDING MY VOICE

by LISA PERICAK

For as long as I can remember the theatre was my obsession. I could not wait until I was old enough to leave home for the glamour of Broadway and eventually to conquer Hollywood, the ultimate coup. I could hardly wait for the day when I accepted my Academy Award, my Grammy, and finally my star on the Hollywood Walk of Fame. With the innocence of a child, I feared nothing. I felt anything was possible. I tolerated the academics of school so I could take part in the more favored aspects: plays, concerts, and chorus.

Aspiring to be "only" a wife and mother was not my idea of living life to the fullest. I had big plans. I rebelled against tradition and everything it stood for. I was not going to be chained to a stove with babies at my feet. I was going to prove to everyone that I could be someone. Unfortunately, my star crashed and burned before my feet ever left the ground.

So impatient was I to get away from what I felt were overly demanding parents that at seventeen (just three days after my high school graduation), I left for the Air Force, only to return ten months later with a newborn son. Everything I had rebelled against was coming to pass. At twenty-three, I was a full-fledged mother and wife. Gone were the days of theatre and fun. Instead of superstar, I was Supermom. I tried my best to be the June Cleaver of the 1980s. It wasn't me. I could never quite make it work, no matter how hard I tried. In my eyes I had failed miserably, and I felt the same sentiment reflected in the eyes of those around me. The songs that once lifted me up died in my heart before a note passed my lips. Novels that had once given me freedom from my doldrums now quietly gathered dust in the corner of my room. I told myself that responsible mothers didn't have time for nonsense. I felt I had sold my soul for a few moments of pleasure.

Panic crept up on me. It was insidious, like a plague. Little by little, I began to suffer health problems that seemed to have no origin. Breathing problems were treated as asthma or allergies. Stomach problems were treated as stress. These symptoms became more significant and prevalent. Not knowing the cause of my failing health, my doctor became more aggressive and tried more tests: upper and lower GIs, and enough blood work to make Dracula envious. The results ruled out all the possible suspects. My job was in jeopardy because of the work time I was missing. Minor things began to irritate me for no apparent reason. My husband was disgusted, my children were terrified, and I was questioning my sanity. Before long, a suicide attempt ensured my stay in a psychiatric ward. By choice or by chance, it was my saving grace. Finally, I was presented with a diagnosis: bipolar disorder and agoraphobia.

At first I didn't know what to feel. I just knew that my life had changed. I spent the remainder of that summer in and out of the hospital for various reasons. Eventually I was able to remain at home, where my marriage had begun to crumble. My husband wanted the woman he had married. I wanted my life back, my kids wanted their mother, and everyone was miserable.

Every time I resolved that a new day was going to be different, it grew worse. I spent my days in bed, exhausted from trying to make my mind work the way it was supposed to. I would call my psychiatrist and beg for his help. He would increase my medication. My flulike symptoms plagued me night and day. Leaving the house was not an option. The more I tried, the more frantic I became. Just going out the door to get the mail from the mailbox was a major ordeal. Paranoid and sweaty, I would approach the door. Trembling, I would turn the knob and open the door. Peeking to make sure no one was around, I'd gather all my courage to step ever so gingerly outside. At this point my stomach would lurch and I felt all my neighbors' eyes upon me. Running to the end of the porch, I'd grab the contents of the box and dash back into the house. This was done to the imaginary laughter of my neighbors. Locking the door and gasping as though it was my last breath, I would sink into the closest chair and sob.

Going to the store was another matter. No matter whether I could muster the courage to go myself, or whether someone physically dragged me out of the house, it was a nightmare. I prayed for death to deliver me from making the trip. I would beg someone else to grocery shop for me. Usually my mother would drag me out, saying that I needed to go and it was good for me. I hated her for it! Often I'd make it through the entire excursion without incident until I got to the checkout. I couldn't understand what the cashier wanted. I knew what she was saying, but for some reason I just couldn't comprehend. Then I felt as if she were looking at me like I was from outer space. I froze. What did she say? How much was it? Suddenly I forgot how to count! I felt the people behind me beginning to whisper and point. I would thrust a fistful of money at the cashier and pray it was enough. Grabbing my cart, I would leave as quickly as possible.

Sometimes I couldn't even get out of the car. I would wait, curled in a fetal position, sobbing until my mother's return. After a few of these excursions, no matter how she tried, my mother couldn't get me to leave the house. I didn't want any more nightmares.

Parties, coffee with friends (either in or out of the house), a few hours out with my husband—all were out of the question. However, nothing compares to the look on children's faces when you tell them you can't attend their school program. A slow, torturous death would somehow feel better than that look of disappointment from your child.

The very thought of leaving the house was terrifying now. My palms would sweat, my heart would pound, my head would throb, my stomach would churn, I'd feel disoriented, and my entire body would shake. It seemed as though everything became amplified. Colors were brighter, voices were louder, feelings intensified. Smells, sights, and sounds were so strong and loud they seemed like a cacophony of an unnatural mixture from a warped fairy tale. People seemed to look at me as if I were an object under a microscope. Paranoia increased to a height eclipsed only by heavy drug users. The need to run and hide was so incredibly strong it was unbearable. So I would run, usually to my bathroom, doubled over in pain, sit for what seemed like hours, and cry. Then I would sleep. My panic attacks were exhausting. Although an actual attack would only last about two to twenty minutes, the "recovery" time could last up to about two hours, including sleeping. To me, it seemed to take much longer.

My illness wore on my marriage, and my husband left. I moved the kids to the country to get away from the stresses of the city. I knew it was a long shot, but it was the only one I had.

I invested a lot of time in studying myself. I got a computer and started researching this disorder via the Internet. I met people in the same position who offered support, encouragement, and information. I made all sorts of changes: doctors, diet, counselors, whatever I thought would help. What worked, I kept. What didn't, I tossed. I got a workbook on anxiety and about facing my fears. I began to see progress. I regressed from time to time, but that only made me work harder. I noticed that my biggest fallback was my inability to speak up for myself. I hadn't even realized that I had lost it to begin with. I learned that the Internet was a great place to let yourself be heard without condemnation. I realized this was the key. I knew the more I practiced, the less frightening it became. My panic attacks came less frequently now. I began to venture out.

Another key was singing. As crazy as it sounds, I found that when I felt panicky, if I sang, the panic would subside. Especially when driving, I would turn the radio up and sing at the top of my lungs! When I sing I have to control my breathing and maintain a regular airflow. This suppresses the adrenaline from increasing, thereby preventing a panic attack.

My sister's wedding was my coup d'état. She planned to hold the reception at a local hotel, and family members were offered a room at a discount. Terrified, I still jumped at the opportunity. It would be my first night away from home, alone, in four years.

On the day of the wedding the priest asked who would do the readings. I hesitated. It had been so long since I'd stood before anyone and spoken. But before I realized what was happening, I'd volunteered. The time came, and the priest called me to the altar for my part in the mass.

Standing, I took a deep breath and blindly made my way to the altar. When I began to speak, the words flowed from a place in my heart I had forgotten about. I had closed myself off for so long, and now it was as if I were home!

After the service my uncle came up to me and asked if I belonged to a church. I replied that I did not and asked why he had inquired. He said he was so moved by my speaking, he felt that I should be speaking in front of more people. I nearly choked! If he only knew!

By the end of the evening I was exhausted but exhilarated. I took a long, leisurely, hot shower, ordered room service, and slept the best I had in a long time. When I awoke the next morning I realized I didn't want to leave.

I will never forget that day. I still try to get away once a year to celebrate, even if it is just overnight at a local hotel. I am back in college, continue to research my illness, and enlighten others whenever possible.

I recently found that the medications I was on (Wellbutrin, Depakote, and Valium) were major contributing factors in my agoraphobia. What was supposed to help actually aggravated my condition! I know now to research any suggested medications and to ask questions all the time, no matter how pointless they may seem. Whatever I find, I take to my psychiatrist. I have become an advocate for myself, and I make no apologies to anyone for it. I am more important to me than anyone I know.

I still battle manic-depression, but the anxiety is gone. I no longer seek the fame I once did as a child. I am now comfortable in the knowledge that I am a good mom. When that fear tries to worm its way back into my life, I sing. In finding my voice I found the freedom to live.

> *I am a budding writer from Blasdell, New York. I am a thirty-three-year-old mom blessed with a loving son and daughter. Their courage and support have given me the strength to battle the illness that has become a part of their lives. In my free time I also write poetry and essays. This is my first publication. Writing samples are available upon request.*
>
> Lisa M. Pericak
> pericaklm@yahoo.com

Commentary by Paul Foxman

Lisa could be the poster woman for panic disorder with agoraphobia. She became a homebound agoraphobic for whom going to the mailbox was an ordeal and going shopping was a nightmare. Naturally, the condition was confusing and frightening, especially when a host of medical tests could find no basis for her breathing problem.

The hallmark feature of agoraphobia is anxiety avoidance. To recover, it is necessary to face the feared situations, but to be successful, you must be prepared with new concepts and skills. Your goal is to have positive experiences in the situations you previously feared or avoided. You will gain confidence by stretching your comfort zone and handling anxiety.

Anxiety disorders are often progressive, and symptoms generally escalate in the absence of a correct diagnosis and proper treatment. For example, panic attacks often lead to a spreading pattern of avoidance. People suffering from the most advanced stages of panic/anxiety can become severely restricted and homebound. For Lisa, a mother, this included an inability to attend her children's school functions.

As do many anxiety sufferers, Lisa developed a number of secondary fears, such as going crazy, dying, and losing control in public. In addition, she became depressed about her inability to control her symptoms, and she actually made a suicide attempt that resulted in a psychiatric hospitalization. Ironically, this resulted in a correct diagnosis and effective treatment.

It is important to become your own advocate or "case manager," because many doctors and health-care professionals lack expertise in understanding, diagnosing, and treating anxiety disorders. Read books or research the Internet as a source of information about anxiety, and look for opportunities to communicate with and learn from others. Follow Lisa's lead and learn to ask questions without fear, shame, or apology. The sooner you adopt this attitude, the sooner you will find solutions that work for you.

Among other strategies, Lisa found that distracting herself by singing aloud helped to control her breathing and prevent panic attacks. Distraction techniques work best when you understand the mechanisms of anxiety and trust that you are not dying or going crazy. Other distraction techniques include talking to people on the phone, visually scanning the roads for certain models or colors of cars, counting objects such as windows, reciting the words to a song or poem, taking a walk, exercising, washing the dishes or car, and making a shopping list. The idea is to focus on something outside of yourself while the anxiety symptoms subside. Another option for coping with a panic episode is the floating technique, which involves four steps: facing (rather than avoiding), accepting (seeing the anxiety as a practice opportunity rather than an enemy), floating (relaxing the body), and letting time pass (trusting that the anxiety will end). (For more on the floating technique, refer to Dr. Claire Weekes's books, listed in the Bibliography.)

CHAPTER 13

FEAR

by GENE GILLIAM

As a child, I did not get off to an especially auspicious beginning. We were a family of very little means, other than owning our house (I think). Things started going wrong in the second grade. I fell and broke both front top teeth. Smiling became a thing that had to be camouflaged. I didn't like school, so that merely added to my feeling of inferiority.

One day when I was about eight or nine, I went crawdad fishing with three friends at a creek above a high school. We saw some older boys, and I walked toward them. My friends hung back—a good move on their part. When I reached the other boys, things went awry very quickly. They were much bigger than I was. They wanted me to give them oral sex. I yelled to my friends for help, which only sped my friends on their way downstream. I refused until the boys held my head underwater a few times and beat the shit out of me. I was forced to do all four of them.

After that, I was not only inferior, but I had an unredeemable, filthy, scummy, smelly soul. I carried that foulness around with me for most of my life. Failing my way through the sixth grade encouraged me to quit school altogether, so I did, adding actual inferiority to my already fully blossomed, but imagined, inferiority. I have never learned the multiplication tables, nor even decent spelling. I left home at age twelve and began working. Then I went into the Navy at seventeen. I got married while stationed in Memphis.

I was twenty-eight and living in Southern California when I left my unfaithful wife and our two daughters (ages seven and twelve) for the girl of my dreams. She was the epitome of all the virtues I thought I lacked. She was also very unhappily married at the time. I'll call her Betsy.

About eighteen blissful months later, we had a son. I opened a TV repair shop in Apple Valley, and she went to work as a secretary. Things were hard money-wise and time-wise for both of us. She wanted to move back to the Midwest, and we did. After a marathon drive, we arrived on a Christmas afternoon. I was introduced, in my exhausted and very emotional state, to more than fifty of her relatives, and I was able to remember all of their names, interrelationships, and most of their jobs—an incredible feat for me.

Work was all but impossible for me to find. It was the 1960s. I had been an engineer at Hughes Aircraft when Betsy and I met. I was told that I was overqualified to pump gas or work on assembly lines, though I would have done that gladly until I could find something better. But I was an alien in a strange land. The people around us didn't change jobs. They retired from the job they'd taken right out of high school. I was failing and I knew it.

Betsy left me, taking our son. I still couldn't find a decent job, other than with a shyster TV shop that I hated working for. The owner insisted that I bring in every other television for a picture-tube replacement, and I detested doing that. One day a customer came in and asked if we did any custom electronic work. The boss said no. I said, "What do you want?" The customer said, "Something that will tell me about my golf swing and that I can use anywhere." After thinking for a minute or two, I said, "A hundred dollars a week, plus materials. I'll work at home. Figure ten weeks." He thought a moment and we shook hands on it. My boss was flabbergasted when I asked for my check and told him I was leaving. The custom work would earn twenty dollars a week more than he was paying me. I thought it was a great idea.

For Betsy, that was the last straw. She saw it as irresponsible. She started divorce proceedings, and I didn't contest anything she wanted. My feelings were at an all-time low. They went much lower when I heard what the judge had to say to me: "I have no proof of your marriage. Therefore, I am annulling it. You are to have no contact with the boy. He becomes the responsibility of her previous husband. There are no alimony or child-support payments. But remember, no contact. Next case."

I just stood there dumbfounded; then I finally made my way out of the building, feeling completely transparent to anyone who cared to look into my slimy, scum-filled soul. That feeling got worse as time went on. I was too ashamed to even go into a bar for a beer. The fear of being around people got to be overwhelming, because I felt they could see into my eyes and find what a worthless, faulty, soiled human being I was.

I completed the golfing machine to the man's satisfaction. He was the only person I could speak to, and even then I kept my head down. I felt I had to be very careful not to reveal too much of myself. My lonely world would have been nearly completely dark without the light of my acquaintance with this man. He asked to borrow my Ruger .22-caliber pistol. I doubt whether he had ever fired a pistol before in his life. His idea of wanting to borrow an unfamiliar firearm seemed fabricated and devised on the spot when I told him I owned a gun, so I assumed he thought I might try to use it on myself. I think he just didn't want to take a chance that I would regress and do something like that, but the thought had never occurred to me. I've seen neither the man nor the pistol since. But that's okay. I miss the man far more than I miss the pistol.

I knew I was in deep trouble, mentally and emotionally. I had always felt inferior, but now I was desperate. It's like swimming with hungry sharks: When you're at the bottom, you have no other choice. You have to swim. You may get badly chewed up on your way to the surface, but unless you're eaten, there is still a possibility that you will have a chance to breathe once again. I wasn't seeking normal. I needed to get a breath or I would die.

My ex-wife made an appointment for me to see a psychiatrist. It took just one visit for him to recommend that I go to a hospital (read: loony bin), but it was full. I bought a dictionary of psychological terms and decided I had damn near every symptom listed in the book.

A job came up at the University of Michigan. I took it, not without a little concern. I would work for Dr. James Olds, in the department of brain research. At the beginning of the interview I told him that I was emotionally screwed up, but that I would do the best I could. He responded, "Wait until you meet my wife."

We succeeded in training a single brain cell in a rat to fire on demand. Meanwhile, I stayed as far away from contact with people as I could. I had no social life whatsoever. When the job was finished, my boss recommended me for a position with the high-altitude research lab. My supervisor at the lab thought I should get out more, so he bullied me. (Okay—it was gentle bullying.) He talked me into attending the Ann Arbor Civic Theater workshop. I went about three or four times and finally read a scene or two, seated in a chair, scared out of my mind.

The next time tryouts were held for a play, the workshop director insisted I go to the tryouts. I had thus far never even seen a play, and I was sure I could not stand up in front of people and do anything but try to hide. Still, I went to the tryouts. I mustered the courage out of a desperate need to rejoin society. I didn't know the name of the play I was trying out for, and I hadn't seen the movie that was made from it. But I ended up playing Richard Burton's movie role in *Night of the Iguana*, a story of a crazed, alcoholic, defrocked priest, reduced to driving a tour bus in Mexico—not a role I would have chosen in my state of mind; I was trying to conceal my inferiorities, not display them.

On opening night, once I was onstage, my knees trembled until I said my first lines. At that moment I actually felt the audience joining with me, an astonishing feeling. To my utter amazement, the production was a success, and I was hooked on banging the boards. I tried out for every play that came along, and I got into most of them. I even joined the Ypsilanti Players and appeared in a few of their productions.

At one point I was in two simultaneous productions and rehearsing a third. My fears of people seeing what a sullied creep I was began wilting. The praise I received about my performances greatly improved my self-esteem.

I began oil painting about the same time. Then I discovered stone and metal sculpture. These successes built on each other to begin shoring up my rock-bottom self-esteem. But it was slow going and tedious. It took about four years before I could finally feel somewhat at ease around other people. My swim to the top of the shark tank was nowhere near as direct as I would have hoped—I was gnawed on often—but I made it. Now I'm fortunate to call many people friends and to have them call me the same. My son found me after thirty-five years. His mother did, too. We all keep in touch often and happily. They live near Orlando, Florida. I live in Point Arena, California.

My old fears are gone. New ones have taken their place—generally, the same ones that affect most ordinary people (but I have to say I don't really think I'm very ordinary, and I don't know anyone who is). Although going onstage still terrifies me, I do it. It has proved good for me, as has expressing myself in other arts. I've sold just about every painting and sculpture I've made. In my early sixties I started writing. I haven't made a dime from it and I don't care. I've found that it's far more exposing than any other art form I've tried.

To anyone who is ashamed, or feels inferior, or feels unworthy of calling yourself a person, I heartily recommend just sucking it up, being prepared to fall on your face harder than the law allows, and getting out there through whatever means are available—even if, and especially if, you're trying something brand new. You will find the real you—not the "you" that has been your fear, but the "you" that has unstoppable potential for enjoying yourself and others. I can say this with more than a little authority: Get up! Go out! And *do* it! So what if you fall down? That's why they invented getting up.

You may not notice the immediate rewards, but then along will come a day when you wake up in the morning, the birds are singing, the sun is coming up brightly, and you actually feel like singing. But don't try singing loudly unless you're pretty damn good at it. On the other hand, have at it. It's your day, after all. You're no longer crippled by fear.

Bless you and sleep well.

> *For the past twenty-five years, I've been moored snugly in Point Arena, California, graced by many friendships and learning about various arts when I'm not working at being an electrician. I'm living my bliss with friends and my cat, Show Time, who may be more blissed than I, but not more blessed.*

Commentary by Paul Foxman

As a victim of violent sexual abuse in childhood, Gene suffered for many years from damaged self-esteem. Sadly, he viewed himself in harshly negative terms, as having an "unredeemable, filthy, scummy, smelly soul," and as a "worthless, faulty, soiled human being." It is understandable that Gene quit school, struggled with underemployment, suffered from a host of symptoms, and avoided people and social situations to an extent bordering on agoraphobia. It is unfortunate that he did not receive help earlier in life.

Damaged self-esteem is the basis of self-sabotage in relationships and career. People with low self-esteem tend to compromise easily and settle for less than they deserve. They put themselves down, shy away from learning for fear of making mistakes, and avoid the risks inherent in close relationships. If you fit this description, you need to improve your self-esteem in order to enjoy a fulfilling life. How can this be accomplished? How does self-esteem develop?

Under normal circumstances, good self-esteem begins to develop in childhood as a result of praise and positive input from parents, teachers, and other significant caretakers. We internalize this positive attention, which becomes the basis for recognizing our strengths, talents, and other unique attributes. Ideally, we also learn that love and attention are not contingent on achievements alone—that we are worthy no matter what. Self-esteem continues to develop throughout life, as a result of mastering new skills and achieving personal goals. Without the necessary positive reactions in childhood from significant adults and other children—or worse, when we experience negative input or trauma—we fail to develop the attitudes that enable positive self-esteem to develop.

Admittedly, it is more difficult to build high self-esteem in adulthood if the foundation for it is weak. Nevertheless, self-esteem can be improved through a process known as *reparenting*. This approach involves being your own objective evaluator and giving yourself the positive, rational feedback that would ordinarily flow from other sources. Here are some specific suggestions for building high self-esteem:

- Talk to yourself respectfully and compassionately, as you would when addressing a friend

- Make a priority of learning new skills, as Gene did (even when he was frightened to do so), in order to experience mastery and feelings of accomplishment

- Keep a diary of your strengths and positive attributes, and add to it periodically

- Invest money in your own self-improvement by attending seminars, workshops, and other learning activities

- Accept compliments by making eye contact and saying "Thank you"

- Avoid comparing yourself to others; there will always be people who have more than you and those who have less

- Do something positive for yourself each day

- Replace self-criticism with encouragement

- Replace thoughts that begin with "I should…" or "I have to…" with those that start "I choose to…" or "I want to…"

- Set reasonable goals and make plans to achieve them; goals are best achieved when the steps toward them are small and within reach (e.g., for the goal "I will lose twenty pounds," you might start with the steps, "I will call Weight Watchers this week, and I will walk for twenty minutes three evenings this week")

- Improve your health through regular exercise

- Treat other people the way you would like to be treated

- Learn how to advocate for yourself, express your opinions, and ask for what you want

- Learn how to say, "No, thank you," without feeling guilty

- Make a list of activities that bring you pleasure or gratification, and do them regularly

- Join a therapy group to learn interpersonal skills and to receive feedback in a safe learning environment

CHAPTER 14

KICKING OUT AN UNWELCOME GUEST

by JILLIAN SANDERS, as told to Jenna Glatzer

Growing up in Winnipeg, Canada, I didn't have a "troubled childhood." In fact, I had a great family life, and I loved my parents and younger brother and sister. My panic disorder seemed to come out of nowhere when I was eighteen years old. I was the lead singer in a full-time band, traveling all over the place and making great money for my age. I was very much in love with my boyfriend, and I was happy with where my life was headed.

Then, one night in September, I was lying in bed reading. I remember the smell of burning fields wafting through the house even though the windows in my room were closed. (Many Canadian farmers burn excess hay in the fall after harvest. They claim it makes the soil better for when they reseed in the spring.) I was reading the book *Flowers in the Attic*, by Victoria Andrews. It's funny how good I am at remembering such detail from fifteen years ago, yet I can't remember what I wore yesterday!

All of a sudden I started to get a heavy feeling in my chest. Then I started to feel clammy. I felt my legs go numb and I wanted to cry out to my mom, but everything went into a state of unreality. I felt like I was outside of my body. I was sure this was what going crazy felt like. I couldn't muster the strength to scream, so I crawled up the stairs and into my mom and dad's bedroom, and said, "Mom, wake up. I think something is very wrong. I may be having a heart attack." (Just writing this, even now, brings back the absolute terror I felt at that moment.)

My mom woke up and put her arms around me. I was shaking like a leaf. She said, "It's okay, Jillian. I think you are just having an anxiety attack." What the hell was "just an anxiety attack" when I felt like I was dying? I could not sit still. She tried to lie down with me and attempted to talk me down from my inescapable rush of adrenaline. I feared that if by any chance I was able to fall asleep I would die. It was like having your foot stuck on a railroad track with a train coming towards you. Once she eventually got me to lie down, she recited a few stories she'd read to me as a young child. The consistency of her soothing voice eventually lulled me to sleep. This was about three hours after the attack started.

After that episode I made an appointment with my doctor. He was sure it was anxiety disorder from the start, but I was still convinced that I was either going completely insane or having severe heart problems. I had many more attacks after the initial one. My brother drove me to the emergency room one night because I couldn't regain control of my body or mind. My heart rate was so out of whack that they admitted me to an observation unit for an overnight stay to monitor my vitals. This scared me even more, but they put an Ativan under my tongue (my first experience with an antianxiety drug), and within fifteen minutes I had calmed down quite a bit. Then I went for extensive testing to rule out any other problems: blood work, echocardiograms, electrocardiograms, you name it.

My doctor referred me to a psychiatrist who pulled out his little pad right away and wrote out a prescription for antidepressants. I told him, "But I don't want to take pills. I want to do this on my own." He said, "My dear, if you don't take these pills, then I can't help you." I never went back to him.

For about two years panic totally ruled my life. I was a full-time musician, on the road most of the time. Other than telling my band members, I tried to hide it from the public. I was afraid that if promoters and agents found out, they wouldn't see me as "dependable," and their opinions would be prejudiced against me. Nevertheless, I ended up having to cancel gigs because of this disorder, which was so bizarre to me, because I have always felt the most secure when I'm onstage. Everyone, including doctors, found it strange that I remained comfortable onstage, considering the grip panic held on the rest of my life. I think it was because onstage I became someone else: "Jillian the singer" instead of "Jillian the girl with panic disorder."

Most of my friends did not understand what panic disorder was, but they were very accommodating. This wasn't always a good thing, because their "coddling" enabled me to give up in a lot of circumstances when I otherwise wouldn't have. My mom was especially understanding. I found out later that she, too, suffered from anxiety attacks. Even now I still receive support from all of my friends and family —except for my husband. He has never understood panic disorder; therefore, he's used the "tough love" route to deal with it. If I felt a panic attack coming on when we were in bed, he would say, "Relax, go to sleep. It's all in your head."

I was prescribed Ativan at a dose of 1 milligram three times a day. However, I am not a big fan of prescription drugs, so to this day I only take it when I absolutely cannot control the attack—that is, when the attack has gone too far. In addition, a psychologist referred me to group therapy for people with panic disorder, a program that was directed by a behavioral therapist. There, I was among people like myself: nurses, doctors, flight attendants—people who I never imagined would "lose control" as I had.

I didn't agree with some of the techniques the therapist used to help us. For example, he purposely got us to bring on symptoms of a panic attack to learn that those symptoms were not the result of a heart attack or of going crazy. We were told to spin around on stools and make ourselves dizzy. This brought on hyperventilation, which triggered a number of the familiar panic symptoms. The only thing I really got out of the group was learning that I wasn't the only one in the world with this disorder.

What finally worked for me was keeping a journal. I wrote down where I went every day, and how I felt, what people said to me, and how I reacted. Then I would write down all of my symptoms. I would read through the journals when I was having a good day, and over time I realized a pattern: I noticed I could easily cope with any situation at hand that needed coping skills. It was only after the situation was no longer a "situation"—when my coping skills were no longer needed and I had let my guard down—that panic would try to overtake me. I also noticed that my anxiety was especially high whenever I was menstruating, which is only about four times a year, since I have polycystic ovarian syndrome.

I still use many tricks of the trade. Since I know I usually get cold and shivery when a panic attack starts, I run my feet under hot water when I sense it happening. If I ever felt one coming on while I was on-stage (which was seldom), I would put an ice cube in my boot. That seemed to "shock" me out of having a panic attack. Some anxiety sufferers wear a rubber band on their wrist and snap it to "jolt" themselves out of an attack; I've used that trick. And I've carried sheets of paper with words of wisdom written on them, like, "What you are feeling is not a heart attack. You will not die. You are not going crazy." These might be silly mental things, but whatever works, right? I have also discovered that aromatherapy and sound therapy help me.

Now I refuse to allow panic to enter into my daily routine. I refuse to make allowances for it. I've learned to listen to the warning signs of an attack coming on. I used to swear they came out of the blue with no warning, but after reviewing my journal entries I realized there were patterns. I now change stressful or anxious thoughts into positive thoughts as soon as they come to mind. This means I think right away of an "alternate route" for my mind to travel. Instead of dwelling on the negative, I try my best to find the positive.

I choose to let the anxiety appear whenever it feels it needs to get out, but I don't fight it; I fly with it! I let it run its course while I remind myself that it will go away. The less attention I pay to it, the better off I am. Life is so much more fun this way. I can travel long distances on planes, trains, buses, and cars. I can be the "me" I want to be and not have to worry about what people would think if they knew my secret. My goals are the same as they were before I acknowledged my disorder: I want to live a healthy life with a healthy mind and soul.

If I were to meet someone today with a panic disorder, the number-one thing I would say is "You are *not alone.*" I would stress that they rule their body and mind, and that they can overcome this. They can be boss. In the beginning, panic takes over your whole life and will remain in control if you choose to let it. Instead, may you soon discover, as I did, that life is too short to live it under panic's rule.

> *I am a full-time music teacher of voice, piano, and theory. I live in the small town of Saskatchewan, Canada, but hope to move back to my hometown of Winnipeg, Manitoba. My husband and I still do the occasional live gig as a duo when we have a free weekend.*

Commentary by Paul Foxman

Jillian was an outgoing musical performer before developing panic disorder. She led a busy life of travel, singing with a band, and active socializing, all with no anxiety. We can safely assume that stress overload was responsible for triggering her panic disorder. Of all the recovery methods she tried, Jillian found journal writing to be the most helpful. What is a journal and how can journal writing be helpful in anxiety recovery?

A journal is a series of personal writings in response to daily life. Going beyond a diary, which typically describes events of the day, a journal includes personal reflections on the meaning of daily experiences. Think of your life as a journey through time and your journal as a travelogue, or an interpretive record of your trip.

Journal writing creates opportunities to see patterns in your thoughts and feelings. For example, you may discover that most of your worries are variations on just one or two basic fears. Or you may find that you become anxious at certain times or under particular conditions. By recognizing the underlying issues, you can deal more effectively with them.

Writing personal reflections in a journal is similar to meditation; it helps clear and slow down your mind, which can be relaxing and can reduce stress. It also trains the mind to be more objective about your thoughts and feelings and allows you to learn from your experiences in ways you might otherwise miss. Furthermore, journal writing helps you recognize unreasonable thoughts and irrational feelings and to become less reactive to or controlled by them.

Although there are many choices, the tools for keeping a journal are simple. Select a format that fits your lifestyle. You can use your computer if it is accessible daily, or you can write in a small book that you can carry with you. Some people like writing on unlined paper while others prefer lined paper. Your choice of writing tools is unlimited and includes fountain pens, colored pencils, interesting gel pens, and more, but consider using permanent ink that will not fade with time. Since your journal is personal and private, find a way to ensure its confidentiality, such as keeping it in a locked location or keeping it with you at all times.

To get started with journal writing, try focusing on the best and worst thing that happens to you each day. Note ideas about what you could have done differently or about improvements you want to make in the way you respond in various situations. Emphasize your feelings, and develop a vocabulary for your emotions. If you feel good about something, write about why it was positive.

Here are some further suggestions for therapeutic journal writing:

- Write on a regular basis, preferably daily
- Date each entry to keep things in perspective
- Write whenever and however you want to, although you may benefit from writing at a specific time of day or in a specific location
- Be totally honest with yourself in your journal writing

CHAPTER 15

WINNING MY BATTLE
WITH ANXIETY

by ELLEN M. DUBOIS

I was very outgoing as a child. Throughout elementary school and high school, I'd stage plays in front of my parents, sing to records, and put on shows. Nothing scared me and my aspirations were high.

I began college as a theatre major and switched midstream to a communications major. I pictured myself as the Next Big News Anchor. I even auditioned impromptu at the Connecticut School of Broadcasting and was accepted.

At the age of twenty, during my sophomore year in college, I lost most of the sight in my left eye. To say I was frightened is an understatement. I was terrified. But I handled it like a trooper, even on those nights when I was alone in the hospital not knowing what was wrong with me. When family visited, I appeared strong. At night, I cried alone.

Shortly after I got out of the hospital I went to see a stage production of *Fiddler on the Roof.* I remember it well because that night was the first of many, many terrifying experiences. It was when I had my first anxiety attack.

During the show, my heart began racing so fast I thought I was dying. My chest constricted and I couldn't get enough air. I hyperventilated. The more I panicked, the worse it got. I ran up the aisle of the theatre and headed straight for the phone. I needed to talk to my parents. I didn't know why, but their voices were what I needed to hear. I thought I was going crazy.

We contacted my doctor immediately to see if any of the medications I took for my detached retina were the cause of these symptoms. The answer was no. I was told to go home and lie down. The subject wasn't brought up again, but I continued suffering panic attacks in agonizing silence.

About seven months after my loss of sight, I was out with my fiancé. Suddenly I couldn't see with *both* eyes open. My heart began to race as we rushed to the hospital. By the time we arrived, my verbal and motor skills were gone and the entire left side of my body was numb. You could have cut off my left arm and I wouldn't have felt it. I was screaming inside, but when the nurse asked me to describe what I was feeling I couldn't form any words (although I knew what I wanted to say). I thought for certain that I was either having a stroke or dying of a brain tumor.

Fortunately, neither was the case. I was diagnosed with what's called a *classic migraine*, which impairs verbal and motor skills. I regained those skills in about twenty minutes, and then I got the worst headache I'd ever had in my life. The doctor said it was stress induced. It hasn't happened since, thank God.

And that was that.

As time went by my attacks came in waves. They subsided for some time while I was in college, but shortly after I got married they seemed to come out of the blue. They didn't happen often, but each time they were frightening. I didn't know then what I know now, and as I reflect back I can see that I literally talked myself into a worse frenzy.

I didn't have the courage to seek help. I thought this was something I just had to live with. Doctors had examined me for additional eye problems and for the classic migraine, and all of the test results indicated that I was just fine. So I went on with my life.

When I was twenty-five, at sixteen weeks pregnant, I suffered a miscarriage. The baby didn't abort itself; it died in my womb and the doctors had to remove it. When I got home from the hospital I wanted to grieve, but my husband and I were on different wavelengths. He thought I should get on with it and over it, but I just couldn't let go of my loss or my grief. That's when my anxiety attacks came back with a vengeance. I endured heart palpitations that were so frightening I thought I'd have a heart attack. I worked for a ski area and commuted to New Hampshire, many times driving several hours alone on weekends. I suffered some horrific anxiety attacks while driving. My husband didn't really understand what was going on or sympathize very much. I can't blame him for his lack of understanding, but it didn't make matters easier. I kept everything inside, where it festered.

When I was twenty-seven, my husband and I split up. My anxiety attacks grew worse; I almost reached the point where I couldn't function. But I forced myself to. I went to work, I drove even when my hands were so numb I couldn't feel them, and I talked to people—when inside it took every ounce of strength I could muster to appear "normal." It was exhausting. I was petrified. I couldn't eat alone for fear I'd choke. I couldn't eat in restaurants for fear of embarrassment. I'd stare at a plate of food and feel starving with hunger—yet unable to get it down.

The advent of my divorce was the catalyst to my seeking professional help. What originally was to be marriage counseling turned out to be individual talk therapy. I knew my marriage was over, but the anxiety needed to be dealt with, and the therapy proved to be the beginning of my journey.

Adjusting after the divorce while also dealing with anxiety attacks, proved quite challenging. The situation was multilayered. I found that talk therapy helped not just with the divorce but also with the anxiety. The talk therapy ended after about a year and a half, when my therapist moved to another state. However, the knowledge and insight I'd gained was invaluable and put me on the path to recovery. I did extensive research on the subject of anxiety and read countless self-help books. I was always reaching for more answers, more assurance. As a result, I learned how to deal with the attacks. The negative self-talk and the fear of loss of control diminished as I developed the ability to handle the attacks with my mind by gently talking my way through them.

They didn't completely go away, however.

In 1996, I met the man who is now my fiancé. One of the biggest challenges he helped me to meet, unknowingly, was facing my anxiety. He is a pilot, and on one of our earliest dates he surprised me with a trip to the airport to take his plane for a flight.

I'd never been on a small plane, and as my heart raced madly, I decided to face my fear. That flight was one of the most beautiful things I've ever experienced. Had I succumbed to my fear, I would never have seen the exquisite moon and stars on that clear and magical night. That taught me a wonderful lesson: I was stronger than my anxiety. I just needed to draw upon my strength.

In 1997, I went to a new primary doctor for severe intestinal pain. She had only a brief idea of my history, but after asking me several questions she wisely came to her diagnosis. She told me that I had a stomach condition caused by chronic anxiety disorder. I began talk therapy again, on her advice, and started taking a small dosage of the medicine Klonopin to relieve some of the symptoms of anxiety.

That year I also became the lead singer of a band that played at weddings. During my audition my anxiety got so bad that I could feel my knees knocking and my lips tingling. Try singing like that! But somehow I made it through and got into the band. At more than one gig I felt my hands and mouth get tingly and my legs begin to buckle. But I made myself perform. I think doing so pushed me further into discovering my own inner strength. If I could handle an anxiety attack in front of three hundred people (and believe me there were moments when I clung to the microphone stand to hold me up), then I could conquer this!

I have continued my research on anxiety. I still read many books dealing with the subject and put into practice many of the psychological exercises that help keep anxiety attacks at bay and/or under control. I no longer use talk therapy, but what I learned in the process will stay with me forever.

The fight against anxiety disorder is not a battle that's won overnight, although the disorder seems to appear overnight. The road is long, and there are many ways to effectively treat anxiety. The most important factors contributing to your recovery are the support of those who love you, your own understanding of the disorder, holding onto the faith that you will overcome it, and the knowledge that you are not alone in your struggle.

Believe me, you are not.

> *I am a Massachusetts writer. I am engaged and have a dog who loves to critique my work. I have several cards in market review with SPS Studios Inc. (the publisher of Blue Mountain Arts), am published in volume two of* God Allows U-Turns *with my piece "The Angel in the Dumpster," am a featured writer in the online magazine SpiritHunter, was a featured writer in the* National Association of Women Writers Newsletter, *and have two books under contract for e-book and paperback publication. One of my dreams is to keep writing so I can continue to touch the hearts of others.*
>
> *Please visit* Writings of the Heart, *my award-winning writer's resource site, at http://writingsoftheheart.homestead.com/index.html, and my inspirational site, http://writingsoftheheart.homestead.com/inspiration.html.*

Commentary by Paul Foxman

It is common for people with panic disorder to experience their symptoms as "coming out of the blue." A sudden "attack" of intense, physical symptoms—such as chest pain, racing heart, or difficulty breathing—is one reason why this form of anxiety is so frightening and why fears of having a stroke, heart attack, or brain tumor come to mind. Unfortunately, these associated fears serve to intensify the physical symptoms and create a vicious cycle of anxiety.

Ellen's symptoms resulted from stress. Consider the loss of vision in one eye at age twenty that preceded her first panic attack. In addition, Ellen experienced a miscarriage and a divorce. No one—including her doctors—recognized stress as the source of her physical symptoms or of the anxiety this triggered, so her anxiety disorder went undiagnosed and untreated. Ellen's condition spiraled downward, and she developed anxiety associated with driving, eating, and being in public.

One of the steps in recovery from panic disorder consists of changing your "inner dialogue." This vital step—which is how Ellen learned to overcome "negative self-talk and the fear of loss of control"—involves a new way of talking to yourself about what is happening. Instead of frightening yourself with fears of dying or going crazy, tell yourself that your symptoms are natural reactions to stress and that they are not life threatening. Begin to trust that your symptoms will go away when you understand this. At the same time, practice methods for calming yourself (such as deep breathing), and focus on reassuring or positive thoughts. Talk to yourself as if you were talking to a friend who was experiencing the same symptoms and irrational fears. Internalize your knowledge of anxiety, and become your own support person who can evaluate realistically what is happening and can reassure yourself.

In addition, I advise gradual exposure to feared situations (also called *desensitization*) for reversing the pattern of avoidance that often develops in an effort to control anxiety. Generally, the best way to approach this step is to make a list of your uncomfortable situations, relax and visualize yourself in each situation (as though watching yourself in a video), and then take steps toward encountering each situation in real life. In both the visualization and reality stages, start with the least uncomfortable situation and work up to the most uncomfortable situation. Expect some anxiety as you face your feared situations, but know that this is necessary to make progress. Focus on situations that you *really want* to overcome, because strong motivation is helpful. It takes only a few exposures to eliminate a particular fear.

For Ellen, this process was accelerated by a date with a pilot who offered to take her on a romantic two-person flight. Her desire outweighed her fear, and she decided to take the risk. Since the outcome was positive, she gained confidence that she could overcome other fears. You, too, can face your fears and conquer anxiety.

CHAPTER 16

I NEED TO TEACH!

by TRAUTE KLEIN

What turned an outgoing person like me into a woman afraid of everyone around her? How did I lose touch with the people with whom I'd had personal relationships, people who used to share my life?

It happened in an instant, in an unpredictable moment frozen in time. A drunken driver plowed into my subcompact vehicle, destroying my confidence, robbing me of my dreams, leaving me unable to comprehend the world. I remembered little of the circumstances, except that I had been involved in an accident. My demolished vehicle offered sufficient evidence of it. I remembered the physical injuries because the constant pain was difficult to ignore. I did not, however, remember that the driver had almost run me over in an attempt to avoid arrest. That detail was simply too painful to deal with, and I blanked it out. I also didn't recall much from the following years, even when I was reminded of specific incidents or when I read about them in my diary.

The physical pain was intense. The emotional pain was unbearable.

I had been an educator with all my heart and mind. Teaching was not only my profession; it was my calling. I loved people, and I loved life. That life faded into a faint memory, like a movie that I had seen but could not quite recall. It seemed unreal, removed by eons of time. The people who had been my friends appeared distant and unreachable. They soon withdrew, unable to relate to the new me. That did not surprise me. I was unable to understand myself. How could I expect anyone else to understand me?

The biggest shock occurred when, during a psychological test, I was asked if I liked children. I answered no. My response stopped me cold. How could I, who had taught every age group from two to eighty-two with great enthusiasm, now say that I did not like children? I tried to erase the answer from the page, because I could not admit my feelings, even to myself.

In the years following the accident I received no help with either the physical pain or the emotional turmoil. Various health-care providers diagnosed me as suffering from post-traumatic stress disorder, but no help was offered. The insurance company that should have been paying for therapy was intent on proving that I was putting on an act in order to defraud the system. It refused to pay for my living expenses, insisting that I return to teaching. Deprived of my means of survival and unable to receive help, I sank into dark despondency.

Eventually I found a chiropractor who took my injuries seriously and provided me with effective treatment, even though he received no payment until years later. He saved my life by giving me hope.

As soon as the physical pain abated, I started to search for ways of pulling myself out of the quagmire of despair. I no longer looked to the medical establishment for help. I knew that I would have to find my own way back to at least a semblance of the life I had known, and that life meant teaching. I also knew that I did not have a snowball's chance in hell of ever being hired again as a teacher or university lecturer. All my medical reports stated clearly that a teaching position was out of my reach, yet I was uninterested in any other job. Where would I find a teaching opportunity that I could handle?

A senior center near where I lived needed a volunteer German teacher for a weekly ninety-minute class. I had to try it, and I did. The seniors were most appreciative. Volunteers are hard to come by, and they are treated gently. I proved to myself that I could handle that situation, but I was not yet satisfied. To regain my confidence I needed to be with an age group who would be less considerate of my handicaps than the seniors had been. I had to be with children. They would treat me as they would treat anyone else, making no allowance for personal problems. I felt such an overwhelming need to be in a classroom that I devised an alternate plan. If I could not be a teacher, I would become a student. That would at least get me into the environment I loved.

After having taught at the university level for almost a quarter of a century, I enrolled as a regular student in the local high school, taking one course at a time. Schools now offer a great variety of interesting subjects that no one had ever heard of during my school days. I delved into creative courses like graphic arts and woodworking. Classes lasted for just over an hour a day, and that was about the limit of my ability to concentrate. I loved it. The teachers enjoyed having me. My classmates treated me like one of them. They had no idea I had been a teacher myself. For all they knew and cared, I could have been a high-school dropout who had come to her senses late in life. None of them knew of my post-traumatic stress disorder. It felt good to be accepted as a peer, even if it was by students a third my age. I knew that I had received full acceptance when one of the teenage boys shared his fears with me. Thinking that his girlfriend might be expecting a baby, he asked me whether I would tell my mother if I got pregnant. I told him, "I don't think I need to worry about that anymore."

My success in school made me bolder. Was I ready for the next step? Would I be able to handle a classroom of children? After years of avoiding social situations I started to attend a neighborhood church where no one knew about my former life and I was able to make a new start. When the Sunday school needed someone to launch a music program, I was approached, and with the cooperation of the other teachers I was well able to handle the new endeavor. That task was soon enlarged when the preschool Sunday school teacher unexpectedly resigned shortly after the beginning of the season, since I was the only person who could possibly replace her. I had no choice. I was needed. I agreed to fill in just until someone could be found to perform the task on a regular basis, but things went so well no one bothered looking for a replacement.

The group was small enough to present no discipline problems. All the children knew me from having sung with me. That class gave me back my dream. The emotional pain I had suffered had given me a compassion I had not known before, and the children responded to it with an outpouring of love. I became more than their teacher. I became their substitute grandma. They went home Sunday after Sunday and shared with their families whatever they had learned in class, and soon parents were telling me of the changes they had noticed in their children's lives.

I now know that I was and always will be the teacher I wanted to be. Granted, my dream has not turned out as planned. Maybe it has surpassed my expectations. I dreamed of being a successful educator. I dreamed of teaching people how to learn. I did not dare to dream of changing lives, but that is exactly what is happening in this small class of preschoolers, as well as in their families. My dream has not only come true, it has reached a higher level than I dared to expect.

The road back to life has been hard, but by taking one little step at a time I have learned to conquer the despair of post-traumatic stress disorder through faith and determination. I don't know where the road will lead me next, but I know that I don't want to turn back.

My name is Traute Klein, a.k.a., Traute the BioGardener. I grew up in a Europe torn apart by World War II and its aftermath. Surrounded by a loving family, I overcame the horrors of hatred and destruction by concentrating on the beauties of life: art, music, and faith in the goodness of God. My family escaped to Canada to live in peace. In my teens I felt a definite call to teaching, and that call has been a compelling force in my life. My teaching career was cut short by a traumatic car accident, but I now reach as many people on the Internet daily as I ever taught in the classroom. All my life I have felt a commitment to living in harmony with the creator and his creation. My teaching is now focused on passing that commitment on to the next generation. I write regular columns on holistic living, natural remedies, and organic gardening. Visit my Healing Hug website at www.healinghug.com.

Commentary by Paul Foxman

The severity of Traute's physical injuries makes this a complex case of post-traumatic stress disorder (PTSD). Without more details, I can only speculate that Traute sustained a brain injury in the car accident that affected her memory, concentration, general comprehension, and other cognitive functions. As a result, her road to recovery proved long and frustrating.

In spite of her physical pain and cognitive deficits, Traute's story illustrates the gritty determination of the human spirit. She had a burning desire to teach again, and this sustained her through many years of despair and painfully slow recovery. We can all take a cue from this woman's faith and creative problem solving. Even when the odds seem overwhelmingly against us, we must never lose hope.

One unfortunate reality of post-traumatic injury resulting from auto accidents is the adversarial nature of the liability-insurance and legal systems. Insurance companies usually attempt to determine who was at fault and to control the cost of damage repair. Damage to a vehicle is one thing, but the cost of personal injury, where pain and psychological symptoms are involved, is much more difficult to establish. Naturally, the insurance company representing the "at fault" driver needs to be sure that the injured victim is not "malingering" or exaggerating her symptoms for financial benefits. However, when a victim's credibility is challenged insensitively, as in Traute's case, the settlement process can become another trauma.

Traute used the gradual-exposure process known as *desensitization* to approach her goal of returning to classroom teaching (desensitization is also described in the text and commentaries of Chapters 15 and 20). She sought opportunities to test her abilities under controlled conditions, such as taking one-hour classes as a student, working as a volunteer teacher with seniors, and teaching a small class of Sunday school children. Her confidence increased through this "one little step at a time" approach. This method is appropriate for reentering any anxiety-arousing situation, including socializing, driving, traveling, public speaking, and many others.

In addition to memory loss and impaired concentration, a host of other symptoms are typically found in post-traumatic stress disorder. These include nightmares, intense distress on exposure to reminders of the traumatic event, sleep disturbance, emotional numbing, flashbacks, avoidance of anything associated with the trauma (such as thoughts, feelings, or conversations), irritability or outbursts of anger, depression, and feelings of detachment from other people. Steps toward recovery include relaxation practice, cognitive-behavioral counseling, and medication.

A recent development in treatment of post-traumatic stress disorder is EMDR (eye-movement desensitization and reprocessing). This technique is used in psychotherapy and involves making rapid, back-and-forth eye movements while mentally picturing the traumatic event. A growing body of research substantiates its effectiveness—often in a few sessions—in reducing symptoms. This form of treatment has been used for a wide range of survivors of trauma, including combat veterans, crime victims, sexual abuse victims, and accident victims, and some insurance companies have approved its use.

CHAPTER 17

GROWING UP FAST

by CHRISTINE EVANS

I'm a thirty-four-year-old mother of three from Sydney, Australia. When I was a toddler my family moved to the outback, where my parents owned country pubs (hotels); we returned to city living when I was eight. Throughout my teens we lived in the eastern suburbs of Sydney, where I became quite rebellious. I moved out of my home at age sixteen and was pregnant the next year. The father of my baby girl stayed with us for a few years. When that relationship came to an end I moved in with my sister and her husband. I had my first panic attack when I was twenty-one. Following the attack I was agoraphobic for three years.

My life now is wonderful. I'm recently divorced, but I have found a wonderful partner whom I love dearly. My children are the light in my life, and they bring joy and meaning to it. I am a nail artist, and I enjoy creating unusual nail-art designs. I also love reading, meditating, and listening to music. I'm very optimistic about my future, but things didn't always look so bright.

When panic struck I was young and in the prime of my life. It was 1988, and life was about going out and having fun. But that soon changed!

One night my friends and I went out nightclub hopping. We started the evening at a club near my home, and we were enjoying a few drinks when—BANG!—something hit me. I thought, "What the hell is going on? My ears are ringing and I feel like I'm going to pass out! Oh my God…my heart! I think I'm having a heart attack. I have to get out of here!"

I left my friends and headed for home. I don't remember how I got there. I went straight to bed, but could not sleep. The room was spinning and I thought I was going to throw up. "Ohhh, please, God," I prayed. "Let me get through this night!"

The next morning I woke up with the ringing still in my ears. I figured I definitely had some awful condition. I woke my sister early and said, "You need to take me to the doctor. Something is terribly wrong with me!" We arrived at the doctor's office and he examined me. He said I was suffering from tinnitus and it should pass in twenty-four hours. With that, he told me to go home and relax. But how could I relax when I *knew* I was dying?

Weeks passed and nothing changed. I became a virtual prisoner in my own home, just sitting there in a state of total panic and waiting to die. My family decided it was best for me to start seeing a psychiatrist. I agreed to go, but I knew he could not help me. All he did was prescribe drugs each week, drugs that I never took. Why would I want to feel more dizzy and sick? I knew I didn't need those drugs. I knew I was suffering from some mysterious, deathly illness the doctors had overlooked.

I lived like that for three years. It was a very lonely time; my friends had a hard time understanding what was "wrong" with me, and since I didn't fully understand it myself, I found it very hard to explain to people. I don't know how I got better back then, but my struggles with panic did slowly diminish and I started to live an almost "normal" life again. I hoped it was over for good, but panic disorder wasn't done with me yet!

I met the father of my other two children when I was twenty-three, and we married. Daniel, my youngest child, was born with multiple problems and was diagnosed as having a developmental brain abnormality. His troubles prompted me to learn about child development and behavior. Daniel required constant medical attention and spent the first two years of his life in hospitals. Maybe the strain of these extra duties led to the breakup of my marriage.

The panic and anxiety returned a couple years ago. Strangely, it wasn't at the time of all the added stress in dealing with my son's issues and with a failing marriage, but rather when things started to calm down (which, apparently, is quite common). My children knew their mom was "sick," and I was determined to get better. I decided to learn about this disorder, and I started a website, which continues to grow as I learn more.

I believe my disorder to be genetic in nature, as some of my family members (my mother, my aunt, and my daughter) suffer the same affliction. My research has taught me that I do not need to suffer. With a combination of techniques including meditation, breathing, and positive affirmations (described in more detail on my website) and with the help of medication (which I'm no longer terrified to take), I no longer live in a world of terror. I've conquered the agoraphobia, and although I still have some phobias (fear of flying and claustrophobia), each new day feels like a blessing.

I have found an inner peace, and I thank God for allowing me to experience the "bad" times, because without them I probably would not have developed the compassion for others I feel today. We really do learn the most about ourselves during our trials. I believe everything happens for a reason. For me, the "reason" has been the opportunity to become a stronger, more loving, and more spiritual person. I have started a journey to discover my purpose and meaning in life, and I'm learning the true meaning of inner peace. In place of the symptoms of panic and anxiety disorder, I'm striving to achieve the following "symptoms" of inner peace:

Symptoms of Inner Peace (by Anonymous)

- a tendency to think and act spontaneously rather than from fear based on past experience
- an unmistakable ability to enjoy each moment

- a loss of interest in judging other people
- a loss of interest in judging self
- a loss of interest in interpreting the actions of others
- a loss of interest in conflict
- a loss of ability to worry
- frequent, overwhelming episodes of appreciation
- contented feelings of connectedness with others and with nature
- frequent attacks of smiling through the eyes and heart
- an increasing tendency to *let* things happen rather than to *make* them happen
- an increased susceptibility to the love extended from others, as well as the uncontrollable urge to extend it

Wouldn't it be nice to achieve all of these qualities?

I enjoy working on my website, reading, arts and crafts, and romance and comedy movies. My dislikes are scary movies (I have enough adrenaline already), flying (because I'm such a chicken), and crowded shopping malls (they freak me out). You can visit my website at www.anxietyselfhelp.com to learn more about the methods and techniques I have used to combat anxiety. I feel that my mission now is to offer education and support for those experiencing persistent anxiety, panic attacks, phobias, fears, and obsessive worry.

Commentary by Paul Foxman

Christine's anxiety story could be renamed "Finding Inner Peace," because it illustrates some of the special benefits of anxiety recovery. In dealing with anxiety, she discovered inner peace and became a stronger, more loving, and more spiritual person.

As with many cases of panic disorder with agoraphobia, Christine's condition developed as a result of multiple stresses. Indeed, her "growing up fast" refers to a cumulative history of stress and responsibility that included a teenage pregnancy, a divorce, and a special-needs child. One important point about stress is that its impact doesn't always hit during the stressful times, but often after things calm down. This happens because during stressful periods we rally all of our energy and resources to cope with immediate issues, but then pay the price later when things stabilize. This is one reason why anxiety symptoms sometimes seem to appear out of the blue.

Stress management is an important part of anxiety recovery. Of course, it is better to manage stress at the time it is occurring; doing so will help to prevent the impact of stress and anxiety symptoms. I recommend three steps for stress management, which I call the Three-S approach:

Step one is recognizing the early warning *signs* of stress. These include tension, fatigue, sleeping difficulties, and moodiness or irritability.

Step two involves identifying the *sources* of stress, such as life changes, work problems, relationship issues, and so on.

Step three consists of adopting appropriate *solutions* to stress. This means making the necessary adjustments to reduce stress and engaging in stress-recovery practices that will address the sources of stress in your own specific case. Christine used reading, meditating, breathing exercises, nail art, positive affirmations, and listening to music for stress reduction. Other stress reducers include exercise, increasing rest and sleep, hobbies, outdoor recreation, gardening, writing, or whatever activities give you feelings of relaxation, positive energy, and a sensation known as *flow* (when you become one with the activity and lose awareness of time, or as it's stated in one of the "Symptoms of Inner Peace," "an increasing tendency to *let* things happen rather than to *make* them happen").

What comes to mind when you think about the *opposite* of anxiety? Most people think of qualities such as peace, serenity, confidence, and freedom, many of which are the goals of spiritual or religious practice. Furthermore, some of the methods for counteracting anxiety are similar to spiritual practices such as meditation, quiet reflection, study and reading, participating in a supportive community, and spending time with nature. Thus, as Christine noted, there is an interesting overlap between anxiety recovery and spiritual development.

Christine's physical symptoms—ringing in the ears, dizziness, and perceptual distortions—frightened her. These sudden, unexplained, and disorienting symptoms created additional anxiety and a fear of dying (from a "mysterious, deathly illness the doctors had overlooked"). With good cause, you, too, may lack trust in your doctors when they tell you there is nothing wrong. After all, when suffering from anxiety, you know something is wrong. But what is wrong is not what you fear. While it is important to rule out a medical basis for your symptoms, it is equally important to diagnose the anxiety disorder so you can begin the process of recovery as discussed throughout this book.

CHAPTER 18

A PRISONER FOR LIFE: MY PHOBIC EXPERIENCE

by TERESA ROBBINS, LPN

The First Half of My Life

My name is Teresa. I am a lifelong, recovering agoraphobic. I have lived with anxiety for more than fifty-three years. I am grateful for the opportunity to share the account of my struggle. I hope recounting events in my life will comfort individuals who may be experiencing feelings of isolation.

People suffering from agoraphobia, anxiety, and panic disorders can learn to live more independent lives. The achievements I have reached have proved to me that a person can indeed get better. Over the course of my recovery I was able to create another version of myself that was better able to handle stress and better equipped to go out into public and hold a job.

I did not experience one particular incident that triggered my problem with anxiety. Instead, I believe that I was born with the tendency to be extremely shy and withdrawn. I seemed to always have been sensitized to outside people and places. For me, there was only one safe place: home.

When I was taken outside of my safe place, I would go into a trancelike state. I remember as a young child trying to ignore the people around me. I focused on playing with little toys and making up elaborate stories in my head. I would often sit in the corner with my back to everyone. I refused to talk even though I had an enormous vocabulary. I looked calm on the outside, but inside I felt like running away. I was usually frozen to the spot. I had trouble hearing at these times. I could tell that my parents were speaking to me, trying to get me to say hello to people or to smile or answer questions. I wouldn't respond. I hated being focused on and wished that I were invisible.

The first panic attack I can recall happened on my first day of grade school. I felt like I was going to die. My dad took me into the classroom, but when he pulled away from me to leave I started to hyperventilate, almost fainted, and threw up in front of the whole class and my teacher.

By fourth grade I had been put on some green liquid medicine for "my nerves." I had a constantly upset stomach. I now think I was developing an ulcer. I either couldn't eat or I threw up my breakfast every single morning. My stomach was empty most of the time. Things got worse when I had to go to high school. I ended up in the hospital within three months. I was tested for every known medical condition. No physical problems were discovered in all those tests.

The doctors decided that my problem must psychological in nature, but I was discharged from the hospital with no diagnosis. In 1961, you did not see television ads about social anxiety and medications like Paxil. People were afraid to go to psychiatrists because only "crazy" people went to head doctors. My parents did not believe in "shrinks" and had no intention of taking me to see one. I was given the advice to "snap out of it!"

Looking back, I can see how this disorder affected every decision I made throughout my whole young life. The agoraphobia held me back from living a full life, limited my education, trapped me in an unbearable marriage, and even brought on a depression that lead to my being suicidal. I was unable to attend college, hold a job, go out with friends, drive a car, go grocery shopping, or take myself to a doctor or dentist. During the entire period I would take the phone off the hook and refuse to answer the door.

By age twenty-seven I had decided that I was a terrible person who deserved exactly what I was getting, because I was weak and lazy. I forced myself to enroll in a nursing program and took the bulldozer approach to going to school. The classroom work was bearable because it was a small school and I was a good student. The clinical days, however, were a living hell. It was like I was right back in first grade again with the nausea and vomiting every morning. In fact, my stomach symptoms were worse than in my schooldays, because I was also pregnant at the time and endured extreme morning sickness along with my regular "phobic stomach." This pregnancy ended in miscarriage.

I became terrified that I would make a mistake that would harm a patient or cause someone to die. Due to visual distortions I had trouble reading directions in patients' charts or on labels. It was hard for me to think straight enough to make a decision or to concentrate or remember medical facts and information. It did not help that our instructors rode us like drill instructors. They found every little way they could to criticize us, and the criticism always took place in front of an audience such as a group of doctors or other nurses. This scrutiny made me feel like a bug under a microscope. I couldn't breathe.

I was frequently ridiculed about my nursing uniform being wringing wet with sweat. My legs wobbled and my heart seemed about to jump out of my chest. I always felt like I was going ninety miles an hour. I endured a continuous panic attack each day of my clinical training. Finally I graduated and got out of that living hell.

I thought I would go to work in one of the hospitals after graduation. Instead, I immediately took to my bed for the next four months. I was unable even to think about taking a job as a nurse, especially in a hospital. I stayed in that bed, didn't get dressed, didn't read or watch television, didn't eat, never talked to anyone, and just looked at the ugly lavender wall in my bedroom-slash-prison. I had worked so hard to get through nursing school, yet now, for reasons unknown to me, the task of getting a job seemed impossible. I felt like a fake and was scared to death I would be found out as a fraud. I lacked absolutely any confidence.

After four months I called a psychiatrist who had been recommended to me by one of my nursing instructors. He was a wonderful and caring doctor. He rescued me from my depression by prescribing Elavil, and he diagnosed me with agoraphobia with anxiety/panic disorder. He convinced me that I was not at fault for how I was feeling and acting. He said I had something wrong with the chemicals in my brain. He told me the chemicals were out of balance and that I should stop blaming myself and feeling guilty. There was a physical reason for my depression, and it was not my fault. He gave me medication to correct the imbalance.

I was now twenty-eight years old, and finally I had a name for what was wrong with me. This knowledge gave me tremendous emotional relief and was the beginning of my recovery from phobia. My recovery has been a very individual process and I have employed many diverse approaches. Some worked for me and some didn't. Positive self-talk and refusing to project an outcome have been the most valuable tools I've learned to use.

The Second Half of My Life

After about three months of drug treatment with Elavil, I began to experience some improvement from my depression. However, the drug also produced weird side effects. I was unable to drive because my perception of the width of the street was very distorted. I slept twelve to sixteen hours a day and suffered constant dry mouth and terrible constipation.

On the positive side I began to experience some good days, felt less fatigued, and became interested in my life again. I embarked on weekly therapy sessions with my doctor with very positive results. He introduced me to the idea of using support persons and of making dry runs to practice going to new places. A dry run consisted of driving to the new place a few days before I actually needed to go there, in order to find out exactly where it was located, to discover what parking was available, and to note landmarks around the site. All this would make the place easier to find later, when I'd be feeling anxious. During a dry run

I could also note the amount of traffic at the time of day I would be arriving and needing to park, find the most accessible and least frightening entrance to the building, enter the building with the help of a support person, and locate the reception area, water fountains, bathrooms, and closest exit.

Around this time I became pregnant with my oldest daughter and stopped taking my medication. Because I had suffered several previous miscarriages, I remained at home during the pregnancy. My therapist had cancer and died just before my daughter was born. It was a big blow to me and my recovery. I knew I was having a relapse. After the birth of my baby I again had trouble leaving the house on my own.

I started seeing another therapist, who put me on Tofranil. The medication worked well for me, but the therapist knew little about anxiety disorders. I took a job in a small nursing home. Since I had been unable to work right after graduating from nursing school, I didn't feel current in my medical knowledge. I quickly discovered that this made me feel overwhelmed and incompetent. I stayed in that job for almost two years, but I was just as stressed as I had been in nursing school. My weight dropped to ninety-eight pounds, and my marriage fell apart.

I tried three more times to work in a nursing-home setting, but my stay at each job was shorter than the last. Although I had an aptitude for nursing, I believe I should never have entered the medical field. When I finally accepted that, I started looking for a way to use my nursing knowledge in a different way.

I also searched for a new therapist—one who had actual experience working with people who suffered from anxiety disorders. I continued on my medication, with Xanax added for panic attacks. My goal with my new therapist consisted of working only on being able to keep a job. I put everything else on hold.

A position for a nurse as a community-health instructor became available. My therapist helped me to apply for the position. I was hired and immediately had to learn a lot of information in a short period of time. Instead of being nervous I was excited. I enjoyed the feeling. This was a new experience for me. I was to teach sex education at a different school each week. I had to drive a staff car some of the time. I had to go to new places and do health screenings and teach other classes during the summer. It was definitely a challenge. I used support persons, including fellow students, teachers, friends, family members, and coworkers who were aware of my problems with anxiety. I informed my supervisor that I suffered from a mental disability and asked for accommodation. I made dry runs to the school locations on the weekends so I would know where I was going. I spent many hours before a mirror practicing teaching the material.

I'll never forget the first class I taught. My mouth got so dry that my tongue stuck to the roof of my mouth. The teacher whose class I was instructing left the room and got me a glass of water. It turned out that I was a natural with the kids and fell right into the job. In no time I was receiving wonderful evaluations from the teachers whose classes I taught.

I performed that job for more than seven years, which was the longest period of continuous employment during my adult life. I used skills I didn't even know I possessed. I wrote several training manuals and developed handouts, transparencies, and flip charts. I taught others how to be instructors and gave speeches to business groups on health issues. One of my proudest days in that job was the day I taught in one of my own daughter's health classes.

Today I am retired due to health problems that resulted from a heart attack I suffered in 1998. I am still interested in health issues, so I write articles for several online publishing communities. I am also very interested in web design and have designed sites for myself and others.

My recovery has consisted of antidepressant medication, professional counseling, establishing a spiritual relationship with the God I believe in, prayer, attending support groups, and reading and using self-help guides on coping with anxiety. I am currently taking Paxil, but I am not seeing a therapist at this time.

The most important thing I have had to remember is that recovery is an ongoing process. Like those who attend AA meetings for alcoholism, I prefer to say that I am a "recovering" agoraphobic. As long as

I keep the fact that I have this condition in the very front of my brain, I am better prepared to deal with any situation where my anxiety may again rear its ugly head. I must challenge myself to retain my abilities. I must prepare for new experiences and use what has worked for me in the past. The day I become complacent about my phobia is the day it will sneak up behind me, catch me off guard, and produce a panic attack. That seldom happens today.

I am a fifty-three-year-old nurse and teacher who has taken early retirement due to health problems. I am married to a truck driver, and we have two grown daughters. Our home is in Missouri, where we also live with a Lhasa apso and a yellow tabby cat named, of course, Morris.

I have written articles and stories for online publishing communities for the past year and a half. You can find my writing on these two sites:

My Editor Site at Suite101.Com: www.suite101.com/welcome.cfm/death_and_dying

My sex education website: www.sexualityedu.com

My main areas of interest include writing articles on health issues, sexuality education, self-help, recovery programs, and death and dying. I also occasionally enjoy writing children's stories based on my own childhood experiences.

My hobbies include interior design, gardening, pet care, Southern cooking, American cultural history, online research, and web design.

I have designed and managed the following personal Internet sites:

My original site: http://pages.ivillage.com/resa526/index.html

Teresa's Online Journal, Struggling with Multi-Infarct Dementia: www.geocities.com/resa526/journal2002a.html

Commentary by Paul Foxman

There are fewer lifelong anxiety "prisoners" today than in the past due to increasing medical awareness, new treatments, and social acceptance of mental-health services. Nevertheless, as Teresa did, some people have endured anxiety for many years as a result of receiving improper medical care or none at all. Until relatively recently you might be considered "crazy" if you sought psychological counseling or psychiatric treatment. Twenty to fifty years ago many of the anxiety disorders we can treat successfully today did not even have names, and treatment was often limited to hospitalization or powerful tranquilizers with unpleasant side effects.

Fortunately, through her nursing-school instructors, Teresa's anxiety was identified. She was referred to a psychiatrist who diagnosed her condition as agoraphobia with panic attacks (now known as panic disorder with agoraphobia), along with depression. She was treated effectively with a combination of medication and cognitive-behavioral therapy.

Teresa also found that developing her spirituality, reading about anxiety, working through self-help guides, and attending a support group helped her cope with anxiety and live a satisfying life. Group support in particular is invaluable in providing inspiration and hope, and for sharing new skills and knowledge. Ideally a support group should have an experienced leader who can keep a positive focus on useful skills and information and discourage "symptom swapping."

Teresa regards herself as a "lifelong, recovering agoraphobic." What does she mean by this, and what can you expect in terms of recovery? Must you always suffer from anxiety, or can you put it behind you and live a "normal" life?

Anxiety recovery can be defined as having the skills and confidence to handle anxiety, whenever and wherever it might occur. Anxiety recovery does not require a change in your basic personality or disposition, although it is necessary to modify the way you think, handle feelings, communicate, and interact with others. Nevertheless, due to the biological sensitivity factor, you will always be somewhat at risk for stress symptoms and strong reactions to outside forces. In order to maintain your recovery you must continue to use what you have learned, particularly as it pertains to stress management. For example, exercise, adequate sleep, and proper diet are important on an ongoing basis. Many people go beyond *recovering* to *recovery*, where they are able to function without giving a thought to anxiety.

Teresa indicated that she was born with a tendency to be shy, withdrawn, and sensitive to outside influences. These traits are examples of the genetic or biological component in anxiety. While Teresa's basic disposition did not change, she learned new skills that enabled her to deal more effectively with life. She can realistically expect to control or eliminate her symptoms, including the avoidant (agoraphobic) patterns used to protect herself from anxiety. Having been familiar with anxiety for so many years might make it difficult for Teresa to trust her new level of recovery, but she's made great progress, and with time she may feel more comfortable with the knowledge that anxiety never has to inhibit her life again.

CHAPTER 19

IN THE RING WITH OCD

by JOHN WELDON

OCD (obsessive-compulsive disorder) entered my life in 1989, one year after high school, at a time when my life conditions were rapidly changing. It started with horrible thoughts of violence, like scenes from an action film. In my mind I would see machine guns appear in the air and fire off wildly by themselves, mowing down anyone who was in their way, even in church. I was not holding the guns in these scenes; I only witnessed them. I also had thoughts of committing violence against my family, mostly my mother. On rare occasions they were so powerful I would throw up. One night I locked myself in my room just to get rid of the anxiety, but I found myself in an anxiety attack and I threw up five times.

I also had thoughts related to religion. My mind would blaspheme God, Mary, Jesus, and the church. Around Thursday of every week I began to fear going to church on Sunday, knowing I would have an anxiety attack and wondering if I could stand it.

Over time I ran the full gamut of obsessions: thoughts of cancer, of gaining weight, superstitions, fears of dirt and germs, sexual thoughts, and probably at least a few dozen more I cannot even remember.

In 1990 the first ray of light came through. After going through numerous counselors I was at my wit's end wondering what was wrong with me. In desperation I went to a bookstore, and after two hours of searching for anything that might shed light on my condition I found on a bottom shelf a single copy of *The Boy Who Couldn't Stop Washing*, by Judith Rapoport. It was like opening a door with the sun right behind it. Brilliant light shone on my situation. I bought the book immediately.

But upon reading it that night I became disappointed, because the book spoke about numerous types of rituals: washing hands repeatedly, checking locks, counting things—all behaviors I hadn't experienced or even heard of. For the next several months I wondered if I had OCD. I felt lost.

The next year I finally received an official diagnosis, and some time later I entered a major hospital program. There, I received training in cognitive-behavioral therapy, but at first it failed to really take. Six months later my father died, and a series of unrelated events made 1992 one of the worst years of my life. I continued with the behavior therapy, but only made halfhearted efforts at it.

In the spring of 1996 I decided to take greater action. This period marked seven years of OCD, and that was important to me because that made it the problem I'd had longest in my life. I determined to tackle OCD head on, and so I began a thirty-day intensive self-treatment program. I didn't require supervision because after seven years I knew what I was doing.

The "thirty-day program" lasted nearly seven months. It was a day-to-day, toe-to-toe slug match between OCD and me. The makers of the *Rocky* films couldn't have staged a better fight. I attacked all of my obsessions repeatedly in daily sessions lasting thirty to sixty minutes or longer. I used endless loop audiotapes to record the obsessions over and over again, a technique of exposure I had learned some years earlier. I also put myself in places where I knew obsessions would occur. For example, to fight blasphemous obsessions I would spend time in church, often listening to the audiotapes at the same time. Between April and November I didn't miss a single day of battling this disorder.

At the end, both the OCD and I were like exhausted boxers; neither of us had any energy left. But so exposed had I been to my thoughts and fears that there was no anxiety left. The anxiety was "knocked out," and though I've since sometimes dealt with anxiety over real situations, I've not had a single OCD-related attack. While I still catch myself ruminating at times, the obsessions that taunted me for so many years no longer have the energy to even whimper.

Today I have a college degree and teach in a major school district, and I am completing my teaching credentials. I spend my time working, studying a foreign language, volunteering in church-related activities, and going places with friends.

What would I say to those suffering from OCD? *Slug it out until the end.* If you are just starting out, you need professional help. But if you've been through the ropes of behavior therapy for many years, even if, like me, you were previously uncommitted, you may not need additional professional help. In any case I probably would have done even better had I enlisted the support of friends and family. If you need medication, take it, but realize it is not a cure. Also, educate yourself as much as possible about OCD. The famous ancient Chinese general Sun Tzu once said that if you know yourself and your enemy, you will win all the battles. So gear up, arm yourself, and defeat this difficult but defeatable enemy.

My name is John Weldon and I am a native of Southern California. I am a substitute teacher in the public schools; I currently hold a long-term middle-school special-education position. My interests include study of the social sciences and of the Russian language, which I've studied both at home and in Russia. I am a graduate of Cal State University in Los Angeles, with a B.A. in social science. Contact me via e-mail at Jjwmail@aol.com or at ibec756@yahoo.com or by phone at (310) 823-2760.

Commentary by Paul Foxman

Obsessive-compulsive disorder (OCD) consists of either intrusive, recurrent, and unwanted thoughts or compulsive, repetitive behaviors. In some cases both features are present. OCD is a distressing form of anxiety that usually interferes with a person's ability to function comfortably and pro-ductively in daily life.

The primary issue in OCD is control. John's obsessive thoughts about violence, for example, were anxiety arousing because he feared they would take over and he would lose control. The prospect of losing control, of course, creates even more anxiety.

OCD can also be thought of as an effort to control anxiety, especially when it involves compulsive behavior. For example, a need to repetitively check the toaster, iron, or stove is usually driven by anxiety and self-doubt: "Did I really check it? What if I just *thought* I checked it? What if there's a fire while I'm asleep?" In other cases compulsive cleanliness may be used to control anxiety about germs or contamination, or a com-pulsive need to be on time may reflect anxiety about being late. That is why anxiety usually *increases* when the OCD sufferer tries to stop the ob-sessive and compulsive patterns.

It is important to distance yourself from obsessive thoughts. The OCD sufferer experiences objectionable thoughts as virtual reality, whereas the rest of us can dismiss them as unrealistic or simply "weird." The treatment of OCD, therefore, requires a new way of looking at your own thoughts and behaviors. Developing this new viewpoint involves sev-eral steps.

The first step in overcoming OCD is to relabel obsessive thoughts as a manifestation of anxiety. Say simply, "Oh, that's my anxiety acting up" or, "There goes my obsessive thought pattern." Try to avoid identifying with the thoughts, and refuse to give in to the fear of losing control.

Second, practice relaxing every single time you have a distressing thought. It is essential to learn how to tolerate and manage the anxiety that is likely to increase in the early phases of recovery from OCD, when you are experimenting with new ways of reacting to your symptoms. To do this, cultivate the techniques described in earlier chapters to help you relax or "float" through anxiety episodes (see Chapter 2, as well as books by Claire Weekes, listed in the Bibliography).

Third, refocus your attention on more productive activities. This cog-nitive-behavioral approach is described by Jeffrey M. Schwartz in *Brain*

Lock: Free Yourself from Obessive-Compulsive Behavior (see the Bibliography).

Fourth, educate yourself about OCD to help end your fear of anxiety symptoms. This is not a life-threatening illness, and you can overcome it with practice.

In addition, professional guidance is recommended, but seek a therapist with expertise in OCD. The cognitive-behavioral approach in particular has been shown to be effective in changing brain chemistry.

Finally, medication can be helpful when symptoms are so intrusive or distressing that you cannot focus on learning new skills. But keep in mind John's comment: "If you need medication, take it, but realize it is not a cure."

CHAPTER 20

SMALL STEPS

by GAYLENE

I suffered with panic and anxiety for approximately ten years before I was diagnosed. I also suffered from social anxiety and generalized anxiety while growing up. I tried to avoid high school by going to the doctor each Monday morning with a different complaint. If the doctor had picked up back then that I had chronic anxiety, I may have avoided the roller-coaster ride I endured until age thirty-three.

Over the years I suffered a great deal of loneliness and missed out on many things due to my anxiety. I was a shy child, afraid to go to friends' houses because doing so meant leaving the comfort zone of my home. Once when I was about ten and tried sleeping over at a friend's, her mother had to drive me home in the middle of the night because I was terribly anxious about being away from home. I avoided parties because I was so shy and afraid I wouldn't fit in.

I started to "doctor-hop," complaining of a variety of symptoms, in hope that one of them would find a physical cause as to why I felt awful most of the time. They sent me for many tests. I've probably undergone every test that exists, all of which came back negative. Some of the symptoms disappeared after I was told I didn't have whatever I thought I had; but soon thereafter I would produce a new symptom, and it was off to the doctor again. If I had a pain in my leg I would think, "Oh my God, thrombosis." If I had a headache lasting several days I would think, "Oh my God, a brain tumor." I believed that each of the physical symptoms produced by anxiety was a symptom of a serious disease.

When I was about fifteen a doctor suggested that I was "stressed" and prescribed Valium three times a day. *Finally*, I was getting somewhere— or so I thought.

I took the Valium as told, and, sure, it made me feel better, so I kept taking it. But I became dependent on it, and that started a whole new ball game. I was now addicted to the medication that was supposed to help me. I guess it helped that I wasn't strung out with anxiety all the time, but I had to wean myself off the Valium and start all over again. I did this with great trouble, and all my physical symptoms returned. Once again I began doctor-hopping, and once again I got nowhere. I plodded through the days to the best of my ability. I always found an excuse for not going places with my friends, and I was unable to hold down a job for very long. Working was too stressful and only added to my symptoms.

When I was twenty-four, my father was diagnosed with bowel cancer and underwent emergency surgery. I experienced my first crippling panic attack on the stairs of the hospital where he was admitted. I was told that I was very stressed and needed to rest. However, with my father sick and since I was an only child, I refused to rest. My parents had divorced when I was eight, and neither of them remarried, so I took on a lot of extra responsibility. Eventually my father became well again. He went back to work, and I was left to figure out how to "fix" me. Obviously I hadn't taken the best care of myself while I took care of him.

With the stress of my father's illness gone, things settled into some sort of normalcy. I moved about fifty kilometers away from my childhood home and tried to build a life in a more relaxed atmosphere. Being away from home, however, only made things worse. I became even more isolated than I had been, so to rectify that problem I joined a gym, where I met my husband-to-be. We began planning our wedding, scheduled for November 1994, and things were going reasonably smoothly when my father was once more diagnosed with cancer, this time of the esophagus. The roller coaster was off and running again.

During what is traditionally assumed to be the happiest time in a young woman's life, my father was ill and needed me to take him to hospital appointments and doctor appointments. He agreed to be part of a treatment experiment, which entailed a five-week stay in a cancer clinic. A catheter was permanently placed in his heart, and he wore a device (which we called his Walkman) that pumped chemotherapy medication into his body twenty-four hours of every day. I stayed by his side the whole time, knowing how I would feel if I were left on my own during a period of such distress. He seemed to cope well—probably a lot better than I did. The combination of dealing with his illness and planning my wedding was extremely stressful to me.

It soon became apparent that my father's treatment was failing. The doctors put a plastic tube into his esophagus to help him eat and drink, and decided there was nothing more they could do to help him. My father was dying. That was a terrible shock to me, even though I had watched him deteriorate over the months. All hope was gone. He didn't want to die the same way he had witnessed many of his fellow clinic patients die, so my fiancé and I agreed that he would come live with us so I could take care of him.

My father passed away in mid-October, after six weeks of my caring for him. I got through the funeral and related events only because I went numb. My wedding day came five weeks later. I carried many different emotions but went ahead with it anyway.

After we were married I finally broke down. I was working part-time in a geriatric hospital, and I could feel the stress building each day. I knew I wasn't coping well. I would cry upon waking and have to make myself go to work. Then I would have to make myself stay there and do the work to the best of my ability while enduring palpitations, blurred vision, sweating hands and feet, and an inability to concentrate. It was a real battle. I pushed myself too far, and one day I had a panic attack at work. I ended up in a ward hooked up to an ECG machine and being reassured that I was under a great deal of stress and that nothing else was wrong. I found that hard to believe considering the physical symptoms I was experiencing.

I went home wondering what the hell to do next. Then the agoraphobia hit. I was afraid to leave the house in case I had another attack.

I quit my job. I was afraid to be on my own, so my mother came over daily around 6:00 A.M. to be there when my husband left for work. She stayed with me all day, talking to me and urging me to do things and to eat. She left at night when my husband came home from work. The situation was taking its toll on all of us, but I couldn't control it so it continued for the next two months.

I became afraid to take a shower, afraid of food, and afraid to get out of bed. I was having a breakdown. Eventually, with the support of my mother and friends (the ones I had left), I managed somehow to pull myself out of it. I had a fear of medication, so I was unable to take antidepressants or anything else. I had read a lot of books on the subjects of anxiety, panic, and depression. With all my medical tests and with the knowledge that I had been under a great deal of stress, I realized I was suffering from total exhaustion as the basis of all my symptoms.

Starting on the road to recovery required a lot of willpower and strength. I took things at my own pace, day by day, with little steps. I made deals with my mother for her to come over just a little bit later in the morning, after my husband had left for work, to see how I coped. I wrote lists of things to do the following day. I didn't realize it at the time, but I was desensitizing myself to the situations that had caused me severe distress. It wasn't always pleasant, and I endured a great deal of anxiety, but for the most part I did okay. Small steps were the way I eventually made a full recovery.

On those days when I didn't achieve the steps I'd set for myself, I learned how to be kind to myself and not to expect too much. As the months passed I gradually did more and more, and the more I did the better I felt. So I continued to push myself just a little bit harder. Eventually I was doing things without thinking about them and life was actually normal. When I was able to get around on my own I found myself a good psychologist who suggested I learn cognitive-behavioral therapy. This skill has been invaluable for me; it has worked wonders! It has changed my thinking, and I practice it every day.

Unfortunately, the breakdown took its toll on my marriage and we divorced. These days I am living on my own and am very happy. I am lucky enough to be in a relationship with a wonderful, caring man whom I love dearly and someday hope to marry. I have done more in the last two years than I ever thought possible. I have driven miles and miles from my home on my own for vacations, I have climbed mountains (literally), and I have flown in a little plane. I still have a problem flying, but I am working to conquer that fear. I will do it; it will just take some more time, and that's okay!

I now realize that I have to look after myself. I make an effort to sleep well, eat well, and exercise regularly. Most important, I try to avoid stress when I can. All of these habits help to keep me healthy. Recently I learned to meditate, which I am finding a great help with relaxation. It's also helping me uncover underlying issues that can cause me anxiety.

I am living proof that recovery is possible. Please hang in there, take small steps, be kind to yourself, and remember to pat yourself on the back for all your achievements. If you experience setbacks, don't be hard on yourself. There will always be stress that you can't avoid in the world. You just have to learn how to deal with it more effectively. I wish you well—and you will be!

My name is Gaylene, and I'm from Melbourne, Australia. I hope my contribution to this book gives readers hope that recovery is possible. I strongly recommend reading all of Dr. Claire Weekes's books/journals, as well as Bronwyn Fox's Power over Panic *and* Working Through Panic; *you can't go wrong with them. Take small steps with your recovery, follow your own pace, find yourself a good psychologist if needed, and look after yourself!*

I would like to say a very special thank you to my mother, who stuck by me during my recovery. I couldn't have done it without you, Mum! And thank you to my friends, who have also stood by me through some of my darkest hours. And another special thank you to my loving, caring, devoted, and very understanding partner. I will get on that plane one day—I promise!

Commentary by Paul Foxman

Adult anxiety can often be traced to untreated childhood anxiety, and Gaylene's story illustrates this developmental trend. As a shy and fearful child, she experienced uncontrollable separation anxiety. As an adolescent, she frequently avoided high school due to anxiety, and she developed a pattern of anticipatory fear. At her lowest point in adulthood, Gaylene became regressed and housebound with fears of virtually everything, including food, being alone, and even taking a shower.

Gaylene had three strikes against her anxiety recovery. One was use of a habit-forming medication, which resulted not only in a drug addiction but also in an increase of anxiety symptoms when she tried to discontinue the medication. The second strike was the response of her medical doctors, who performed many tests but failed to identify her anxiety condition. Understandably, her condition was difficult to diagnose because she had many anxiety symptoms, including separation anxiety, panic disorder, agoraphobia, and social phobia, as well as multiple physical symptoms of stress. In today's diagnostic language, Gaylene had an "anxiety disorder not otherwise specified," which simply means a mixed anxiety disorder. Strike three was the high stress in Gaylene's life. Indeed, it was the stress overload of planning her wedding and shouldering responsibility for her dying father that triggered her most severe anxiety.

On the brighter side, Gaylene found a psychologist who suggested cognitive-behavioral treatment—one of the most effective therapies for anxiety. This approach replaces worry, negative thinking, all-or-nothing thinking (also known as overgeneralization), and other anxiety-creating cognitions with new thought patterns. New habits, such as focusing on the present, trusting the future, optimism, and nonjudgmental thinking, are practiced daily until they become automatic. For further discussion of cognitive-behavioral therapy techniques, see Chapters 2, 7, and 9 of this book, as well as the books *Cognitive Therapy and the Emotional Disorders*, by A. Beck, and *Feeling Good*, by D. Burns (both listed in the Bibliography).

Gaylene also found that good health habits go a long way toward anxiety recovery. I consider adequate sleep and relaxation, proper diet and nutrition (including discontinuing caffeine and alcohol), and exercise (at least twenty minutes of aerobic activity several times per week) to be the foundation of any anxiety-recovery program. When you have health and energy, you have more control. Furthermore, these lifestyle changes are also necessary for stress management, an essential part of anxiety prevention and recovery. I often say that it is not stress itself that triggers anxiety but rather inadequate stress recovery that does.

Small, manageable steps are the most appropriate approach to behavior change. This method was developed by Dr. Claire Weekes, one of the first professionals to write about the gradual-exposure process known as *desensitization*. Gaylene found Dr. Weekes's books helpful; readers will find more information about her books, and others, in the Bibliography.

CHAPTER 21

LIVING WITH SOCIAL ANXIETY DISORDER

by SUE CLELAND, B.A., B. Soc. Wk., MAASW

I was diagnosed with social anxiety disorder at the age of thirty, after living with it for nearly twenty years. I remember my first experience of feeling more than just shy. I was around age thirteen and was walking across a local park with a good friend. A group of boys whom I knew was standing nearby. They called out to us, and I suddenly felt overwhelmed with an intense need to escape, to run and hide. I could not even turn around and say hello. I felt the heat in my face increase and a sensation that the boys were all staring at me, whispering negative things about me between themselves. I wanted to vanish into thin air. This was the onset of the development of a debilitating disorder that was to rule my life for the next two decades, causing me misery, distress, isolation, loneliness, lack of self-respect, and physical health problems.

During my childhood years I was fairly quiet. I hung around the edges of groups, especially if the groups were made up of people I did not know. School terrified me, especially when I had to get up in front of the class for "show and tell." Although I had lots of close friends and enjoyed their company, as well as that of my brother and sister, I made sure I was never the center of attention. I tended to do what others wanted to do; I let everyone else make decisions for me. I began to develop belief patterns that I was incapable of making decisions and that I was not good enough unless everything I did or said was perfect. As I entered my teenage years, those beliefs became entrenched to the point where I believed I had to be liked and approved of by every person with whom I came into contact. The expectations I placed on myself at a very early age were so extreme and unrealistic that I had set myself up for failure without even realizing it. Since my expectations stood no chance of being met, they slowly ate away at my sense of self-worth, the essence of who I was. By the time I had reached the age of thirteen my self-esteem was incredibly low, and I feared and mistrusted most people, believing they only wanted to hurt me.

Throughout my teenage years the thoughts that preoccupied my mind were mainly concerned with how I appeared to others, how I looked, how I spoke, and what others were thinking about me. These thoughts were all extremely negative and were always accompanied by high levels of anxiety. I had no respect for my body or myself, and as a result I treated myself poorly and allowed others to treat me poorly. I did what anyone wanted me to (apart from my parents) and engaged in some rebellious behaviors throughout my early teens, including drinking heavily. When I drank alcohol my anxiety decreased and I didn't care so much about what other people thought of me.

Alcohol became a major problem for me. I grew reliant on it, especially when I felt I was in situations in which I was being evaluated. I drank heavily throughout my adolescence and early adulthood and tended to socialize with others who also drank. Springboarding from alcohol, I started dabbling in drugs, particularly marijuana, in an attempt to control my anxiety.

I also experienced extreme mood swings that affected my life greatly. My relationship with my parents deteriorated rapidly as I became more rebellious. In retrospect, my mom and dad were very lenient, considering some of the horror I put them through. When I was fifteen my mom took me to a psychiatrist to try to find out what was going on. I was told that my problems were a result of how my parents treated me. This could not have been further from the truth. There was never any mention of anxiety or any exploration of my belief system. I never went back to that doctor, and I returned to living my life in the only way I knew how.

As a young adult my self-esteem remained incredibly low, and my false beliefs and thoughts became so entrenched that I could not imagine thinking any other way. Because I had nursed the same negative thoughts for so long, I now believed them 100 percent. It was as though I were on a train going backward at a very fast pace, and things only continued to get worse. I dropped out of college courses at age twenty because I could not bring myself to give presentations. I was unable to attend a social event without having a few drinks of alcohol beforehand. I could not sign my name or eat or drink in front of strangers, as my body would start trembling.

Every time I walked down the street I believed people were watching me from cars or buildings, waiting for me to trip and make a fool of myself. Every time I entered a room full of people I thought they were all staring at me, judging me and thinking, "What is she doing here?" Every time I spoke with someone, I believed they could see straight through my eyes and into my soul and knew I was a quivering mess inside. As I got older I developed more and more unhealthy coping mechanisms in an attempt to cope with the fear of what people were thinking of me and the high levels of anxiety I experienced as a result of this intense fear. Some of these coping mechanisms included avoiding all situations in which I thought I would be judged, isolating myself from family and friends, continuing to depend on alcohol and other drugs to make me feel relaxed, engaging in binge eating patterns, and constantly relocating from state to state in an attempt to find a place free from fear. All these coping mechanisms were Band-Aid approaches. They only temporarily relieved my anxiety; plus they made my life miserable, further worsening my already shattered self-esteem.

At the age of twenty-two I visited another psychiatrist. At the first mention of some of my symptoms of anxiety, this doctor wrote me a prescription for Xanax, with instructions to take it when I felt anxious. There was no exploration of how long I had been experiencing high levels of anxiety, or in what situations it occurred, or any type of therapy to assist me in learning to control it. As with the earlier psychiatrist, I never went back after my first visit. Xanax became just one more unhealthy coping mechanism that only relieved my anxiety on a temporary basis. I became dependent on the drug very quickly; I found it useful during tutorials and lectures at the university. The more I took Xanax, the greater the dose I needed to achieve the same calming effect. When I wasn't engaging in the use of all of my coping mechanisms, my fear and anxiety returned.

To my friends and my family I was just Sue—sometimes moody, impulsive, always on the move, often quiet and a bit of a recluse, and a person who enjoyed a drink. But inside, I was ready to give up on my life. I often contemplated suicide. After my experiences with psychiatrists I shied away from seeking medical help, even though I desperately needed it. I believed that if I visited a doctor and told him or her what was really going on in my mind, I would then be labeled as weak, pathetic, and a failure—my worst fear come true. Or they would tell me there was nothing wrong with me, to wake up, "think positive," or "get over it." I had already tried these things—maybe not in very healthy ways, but in the only ways I knew how. I needed someone to help me find an answer, to give me guidance and set me on the path to understanding where my fear and anxiety came from, to inform me of correct treatments, to help me off the train I was riding to destination Self-Destruction.

In the first three months of 1999 I experienced panic attacks every day. I became barely able to function. I was living by myself on the Gold Coast of Australia, fifteen thousand kilometers away from my family and friends. I had totally isolated myself. I was working as a social worker in a psychiatric unit, which just intensified my belief that there was something terribly wrong with me, as I could identify many of my patients' symptoms in myself: I was withdrawn, preoccupied, and fearful. In the evenings I would come home and drink alcohol and smoke marijuana, dreaming of another place, another life . . . any life but mine.

I was in the depths of despair, but this fact remained unknown to anyone else because I continued to pretend to my family and friends that everything was fine. In fact, things had never been worse.

March 16, 1999, was the turning point of my life. I was hospitalized for three weeks after being diagnosed for the first time with social anxiety disorder and other co-morbid conditions, including severe depression, avoidant personality disorder, and potential alcoholism—all offshoots of living with intense fear twenty-four hours a day for almost twenty years. With a diagnosis finally in hand, and with support from my family and friends, I embraced a strong determination to beat the fear and anxiety I had endured for so long.

Treatment included many different therapies, including anxiety education, cognitive-behavioral therapy, antidepressant medication, self-esteem therapy, reality testing, relaxation techniques, perception/assertion training, interpersonal-skills training, public-speaking courses, focusing skills, education on the importance of a balanced lifestyle, and more. The main motivation behind my recovery was my resolve to never again have to visit that lonely, miserable, and fearful place in which I had been trapped for so many years. I wanted to live a more enjoyable life free from fear, to develop a sense of self-worth, and to learn to understand and take control of my emotions.

I am now thirty-three. It has been two and a half years since I was admitted to the hospital. It has been two and a half years since I was diagnosed with social anxiety disorder. Nine months after my discharge from the hospital I overcame all of my major fears and anxieties and started living my life to its full capacity. I replaced unhealthy beliefs with healthy, rational beliefs and started trusting again. I replaced unhealthy coping mechanisms with realistic, evidence-based thinking patterns. And for the first time in my life I developed a sense of self-worth and an appreciation for the person I am.

I now run the Anxiety and Stress Management Service of Queensland, based in Brisbane, Australia, where I provide both individual and group recovery programs to people whose lives are affected by social anxiety disorder and other anxiety disorders. In addition, I have founded Social Anxiety Australia, an Australia-wide community service that provides information, education, and support to people who live with social anxiety disorder, as well as to their caretakers, relatives, and other health practitioners. Some of the services offered by Social Anxiety Australia include an extensive website full of information and resources available in Australia, an Internet-based message board, telephone support, advocacy, workshops and seminars, and a fortnightly support group offering hope, support, and encouragement.

I have also established another Australia-wide service, Anxiety Network Australia, which provides information and assistance to people who live with any of the major anxiety disorders, including panic disorder, agoraphobia, generalized anxiety disorder, post-traumatic stress disorder, obsessive-compulsive disorder, and specific phobias. Both these services fill a gap in our health system for easily accessible information on all aspects of anxiety, including where to find local support and assistance.

Social anxiety disorder is very common in our society. It is related to severely low self-esteem, and it is characterized by negative, unhealthy beliefs and entrenched thought patterns in which you believe that other people are judging you, criticizing you, and scrutinizing your every move. These belief patterns generally develop due to a combination of a genetic sensitivity to "worry," the way you were raised, and/or certain environmental experiences. It is also related to extremely high expectations of yourself—a belief that unless you are perfect in everything you do and say, those around you will disapprove of the person you are. Social anxiety disorder usually develops in childhood or early teenage years; it impacts the essence of who you are and your sense of self-worth. As a result, it has an extremely debilitating impact on all areas of your life, including interpersonal relationships, social life, career, and physical health. Social anxiety disorder is thought to be the world's third-largest mental-health problem, behind depression and alcoholism. It is an illness that creates a significantly negative economic impact on our community resources, in addition to the impact on the individual's personal life. Due to the early onset of social anxiety disorder and its chronic nature, it is essential that we dedicate more time, energy, and resources to recognizing and understanding the illness in its early stages in order to prevent a lifetime of suffering and isolation in its victims.

Social anxiety disorder is a treatable condition. If you believe you may have social anxiety disorder, tell someone how you are feeling. Support and treatment are available to help you overcome your fears and anxiety and start living as you choose. With the right information, guidance, and support, fear can be replaced by healthy anticipation. Lack of self-worth can be replaced by self-acceptance and confidence. Isolation can be replaced by a sense of belonging. Lack of control can be replaced by choice. And your dreams and goals can become a reality.

> *For more information on support and treatment for social anxiety disorder, contact Sue Cleland at Social Anxiety Australia or the Anxiety and Stress Management Service of Queensland; tel. +18-07-33-696-090; e-mail sue@socialanxiety.com.au. Or visit the websites of Social Anxiety Australia (www.socialanxiety.com.au) and Anxiety Network Australia (www.anxietynetwork.com.au).*

Commentary by Paul Foxman

Sue's story about social anxiety explains the condition more vividly and comprehensively than any textbook on the subject. She emphasizes a number of key features of social anxiety, and her website provides more helpful suggestions than many therapists have in their repertoire.

Technically called *social phobia*, this anxiety disorder is characterized by excessive concern with one's appearance, behavior, and speech in the presence of other people who one anticipates will make negative judgments about him or her. The basis of social phobia is unrealistic beliefs,

such as the idea that you need to be liked by everyone, that you are inferior to others, and that you must please others in order to be accepted.
Shyness and low self-esteem are also key factors in social anxiety.

As an adolescent Sue began using alcohol to control the anxiety she
felt during social interaction. This is a common coping mechanism, and it
is estimated that up to 40 percent of anxiety sufferers have a coexisting alcohol or drug problem. Alcohol helps many people feel less inhibited and
more gregarious. I find it interesting that alcohol—a widely available legal
drug—plays such a large role in social interaction throughout the world.
Could it be that social anxiety is actually *the* most prevalent emotional
condition and not merely the third most common, as Sue's research has
suggested?

Unfortunately, like many others who rely on alcohol or drugs for anxiety control, Sue developed an addiction problem that made her recovery
more complicated. Her alcohol and drug problem—she "dabbled" with
marijuana and other drugs—was further complicated by a prescription for
Xanax, which led to a dependence on that habit-forming medication. Prescription drugs for anxiety involve special risks in some cases, such as potential for addiction and harmful interactions when combined with alcohol.

Another common coping strategy for social anxiety is avoidance. Like
drugs or alcohol, avoidance does result in temporary relief from anxiety,
but at a high price. Social avoidance leads to isolation, loneliness, and depression. Furthermore, these coping efforts postpone the process of
change and true recovery. In Sue's case, twenty years of temporary relief
led to a complex condition with multiple features, including severe
depression, panic attacks, avoidant personality disorder, and alcohol
dependence.

A variety of treatment interventions can be helpful for social anxiety,
and Sue mentions many of them. However, she does not mention the
value of group therapy. Group therapy with a professional therapist, or in
a support group with knowledgeable leadership, is one of the most cor-
rective experiences for this disorder because it involves facing the very
essence of what is feared in social anxiety. Developing rational beliefs

about people, "evidence-based thinking," and more effective communication skills can be accelerated in group therapy, which provides opportunities for immediate feedback. One learning activity I suggest in my groups is to do two things whenever you receive a compliment: make eye contact and say simply, "Thank you." It is amazing how such a simple social grace as accepting compliments can be so difficult for people with social anxiety, and it is equally miraculous how pushing through fear to practice such a skill can support recovery in the same individuals.

CHAPTER 22

LIVING LIFE WELL

by JACQUELINE HAMPTON

As I get off the plane in Canada I'm struck by the realization that it would be impossible to measure this journey by time and space alone. I've come here to learn how to dogsled—a dream I've had since childhood.

Before arriving, all I knew about the great white north was what I saw on *Sergeant Preston of the Yukon*, circa 1955. But the romantic sense of adventure I felt watching him mush his trusty husky, King, and a team of dogs lunging across the snow was something I never forgot. I was a child bound by an anxiety disorder, and the TV show's swift huskies gave me a sense of freedom and elation. By the time I found myself poised between the sled's runners, ready for my first lesson, I'd spent the majority of my life living in fear, sometimes unable even to leave my house. And now, miraculously, my journey had delivered me safely face-to-face with my dream.

The dog handler tells me that the word *mush* is a Hollywood artifact that stuck. The dog handlers on the set were French Canadian and were actually saying *"marche."* The English equivalent, I learn as I am being prepped for my maiden voyage, is *hike*. Left is *haw* and right is *gee*.

The handler has finished instructing me on the salient points and is showing me the lead that I'll release when it is time to go. Until that time, he tells me, the driver must stand on the brake with both feet. The huskies' signature yowling is getting louder as the handler continues hitching the teams: They love this and are anxious to be underway.

I have wanted to do this my entire life, but still I am scared. The dogs are barking and jumping a foot in the air, straining at their harnesses. The handler looks back to see if I am ready, then turns and yells, "Hike!" I know I'm as ready as I'm going to get. Holding on for dear life, I yank the tie loose. With a sharp jolt I am launched at full dog speed onto the trail.

What do you say when a lifelong dream comes true? I am feeling childlike joy, grinning from ear to ear. As we make our way through Moose Valley, all I can hear are the runners of the sleds and the footfall of the dogs. I am Queen of the Yukon, traveling with my trusty team. I alternate between running behind the sled to help the dogs up hills and mushing, balanced on the runners as we travel. My fear is left behind in a heap with the snow we are crossing. I feel blissful, at peace, and somehow wiser.

I had my first full-blown anxiety attack in 1984. I was boarding a plane to make a visit to a client. My fiancé had dropped me off at the airport. My parents and he didn't get along. I was in denial that the love of my life was in reality a violent alcoholic and drug addict. It took supreme effort to keep my anxiety and any sense of reality about our relationship at bay, but I managed to. Like Scarlet O'Hara, I lived by the mantra that "tomorrow will be another day." While I was sitting in the waiting area, a fellow traveler started to talk to me. A man. I was instantly triggered. I was sure he was trying to come on to me. I wasn't a stranger to anxiety; I'd struggled with it from early childhood, probably a combination of genetic luck of the draw and the result of violence I'd experienced as a child. Born into a family with a multigenerational history of alcoholism and abuse, I'd been sexually molested by the age of six. As I grew older I was beaten until I was big enough and brave enough to fend off the striking hand and the brass belt buckle. Hypervigilance, social anxiety, and obsessive checking of door locks, window latches, attics, and basements became part of my daily routine. I didn't know what I was scared of or what I expected my constant reconnaissance to reveal. Fear was the only thing that mattered; it was the only feeling I could recognize.

The man's innocent remark triggered a cascade of feelings, and suddenly I lost control. Chronic anxiety escalated into my first real panic attack just as the flight attendant announced the beginning of the boarding process. My heart began racing, my palms became sweaty, and I started shivering. I reminded myself to breathe, but my lungs seemed unable to draw in enough air. I remember the traveler asking me a question. I couldn't look at him; I waved him away and stood up to board the aircraft. I felt as though my nearly six-foot frame had been reduced to about three feet tall. My vision started to tunnel, and I had the odd feeling that I was leaving my body through the top of my head.

Walking down the jet way, I had to concentrate intensely just to get my feet to move. I managed to make it to my seat, unsteady and unsure of what was happening to me. I felt like a cornered animal; I looked around the plane wildly. I'd never liked flying, and with every passing second I grew less sure that I could make it through this five-hour flight. The decisive moment came when the man I'd encountered in the waiting area turned up in the seat next to mine.

"Oh, look," he said cheerfully, "our seats are together. Now we'll have a chance to chat."

I bolted. "I can't do this," I muttered, grabbing my carry-on and pushing past the other passengers up the narrow aisle to the door of the plane. I interrupted the flight attendant, who was collecting boarding passes.

"I have to get off this plane. I want my boarding pass back. I can't go on this flight." The panic in my voice caught the attention of nearby passengers. It was like the "Twilight Zone" episode "Room for One More." The flight attendant glanced away nervously and started to explain why I couldn't leave the plane and how returning my boarding pass would mess up their paperwork. I cut her off in midsentence. My voice sank to a gravelly pitch, low and threatening, almost a growl. Even as I spoke, I was shocked at the voice coming out of my body. The flight attendant's eyes went wide. She quickly pulled the boarding pass out and handed it to me. I ran up the jet way and into the terminal.

Standing there, feeling and acting crazy, I didn't know what to do next. I made it to a pay phone and called my fiancé, crying hysterically. I took a cab to his house, ate some ice cream, and passed out on the couch, sleeping like a dead person until he came home from work. I still had no idea what had come over me.

The next day I hopped a flight to visit my client, but I was no longer alone. Once released from its confinement, acute anxiety became a constant and ever more demanding companion, looming larger than my life and finally taking over nearly all aspects of my existence. Like the Cheshire Cat from *Alice in Wonderland*, I just kept smiling as I faded away.

I saw traditional therapists and even sought out psychics and healers of various sorts. No one suggested a psychiatric referral or drug therapy. Over a period of twelve years, each one worse than the previous, it wore me down to tell my story over and over to the next person I hoped would save me. Even *I* couldn't stand to hear my story one more time. Worse, as many times as I told it, there wasn't any improvement. I felt like Neil Young's blind man, "running down the alley at night with the answer in his hand, come on down to the river of sight and you will finally understand." No one understood anything.

Undiagnosed, I created ways to cope: compulsive overeating, spending money, drinking, sexing, drugging. Anxiety was a patient tormentor, keenly aware that my self-destructive efforts to get rid of this loathsome parasite would only make me weaker and more vulnerable to the next attack.

Anxiety drives your nerves like lemmings to the edge of a cliff. When they finally fall over, depression sets in. My first severe depression hit in 1993. Weekends and evenings, I didn't answer the phone, and if someone knocked at my door I hid in the bathroom. I slept most of the day, watched television, and ate compulsively in an effort to find relief and a sense of comfort. Eating got me through my work day. I gained weight. Lots of it. Two years and nearly eighty pounds later, anxiety decided it was time to up the ante.

I was sitting at home, watching television and eating a taco salad. In mid-forkful, I dropped to the floor on my knees in the grip of an overwhelming anxiety attack. I couldn't cry or scream. The only sound I heard coming out of my mouth was literally a horrible, howling wail. I managed to crawl to my phone. Hands shaking, I called my therapist. She was, of course, concerned, so she began making arrangements for me to come and see her immediately. I stopped howling. I will never forget the blanket of chilling fear that descended over my body. I felt myself take a deep breath.

"I can't leave the house," I told my therapist. She asked if I was sure. This sparked another onset of hysteria.

"Yes, yes, I'm sure, don't talk about going outside. Don't say it. I can't do it." She calmed me down and told me it might be a good idea for me to go on medication.

"No," I refused.

"Can you take a walk?" she asked. I thought this over. Oddly enough, the thought of walking didn't make me feel panicked.

"I can walk if there are no people," I said. My therapist remained quiet on the other end of the line. My anxiety disorder was beyond her realm of experience. I know she was doing the best she could. "I'll walk early in the morning and late at night," I offered.

"What are you going to do about work?" Good question.

"I'll have to think about that and let you know tomorrow," I said. I ended up taking a six-week leave of absence. I walked for an hour or two twice a day, early and late, and only when there was little likelihood I'd run into anyone. If I encountered another person I just looked down, avoiding eye contact. I guess I managed to generate enough natural endorphins that I was able to go to the store in the middle of the night and buy food. At the end of six weeks I went back to work. Nothing about the prolonged attack was resolved or answered, but my anxiety disorder had made significant strides during those six weeks.

For the next five years I didn't answer my phone or my door. I'd make plans with friends and cancel at the last minute. I lied constantly to get out of obligations, conversations, and family gatherings. Soon the only people I interacted with were those I paid to clean my house and tend my yard. I continued working; as long as there was food to eat I could put in a decent workday. I gained more weight.

In 1998 another severe depression hit. This time I stopped sleeping and became almost manic. I finally went to my doctor after three days of running around my house nonstop. He prescribed something to help me sleep and also suggested an antidepressant. Finally, for the first time, I listened to the advice to try medication. Life started getting better. I could sleep, and I felt more like myself. However, I continued to keep my phones turned off, lived like a hermit, and couldn't stop eating.

My anxiety was finally unmasked as a result of a series of medical issues that started with a mistake. My lipid profile showed me to be at high risk for coronary artery disease (CAD), so my doctor prescribed medicine to lower my cholesterol. And he asked me to lose weight. Yeah, right. I'd leave his office and drive straight to McDonald's. He booked an appointment for me to have a treadmill test. Afterwards, when he came in with the results, he was unusually quiet.

"I'm going to refer you to a cardiologist," he said. "Are you still exercising?"

"Yes," I replied.

"I don't want you to do anything that raises your heart rate over 120 beats per minute," he said.

My blood ran cold. I was very, very scared.

It turned out that the first treadmill test was faulty. The technician had placed the electrodes incorrectly. The heart scan and the repeat test were fine. But, still, the cardiologist told me it wasn't a matter of *if* I'd develop CAD, but *when*. He recommended that I enroll in a two-month program available to patients interested in preventing heart disease. My fear stripped away enough of my denial that I knew I had to do something to change how I lived—or face the unpleasant consequences. I enrolled.

The first person to arm me with a weapon I could use to counter my anxiety disorder and fight my way back to wellness was the nutritionist affiliated with the cardiac program. I showed up for my consultation with her expecting to hear more of what I already knew about how deplorable my diet was. Instead, after introductions, she looked at me and said, "You're hanging on by your fingernails, aren't you?" Defenses breached, I started crying.

She listened as I recounted the years of depression, anxiety, and eating. She picked up her Rolodex and took out a card. "You need to see this woman," she said. "She isn't taking new patients, but we are going to call her until she agrees to take you." I could only nod and watch as she called her colleague. I didn't realize at the time that in taking this fork in the path I was finally on the road to recovery.

I'm smiling as I write this. I still have work to do, but I'm living my life well. I continued to work with the nutritionist and the psychologist to whom she referred me. I owe them my life, literally. The psychologist instantly recognized my anxiety disorder and called it on the carpet. She referred me to a psychiatrist who specialized in mood disorders. Nine months later we had established a working foundation of medication that reduced my raging anxiety to a manageable level. I continue therapy today to deal with other issues that were masked by the anxiety. I have good days and bad days. But now I know I can do it. And I know I don't have to do it alone. I have my medical support team, some new friendships, and, most precious of all, I reconnected with my family in a way that surrounds and protects me with love and a sense of belonging.

I still have fear. That is part of being human. I used to think I was the only person in the world who felt fear about doing something new. When I got secure enough to ask other people how they felt, I discovered that even veterans still experience fear. They just name it and move through it. Over time, I came to the realization that the fear itself was much worse than the worst-case scenario I could imagine. Sometimes the best way to conquer fear is to give yourself permission to be afraid of something and then to do it anyway. Sometimes the best way to learn is to do all of the wrong things.

The most difficult thing about anxiety, besides the disorder itself, is recovery. Still, to quote a Zen proverb, "You must concentrate upon and consecrate yourself wholly to each day as though a fire were raging in your hair" (Taisen Deshimaru, in *Preparation of a Samurai*).

When it got really bad, I'd remind myself that God didn't bring me this far to drop me like a hot rock. I just kept going. Does it sound like I'm talking about a war? It *is* a war, and you are fighting for your right to live well. And you can. You owe it to yourself to get the help you need to put this ill humor back in Pandora's box. Lock it up and throw away the key!

On the dog-sledding trail, there are turns and corners. Not severe ones, but challenging enough for a first-timer. On the first corner I tried to take, I did everything possible wrong, and I found myself launched face first into the dry, powdery snow. After the fall I knew exactly what to do and executed each of the next turns flawlessly. I was aware of each moment, focused on the bits of learning and confidence that seemed to effortlessly adhere to me as I passed from one moment into the next. This is the feeling of a life lived well. A life no longer crippled by anxiety.

> *"Dying is easy, it's living that scares me to death."* —From *"Cold"* on Diva, *by Annie Lennox*
>
> *I remember standing on the brink of suicide and the incredible people who pulled me back. You know who you are; thank you. These days I'm thankful to be alive and not living in constant fear. I understand what the Zen proverb quoted in my story means. I live it every day.*
>
> *Recovery for me has meant the courage to return to my first love, writing. Now a successful writer, I created my own company, Barking Cats Freelance, and can be reached at jrjax@yahoo.com and at www.barkingcats.org.*

Commentary by Paul Foxman

Once again, we read a story by an intelligent and creative person who developed panic disorder with agoraphobia, but who suffered needlessly for many years due to improper diagnosis and treatment. After hitting bottom, Jacqueline was finally referred for proper anxiety treatment. However, I am intrigued most by Jacqueline's spirituality and how it helped her recover.

Jacqueline's spirituality is revealed in her comment "When it got really bad, I'd remind myself that God didn't bring me this far to drop me like a hot rock." Similarly, one of my patients was able to face his flying phobia after his priest remarked, "Do you think God has to wait for you to get on an airplane to get you?"

At the heart of all religious and spiritual systems is the belief that it is never too late for change and renewal. This is the essence of hope: No matter how bad it gets, it is always possible to turn things around. For anxiety sufferers, it is essential to know that change is possible, no matter how disabling the condition becomes.

Anxiety can be understood to a great extent as resulting from a lack of faith or trust. You can place faith in yourself, based on knowing you have the skills and resources to handle whatever may happen. Or you can place it in a higher power to which you can turn for inspiration and guidance. With faith comes security and safety, as well as a reassuring conviction that things will work out according to a higher plan. Faith allows you to trust that whatever happens was meant to be. From the viewpoint of faith, there is only one basic fear, and all anxiety symptoms stem from it. Lack of faith is the root of anxiety and fear.

How can you increase your spiritual awareness and cultivate a personal relationship with a higher power? Here are some suggestions for developing your spirituality:

- Practice meditation daily to experience quiet stillness and divine inspiration
- Spend time in nature to increase your awareness of larger forces

- Read spiritually uplifting books, or study holy texts
- Practice relaxation and become more open and receptive
- Pray or ask for guidance with decisions and choices
- Be grateful for what you have
- Participate in a social-support group, or develop a network of friends
- Volunteer or do some community service
- Practice a loving attitude toward yourself and others

The reward for having faith is a feeling that Jacqueline describes as "blissful, at peace, and somehow wiser." About her childhood dream (dogsledding in the Yukon) she asks, "What do you say when a lifelong dream comes true?" What would *you* say? When you are grateful, to whom or what do *you* give thanks?

CHAPTER 23

LETTING GO

by ELAINE MACKIN SCHWEIZER

When I was twenty-seven I left my native Texas and traveled to Washington state. My father and stepmother had migrated to Olympia four years earlier, and I looked forward to spending time with them. Not long after the move I found a perfect job as a graphic designer in Seattle. I settled in relatively quickly and loved my work. I was at the job no more than three months when I came down with symptoms of appendicitis. I went to the clinic, but the doctors found nothing wrong. They told me to just watch and wait. That was at Christmastime.

The pain went away and life returned to normal. I visited my father —about a two-hour train ride away—on some weekends. But I wasn't making any friends besides my office mate at work. She would sometimes show me around the city, and on weekdays we ate lunch together.

One day in February, after coming back from lunch, I felt a sharp pain in my abdomen. I doubled over and began throwing up. My office mate went to the company nurse, who accompanied me one block to the emergency room. I was there all afternoon and evening (without painkillers) before they diagnosed me with a burst ovarian cyst. My boss had called my father, who came to take me home.

Recovery was quick, and after a few doctor visits I was back at work. My gynecologist put me on birth control pills to take care of the cysts. I suffered bouts of nausea with increasing frequency. And I endured stabbing pains in my abdomen. During my period I would be on the bathroom floor with sweats and chills from the pain. I called the doctor's office and spoke with the nurse, who told me to take more painkillers. She said I could take more than the dosage indicated on the label. I was so miserable I also asked for a referral to a psychiatrist in order to learn biofeedback, thinking it would help me cope with the pain.

Instead of recommending biofeedback, the psychiatrist prescribed two antidepressants. I filled the prescriptions and took the first pill right away. At bedtime I took a pill from the second bottle. I lay down on my bed with my arms stretched above my head. As I was dozing off I felt the sensation of fire burning my fingers and then sweeping down my entire body. I thought I was about to die, so I unlocked my front door and prepared to call 911. Instead, I dialed my father's number.

When I told him what was happening he said, "I didn't even know you were depressed." He told me to call my psychiatrist. While I was talking to him I had to go to the bathroom to throw up, which made me feel better.

I called the psychiatrist, who told me it was just a reaction to the medication and that I should keep taking it and come to see her the next week. I decided she was insane and stopped taking both pills. All right, maybe she wasn't insane, but I didn't feel understood or supported by her. That night, four or five smaller fires consumed my body and then burned themselves out. I sat on the wooden floor outside my bathroom for another hour until I was finally able to crawl back into bed and fall asleep.

Now I had developed panic attacks in addition to the abdominal pain. When I went to see the psychiatrist she gave me a prescription for an anxiety medication and a referral to a psychologist. After my last drug reaction I decided I didn't want to take any more prescription medications. However, I thought the therapist might be able to help me learn biofeedback. I took off work to visit her once a week. I told her how I was going through a really difficult time, dealing with so much pain and experiencing panic attacks more often. They were happening a few times a week, often when I experienced the stabbing abdominal pains. I talked about how difficult it was to be in a new city, without any friends. And I didn't want to try to make any new friends because I was so ashamed of what was happening to my body. I was afraid people would judge me for being in pain, having anxiety, and generally being a "downer." After a few visits the psychologist told me I had borderline personality disorder. I couldn't understand this, but on another level I was grateful for any name a doctor would use to explain what my problems were. And yet the label didn't seem to help me get through the pain or the anxiety; neither the psychiatrist nor the psychologist told me how to cope with the attacks. On the psychologist's suggestion, I bought a workbook about borderline personality disorder, but found the diagnosis just didn't ring true to me. I wouldn't advise everyone to ignore or dismiss the opinions of professionals, but when you search yourself with all honesty and their view doesn't seem true, then keep looking. I knew I had to continue my quest to get to the root of what was really happening to me.

During this time I tried to go to movies, but only once was I able to sit through a whole picture. As soon as I felt my skin start to crawl and the heat start to ignite, I had a sudden urge to run away and get home as fast as I could. I was afraid to take a bath, because the next attack might cause me to pass out and drown. I cut all my hair and bought two-in-one shampoo so that I could spend as little time bathing as possible. I bought a hat to cover my dirty hair for those days I couldn't face the bath at all.

I became hyperalert to anything going on in my body and made note of every pain. My office mate was getting tired of me and my constant pains and troubles. Even though I got a glowing review from my boss, my work was rapidly deteriorating. I couldn't live with the constant nausea, pain, and panic.

I researched all my symptoms on the Internet and in medical books; with new information in hand I called the gynecologist's office and begged for an appointment. I presented all my research to the doctor and told her I believed I had endometriosis, a disease in which the uterine lining grows outside the uterus in the abdominal cavity. It can cause internal scarring, a buildup of adhesions, and a great deal of pain. The only way to verify the diagnosis was with a laparoscopy, an outpatient procedure, to which she agreed. My mother traveled to Seattle to help me through the procedure, scheduled for shortly after my twenty-eighth birthday. Before the operation the doctor told me not to be disappointed if they didn't find anything. Later she told me I had one of the worst cases of endometriosis she'd seen.

I woke up after the surgery in a hospital room. They'd had to perform a fairly extensive operation in order to treat all the scarring, adhesions, and two cysts, one on each ovary. I was released after a few days, and I spent the next two weeks recovering. My mother was the biggest comfort and support. She helped me walk when I had to rest every five steps. She greeted all my fears with love and restored my hope that I would finally be well. But she had to leave after the first week, and because I was still too weak to do everything for myself, I went to stay with my father in Olympia. Unfortunately, the panic attacks returned shortly thereafter. My gynecologist gave me the same prescription for anxiety that the psychiatrist had given me; this time I decided I would take the pills. I had an attack after taking the first one because I was so nervous, but I fell asleep almost instantly—a welcome relief.

My sick leave ended and I headed back to work even though I wasn't fully up to speed. After a few days at the office I knew I couldn't stay at that job—or in Washington, for that matter. I had been sick for so long before the surgery that I needed a longer recuperation period. I needed friends around me as well as family, and they were all back in Texas. I gave notice at work that I would be moving as soon as possible. I had become so weak that my father and uncle had to pack up my apartment after I moved.

I felt on the verge of death; I needed something life changing. I didn't have a fatal disease, but I had a fatal attitude toward that disease, toward my body, and toward myself. Several months earlier, when I was taking one of my shallow baths, I'd broken down crying because I realized that I really wanted to live—fully, happily, and free from these fears. My mother had recently begun to meditate and offered to take me to a class. I knew after my first lesson that it was what I needed. After two months I still had panic attacks, but my strength was returning quickly. I signed up for a seventeen-day meditation retreat in the mountains of North Carolina.

At the retreat I had an incredible experience. As I was lying in bed, energy started building in my head, and my eyes rolled back. I began to panic, but I stopped myself with the thought, "If I'm dying, then let's see what this is like. I'm tired of the other way. I want to let go." All the energy suddenly popped out the top of my head, and I entered the deepest, most peaceful place in the universe. The episode was short but profound. Through that one experience I learned that all I had to do was let go—much easier said than done. But once it was done, I didn't have another panic attack for more than a year and a half.

I also met my future husband, Jean-Marie, on that retreat. He was a big Swiss bear wearing a T-shirt, shorts, and sandals in the snow. He led a small yoga group in the mornings and afternoons. One day he asked me why I wasn't stretching with the others. I told him of my surgery and said I was still recovering. He saw that as an excuse, which it was, my surgery having been more than four months earlier. I did all of the exercises, and afterwards I cried so much—not because of the pain but because of all the thoughts and feelings I had held in. Jean-Marie sat with me, listened, and accepted me exactly as I was. He told me what he saw in me, and although I may have been less than eager to hear some of the things he said, I was grateful for the honesty and openness. We were married a year later and moved to Switzerland.

It wasn't a huge surprise when I began having pains in my abdomen again, because endometriosis can grow back. I was shocked, however, that the feelings of panic returned. Dealing with the pains was tricky because of my tendency to report anything I deem abnormal in my body—my attention goes immediately to the sensation. So when my heart rate soared one evening and wouldn't slow down after many hours, and my breathing became labored, I awakened my husband and told him I needed to go to the emergency room. I was hooked up with electrodes and my heart was tested. The doctors came back with a diagnosis of panic attack with sinus tachycardia (rapid heartbeat). I was embarrassed because I really thought I had conquered the attacks. But the truth was that I really *was* learning to conquer the attacks, because I was finally learning to deal with them. It became much easier to diffuse an attack before losing control to it.

If I feel any pains now, I refocus my attention on my strength and recovery. Instead of going with the thoughts that tell me I'm not okay, I remember that deep down there is nothing wrong with me. Even though I still experience pain with endometriosis, it doesn't affect who I am and how I react to it; I am the one who decides those things. I decide how to live my life, and I decide what actions support my health and well-being. I have learned how to let go of the fear and relax. There is no more nausea or fire to consume me. Instead of panic, now there is comfort and joy. I love and appreciate my life on a greater level thanks to the responsibility these experiences have given me.

> *I am an artist and graphic designer. I live with my husband, Jean-Marie, and my laptop, Bunny, in Switzerland, where I am still learning how to speak with the natives. I shower gratitude on my father, Pat, and my stepmother, Nancy, for their deep love and support, and on my mother, T. R., who shows such courage and compassion in one entirely beautiful human being.*

Commentary by Paul Foxman

Elaine's story describes an anxiety disorder known as "anxiety due to a medical condition," a diagnosis used when anxiety is the direct result of a general medical disorder. In her case the medical disorder was a painful, ruptured ovarian cyst that required surgery. Unfortunately, Elaine's story is also another case of progressive anxiety resulting from improper diagnosis and treatment. Nevertheless, she found her way out of anxiety through meditation, which opened the door to "the deepest, most peaceful place in the universe." What is meditation and how is it helpful in anxiety recovery?

Meditation is a simple but powerful practice whose goal is a quiet, peaceful, and focused mind. Everyone experiences meditative moments, when attention is fully engaged in a single activity. Sitting quietly by the fire, knitting, and boating on a sunny summer afternoon are examples. At these times, serenity and contentment replace a busy or worried mind, and the concerns of daily life are transcended. However, these activities bring only temporary peace during the time they absorb our interest, or perhaps for a short lingering period afterwards. With practice, formal meditation can train our minds to return to that peaceful state at will, or through the use of a simple exercise such as deep breathing.

Every thought has an effect on us. Worry and negative thinking, for example, lead to adrenaline-charged agitation and unrest. Meditation counteracts this mind/body pattern through the practice of selective focus. By focusing on a special word or positive thought, and letting all other mental activity dissolve into the background, the mind becomes still, clear, and empty. In turn, the body relaxes.

As a beginner at meditation a person may have little control over her thoughts, but with steady practice she can succeed in letting go of those thoughts and experience the quiet behind the thoughts. This is an important step, and it confers benefits such as clearer thinking, a more tranquil mind, and stronger willpower. With additional practice, a person can attain a higher level where she transcends her mind and experiences inner peace and equanimity.

The benefits of meditation take time to realize, and they may not come easily. As with any skill, you must practice regularly in order to make progress. As one meditation teacher explains, "A beautiful tree grows slowly. One must wait for the blossom, the ripening of the fruit, and the ultimate taste." Here are some suggestions for beginning a meditation practice:

- Choose a warm, quiet place that is free of distractions
- Relax your body (breathe deeply, stretch your muscles, etc.)
- Sit straight but comfortably, either on the floor or in a chair, with head, neck, and back in vertical alignment

- Focus for five to twenty minutes on your breathing or on a special word or prayer

- Concentrate on your focus point and return to it each time your mind is drawn away by passing thoughts

- Keep a notebook handy and release stubborn thoughts by jotting them down

- Rise calmly at the end of the session, and carry the serenity of meditation into your daily life

- Practice once or twice daily

CHAPTER 24

UNCONDITIONAL HAPPINESS

by ALEX RYDER, as told to Jenna Glatzer

When I was about nine I started having what I call "bad thoughts." For example, I'd think that if I didn't count to ten in my head right away, then my mother would die in a car accident. Whenever I would have a "bad thought," I'd feel terribly guilty and have to tell my parents. Sometimes I'd be sitting in school and have to call home because I had a troubling thought. My parents and I developed a strong trust bond because I told them everything from such an early age.

There were also things I believed I *had* to do. When I'd pray at night I'd have to say "Amen" twice, or I thought God wouldn't hear me. I wasn't very concerned about my habits; at the time I just saw them as things I had to do.

When I went away to college for the first time, I lived in a dorm with communal bathrooms. Not many people are thrilled about sharing bathrooms, but I had a particular problem with it. If I had to use the stall, I felt the need to shower immediately afterwards. I tried to get myself into a schedule where I'd go to the bathroom only at night. I set things up so that if I felt obsessive about being "dirty," I could shower.

I found that if I obsessed about one thing, it took all my mental energy, so I couldn't obsess about anything else. For example, recently I was having obsessions related to blood. If I thought I saw blood on a door handle, I'd think about it over and over. However, if I walked through that door and then thought I might have stepped in urine, I wouldn't think about the blood anymore. I'd have a new worry to occupy my mind instead. Although that may not sound like a positive thing, it helped me to realize that I could deflect my obsessions by focusing on other things. If I could just keep my mind on something else, I couldn't concentrate on the obsession.

I moved back to my hometown for my second year of college. It was cheaper, and I could live at home. I changed majors from physics to dance and music. I was a bartender at one of the top twenty-five restaurants as ranked by *Food and Wine* magazine. I loved my work. It became my social life—I liked the people there, and they liked me. Unfortunately, outside of work, my social life was dwindling. I've always enjoyed my time alone, but whereas before I'd go out to parties with friends, now I withdrew and didn't have as much fun when I did go out.

I got heavily into fitness and nutrition, and that put a damper on some of my social activities. Months earlier, I might have gone out to have a few beers and pizza with friends, but once I became more aware of fitness I began thinking, "I can't have that beer or that pizza—it's not good for me." I continued to meet with my friends for a while, but when everyone else is doing one thing and you're off in a corner doing something else, it stops being social.

I had always liked running and working out, but I'd never been so careful about my food intake. I read a magazine article about counting calories that really stuck with me. For some reason I couldn't get the phrase "counting calories" out of my head. I didn't look in the mirror and think I was fat, but even so, I went from feeling healthy and muscular at 157 pounds to losing weight until I'd hit 128 pounds. I knew I'd gone way too far, and a blood test determined that I was partly anemic.

Over the summer I began what my dad calls "floundering." I was stressed about college and thinking about changing majors again. I worked for my father, and a coworker inquired about a friend of mine. I told the coworker that my friend was doing language studies in the Army. Other coworkers said, "If I had it to do over again, that's what I would do." I started thinking about it. Since I was so worried about college maybe I should consider the military instead. It was kind of a weird switch—last semester I had been studying ballet, and now I was thinking about joining the Army! I had always been impulsive, though, and sure enough it took the Army recruiter just one day to sign me up.

I was excited about the new adventure. Basic training was difficult, but once I got past the homesickness I was okay. In September of 2000, I was moved out to Monterey, California, and that's when my downfall started. In October I got warts on the bottom of my foot. Those little buggers became such a problem for me. I went to a doctor, and he offered to burn them off. Then I did some research on the Internet. Unfortunately, there were a million differing opinions about how to treat warts. One person said to be careful not to touch them, because they were contagious and could spread. That's all I needed to hear! I became very anxious; I thought about the warts all the time. I didn't return to the doctor because I was afraid that if he burned them off a blister would form that could pop and infect other places. I hoped they'd spontaneously go away.

In the Army I again had to share community showers. It was an even bigger problem for me now because of the warts. I tried not to be too conspicuous about why I was taking longer getting ready in the mornings or why I was asking people to pick me up a piece of fruit from the chow hall because I couldn't take care of my foot and still make it in time for breakfast.

I was supposed to graduate to the next level in December, but because of my foot I was unable to take my physical tests. I was told I might be able to get a waiver and move up anyway, but it didn't happen. Now I was anxious *and* angry because I had been pinning my hopes on graduating, which would have meant I'd get my own bathroom and more freedom.

"Great," I thought. "Now I have OCD, warts, I'm partly anemic (which is probably why I got warts; my immune system was run-down), I'm still obsessed with public bathrooms, and I have this generally anxious feeling that there's always going to be something 'out there' to bother me."

When I went home on leave my mom made an appointment for me to see her doctor, who she said was a good listener. She was right. I had an anxiety attack on the way to the office, but once I got there we had a wonderful discussion. I started crying, and she listened. She taught me about my foot, explaining why it wasn't a big problem, and what I should do about it. It was nice to have someone to talk to.

My mother and sister were wonderful strongholds for me. My mother also had an anxiety disorder, so she understood mine. My sister has her own terrific success story; she has Tourette's syndrome. In the fourth grade she would fall asleep in class from the medication, but she went from being a D student in grade school to eventually graduating from college with honors and becoming a teacher. She always had such a great outlook, and she was always the one to pull me out of the dirt. I'd tell her about my lousy days, and she'd tell me not to worry. She'd never mention her troubles, even though her day might have been twenty times worse than mine. Even though we lived apart geographically, the three of us grew closer during the rough times because we could all give each other support. We have Internet "chat dates" now and have helped each other find happiness again.

While I was home on leave I became more mentally focused. I knew I'd have to go back to California and deal with my anxiety, and I was determined to do it. I made an appointment with a counselor and a psychiatrist, and he prescribed Prozac. Despite my reservations about taking medication, I took it, and it has helped me. It didn't change my whole outlook, but it took the edge off my anxiety and helped me deal with things better. I stopped being as concerned with what I "had" to do.

Then my mom bought me a great book, *You Can Be Happy No Matter What*, by Richard Carlson (also known for his book *Don't Sweat the Small Stuff*). I was never a fan of self-help books, because I was always able to talk myself through things. But this book made a big difference in my life. It lists five principles for achieving happiness, and one of the main points is that happiness is not conditional.

In the Army I had been making my happiness contingent on outside forces: When I graduate, when I get rid of these warts, when I get an A on this test, when I finish Russian, *then* I'll be happy. The book helped me to realize that you can't base your happiness on something else; you can be happy with warts, with stress, with the Army, with everything.

All that time when I was putting off my happiness, basing it on other things, what was I planning on doing in the meantime? Just "dealing"? I mentally put my foot down and said, "No." I decided to accept the fact that I have low moods, but I don't have to make decisions at those times. It's a natural tendency to want to figure out your problems when you're low, but instead I found that if I could just wait half a day until my mood was better, I could approach my problems with a clear mind. Then I could figure out what I needed to do, if anything.

Now I have a whole new outlook. Normally I'd make sure my uniform was ironed right after school on Fridays. Today is Sunday, and I'm just getting to it. I'm learning not to worry so much. I want to live life, not just worry about what it is I have to do to live life!

Every morning I repeat the following phrase to myself: "You can only do what you can do." I know that I'm doing the best I can, and even if I recognize I have a problem, I can still live. Notice I didn't say "live with it." Forget about "it." All you have to say is, "I'm going to live." With the right steps, anxiety disorders don't have to last forever. You have to live a life and be happy, no matter what else is happening around you.

This morning I ran five miles along the beautiful Monterey Bay coast, out to Lover's Point and back, stopping only to watch the waves hit the rocks. I'm looking out my window at the ocean right now, and I'm happy. And I plan to stay that way!

Alex Ryder is a pseudonym.

Commentary   by Paul Foxman

Alex struggled with a chronic obsessive-compulsive disorder that affected his social life, his ability to complete college and military training, and even his health. He tried to control his obsessions by changing his focus to new worries. By counting calories and exercising compulsively he could control his contamination worries, but in the process he lost almost thirty pounds and became anemic.

One of Alex's obsessions reflects a key personality trait—suggestibility—common among anxiety sufferers. *Suggestibility* means being easily influenced by people, events, or information, and this accounts for the tendency of many anxious people to "take on symptoms" from outside sources. For example, Alex heard that you should not touch warts because they are contagious and can spread. Consequently, he became anxious about and obsessed with the warts on his feet. He also reacted strongly to a magazine article about counting calories, which led to an obsession about calories and a compulsive-eating pattern that compromised his health.

The suggestibility trait is one reason why Internet anxiety chat groups may be inadvisable for some people. Exposure to other people's anxiety can cause some sufferers to take on additional symptoms or pick up new worries. This can be counteracted by a knowledgeable group leader or facilitator who can prevent "symptom swapping" and maintain a positive focus.

You can use the suggestibility trait to advantage by associating with positive role models. This is especially beneficial when the other people have been successful in anxiety recovery. In addition, one of the advantages of working with a therapist is that you can be influenced positively in terms of motivation, hopefulness, and steps you can take towards recovery. If properly directed, group therapy can also provide opportunities to interact with people who are taking positive action to improve their condition. Ideally, in both individual and group therapy there should be a positive and encouraging atmosphere, combined with structure and skills.

Alex benefited from the positive influence of two key family members. His mother, who understood anxiety from personal experience, offered him comfort and resources, such as a useful self-help book and referral to a doctor. His sister, who had a "great outlook" and enjoyed her own success in dealing with Tourette's syndrome, provided inspiration and ongoing e-mail support. These are examples of how the suggestibility trait combined with positive input can be helpful in recovery. Even the title of the book given to Alex by his mother, *You Can Be Happy No Matter What*, has a positive ring.

Alex was able to change his habits and patterns. He learned to think positively, worry less, and redefine his anxiety as a temporary "mood." In addition, Alex learned that happiness comes not from outside events, but rather from one's own thoughts and personal choices.

CHAPTER 25

A SIMPLE PRAYER

by CORINNA FRITZ

I'll never forget that first one. I was eighteen years old, seven months pregnant, driving my little green Chevy Chevette into town to see my husband, who was incarcerated in the county jail. It came out of nowhere and grabbed me like a burr grabs your socks—hard and painfully. My mouth went dry, but I couldn't stop swallowing, and to make it worse, I was nauseated. My palms were sweaty, my heart was racing, and I was shaking all over—I was terrified!

I pulled over to the side of the road and got out of my car. I was wearing a thin maternity dress my mother had bought somewhere in the tropics, and I remember the cold, Colorado spring wind whipping the dress and stinging my legs. The wind was so cold, but it felt refreshing, like a glass of ice water in the face to revive me from a faint. I remember wondering if I was going into premature labor. I don't remember how long I stood there, not knowing what was going on, but eventually I calmed down enough to get back in my car and go on with my day. I didn't know I'd just had an anxiety attack. I attributed it to being pregnant and all the changing hormones and stress that accompanies it.

When the attacks didn't go away after I had my baby, I wasn't really surprised; after all, hormones can take a while to settle down. I had been going to the health department for my maternity care, where, of course, we were herded through the checkup process as fast as possible. Even if we hadn't been so rushed, I wouldn't have trusted anyone who worked for the state well enough to tell them about this thing that had been happening to me.

My husband was no help; as a matter of fact, when I look back, I'm fairly certain he was the trigger that caused me to start having the attacks. Putting it mildly, he was not a nice person. When I finally came to my senses and started trying to get out of that relationship, I finally learned what was happening to me.

By that time, I was twenty years old, and my baby was about a year and a half old. I was living with my parents again. Every day, I would get ready to go out and find a job, and every day at the exact moment I was ready to walk out the door, I would get a splitting headache that would feel like an ice pick being stabbed into my head above and in front of my right ear. These headaches were so bad that my parents suggested I go to the doctor, and they even paid for it, which was unusual for them. The first doctor I saw told me I had a sinus infection and sent me home with antibiotics. My mom sent me right back with specific instructions to see her doctor instead of the one I had seen. Mom's doctor diagnosed migraines, postpartum depression, and anxiety attacks. He put me on Tylenol with codeine for the headaches and on an antidepressant for the rest.

Of course, he was wrong about the type of depression, but at least the depression and anxiety attacks got diagnosed. Unfortunately, by the time I had taken all the free trial medications and needed a prescription, my soon-to-be ex was back in my life and controlling it fully. I couldn't have gotten more medication if I had wanted to, but the side effects I endured from the antidepressants were bad enough that I really didn't care to take them anyway. Eventually, I managed to get away from the ex for good and have not seen or heard from him for many years now, although I do still have an occasional nightmare that includes him.

I believe I started recovering when I moved in with my grandma. She always had a knack of nurturing those in need. I never did get back to the doctor for any different medications or counseling, but who needs that stuff when you have a grandma? While we lived with my grandma, she took wonderful care of my baby and me. I worked full-time and then some every day, but I knew my baby was being well cared for, I'd have a place to sleep, food to eat, and clean clothes to wear. It was heaven after the abusive nightmare I had just been through with the ex-husband. The panic attacks came less and less often and were usually less severe than they had been while I was married.

Then I met my future second husband, totally by accident. I was not looking for a date, a boyfriend, a husband, or a father for my daughter. As a matter of fact, I'd had just about all I could stand of men at that point. I agreed to let him hang out with me on the grounds that we remained only friends. That worked for about a month. He was just too nice, too much fun, and so supportive. When he graduated from college, he asked me to come back to his home state with him. I agreed, and we've been together ever since.

The anxiety attacks didn't stop overnight, or at any precise time. I had them for about four more years after meeting my husband. Although my husband is wonderful, kind, supportive, and loving, I can't give all the credit to him or our relationship for the lessening of my panic attacks, because we've had our share of serious issues and rough spots along the way. I also can't say exactly when the attacks stopped; it wasn't an on/off sort of thing. It was a gradual tapering of frequency, length, and severity of the attacks in general. I don't know what made them go away, but I'm just glad they did.

The other good news is that there were two things that seemed to be able to stop a panic attack fairly quickly for me. The first one was prayer. I discovered that if I just went to a quiet place and started praying to the Lord about the attack I was experiencing, the attack would fade away much faster than with any other method of relaxation, including progressive relaxation, self-hypnosis, reflexology, aromatherapy—you name it, I probably tried it. The second thing that nearly always worked was to be held quietly in an embrace by my husband, and the beauty of it was that he didn't even have to know I was having an attack for it to work—sometimes he even dozed off and it still worked.

Today, I am thirty-two years old, live in the suburbs, am still married to the same sweet guy, and am now the mom of not one but two beautiful daughters whom I homeschool. I do all the things a suburban housewife and mom does. I haven't had an anxiety attack in so long that I'm sure I don't remember all of the terrifying details.

My hope is that I don't ever experience another attack, but my consolation is that if I do, I'll know how to deal with it. Just knowing that there is a way to gain control of an attack is probably more than half the battle.

My advice to those who feel imprisoned by panic is to reach out for help whenever and however you are able to. There are lots of good strategies out there from people who have been there and from professionals who treat anxiety. Use whatever means you feel comfortable with—books, computer, videos, or whatever works for you—to learn everything you can about panic attacks. Try everything you think might help alleviate or lessen the attacks. I personally believe that an important part of getting over panic is gaining a sense of control over your initial reactions to stress.

There's no shame in going to your doctor and asking for help. There are nonnarcotic antianxiety drugs that have worked wonders for some people, and they are probably worth a try.

In my humble opinion and spiritual view, you are a precious human being who was created in the Creator's image and are loved by Him and many others.

Matthew 29:31 says, "Are not two sparrows sold for a penny? Yet not one of them will fall to the ground apart from the will of your Father. And even the very hairs of your head are all numbered. So don't be afraid; you are worth more than many sparrows."

You deserve to be well, and you are worth the effort to get there. Talk to your preacher or spiritual counselor. The best thing I've ever found for anxiety attacks is prayer. The best thing I've ever found for improving my quality of life is regular church attendance. The attitude that maintains my happiness is the attitude of gratitude.

I'll be praying for you.

> *I'm a thirty-two-year-old happily married, so-called stay-at-home, homeschooling mom of two beautiful girls. My hobbies include reading, writing, singing, crochet, and drawing. Some of my drawings are posted at http://www.zing.com/album/pictures.html?id=4294850765. Once a week I drive into the heart of downtown Portland, Oregon, to take guitar lessons, which is something I never could have done a few years ago. One of my absolute most favorite hobbies is riding my dirt and street motorcycles. I've come a long way from where I was at my worst.*

Commentary by Paul Foxman

It could be said that Corinna was cured of panic disorder by good old-fashioned grandmotherly love. Living temporarily with her nurturing grandmother was certainly a healing experience, and it points to the importance of supportive relationships for anxiety recovery.

Corinna's grandma provided a safe, secure, and caring environment that enabled her to get back on her feet following an abusive marriage. But her grandmother offered something more intangible: an intuitive understanding about the emotional needs of someone who was trying to get a handle on anxiety. What can family members do to help loved ones recover from anxiety? Are there any "dos and don'ts" for family members?

Anxiety recovery, which often involves a feeling of starting all over again, requires a safe and supportive atmosphere. The ideal family environment would include understanding, patience, acceptance, and unconditional love. Here are some guidelines and suggestions for family members who wish to encourage and support a loved one's anxiety recovery:

- Read about anxiety to further your understanding
- Ask how you can help; don't make assumptions
- Be patient and accepting but don't fake it
- Be consistent and predictable

- Find something positive in every effort

- Don't enable avoidance; negotiate steps in facing the fear. Gently resist any pressure or temptation to rescue

- Don't get too involved unless asked

- Don't motivate with guilt ("We're wasting our money if you don't recover")

- Realize that setbacks are inevitable in learning new behaviors and facing challenges

- Verbalize your support and encouragement with comments such as "I love you no matter what"; "Go ahead and feel the anxiety, I'm here for you"; "Stay in the here and now, don't anticipate the future"; "Face the fear and it will slowly disappear"; "Don't worry about 'what if'"; "Don't fight it; float through it"; "I'm proud of you—you're courageous."

The CHAANGE program, a self-help anxiety-recovery process discussed at other points in this book, includes a "Dear Family Member" letter to be given to loved ones early in the program. The letter provides an explanation of anxiety as well as some dos and don'ts similar to the ones listed above. Interested readers will find the complete letter in my book, *Dancing with Fear* (on pages 342–344).

We must recognize that family members may have their own feelings about residing with a highly anxious person. These feelings may include frustration, resentment, anger, loneliness, helplessness, guilt, and fear. It is important that these feelings be handled maturely and not acted out towards the anxious person. They should be discussed openly, without any assignments of blame. Affected family members may need their own support, and it is advisable in some cases for them to seek counseling. They need to keep their own lives in balance and to pursue their interests without abandoning the person dealing with anxiety. Family members need to take care of themselves physically, emotionally, and spiritually so they can be there for their anxious loved one.

CHAPTER 26

THE GIRL WHO USED TO BE ME

by RENEE DECTER

It's 8:00 P.M. and I'm writing this as I try to remember "the girl who used to be me." That's the title of a song from the movie *Shirley Valentine*, one of my favorites, though I didn't know why until today. Today was a full day, for I taught my first college-credit English class and was gone from the house for six hours. The girl who used to be me twenty years ago couldn't have done that. Teaching a college course would have been ridiculous to even consider. And being away from home for more than six hours, driving on freeways, going to new locations, and getting lost—well, those things would have gone beyond ridiculous in 1981. They would have been impossible. You see, I was housebound at the time, frozen in my tracks with agoraphobia.

I returned to college in 1980. My plan was to take one or two classes per semester and then transfer to the university to finish my bachelor's degree. One day in a psychology class—a prophetic environment, I was soon to learn—I felt an overpowering force swell within my gut. The stomach flu! The feeling slowly crept into my chest. Oh, I thought, I'm too young to have a heart attack! Then a burning sensation crawled into my throat, and heat like the Sahara Desert's spread into my cheeks and forehead. Could this be the beginning of menopause?

When the sensation encircled my brain, I bolted out of the room. The professor followed me as I ran to the ladies' room. "Are you okay?"

he called from outside. I couldn't answer. I didn't know what had happened. Finally I yelled that I was okay, and eventually I returned to the classroom. This happened on several other occasions, sometimes during a lecture, other times during an exam.

A few months later, I was on my way to the first day of classes. I'd been getting dizzy a lot and found that I felt more comfortable carrying food and water whenever I went out, so I was laden with not only my notebook but also water bottles and food. I went through registration (in the days when doing so involved standing in long lines for a good part of the day) and was on my way to my first class when my feet slowly stopped functioning. I felt so dizzy that I leaned against a tree, the nearest solid object. Then my knees seemed to melt into my ankles. I started quivering uncontrollably, and by this time the same force that had overcome me in the psychology class had returned full-blown. I couldn't catch my breath, my chest hurt, and I felt like I was going to be sick to my stomach. Every muscle in my body was locked tight. Still, I was able to run to my car. Ten minutes later I was in my living room. I couldn't believe I hadn't hit a pedestrian or another car, for the drive home from the college normally took at least twenty minutes when there was no traffic, and there was heavy traffic that day.

My gynecologist had given me some tranquilizers, and I took one. I called in sick to my part-time job and tried to pull myself together before my eleven-year-old daughter got home from school. After a nap, I attempted to comprehend what had happened. I loved college, was doing extremely well, and somehow had quite smoothly made the transition from a single mother working full-time to a single mother working and going to school part-time.

I didn't return to college that semester, nor the next, nor the next. Actually, I didn't return to college for many years. The overpowering force happened more frequently and with more intensity. After a few months I stopped going to the mall, and then the bank, and then the market. I missed so much time from my part-time job that they replaced me. Finally, by June of 1980, I couldn't even walk out of my front door. I waited until midnight to walk down the stairs of my apartment building to get my mail. By this time I had concluded that it wasn't menopause. It was insanity. I didn't want anyone to see this crazy lady I had turned into, and I knew that by midnight my neighbors would probably be asleep.

Soon I found myself spending hours sitting on the floor of a closet. I rarely showered or dressed and was able to eat once in a while only through the kindness of my parents, who shopped for me. When my daughter was in the house, I tried to put on a show for her, but eleven-year-old kids are pretty smart. Eventually she moved to her father's house. The thought of losing my child triggered something in me. I called a family friend, who was a psychiatrist, and made an appointment. Somehow I managed to walk out my front door, drive the few blocks to his office, and slither along the brick wall of the building to the front door.

This doctor had known my family and me for almost thirty years, so I didn't have to talk too much. I couldn't, because my throat tightened up. He gave me a hug when he saw how I looked and sat me down in his inner sanctum. He asked why I was there, and I searched for the words to explain insanity. I heard myself saying, "I'm here for you to commit me to the state mental hospital." He laughed, not really at me, but as one would who hears something he knows is impossible—my being insane, that is. No, I insisted, I must be crazy. He gently prodded, and I told him about the past six months of my life. At one point I stopped talking in midsentence and started sobbing. I told him I couldn't go on. He said I didn't have to, and he picked up my story where I had dropped it.

He filled in the details about the past six months of my life, and then he told me about the past forty years of my life. "What are you, a fly on my living-room wall?" I asked. It felt good to laugh when I said that. He went on to explain what my problem was. He gave it a name, a word I'd never before heard: agoraphobia. He told me what it is, how I got it, how my parents raised me, how sensitive my personality is, and yet how intelligent I am. After a deep breath, my first in several months, I asked him what we should do about it. He recommended an educationally based behavioral program for treating agoraphobia and related disorders. The group met once a week. I told him I couldn't drive to any group and that I'd rather see him for therapy anyway. So he bribed me. He said he'd see me every week if, and only if, I entered the program.

Here was a person telling me I wasn't insane, a person who knew me—I mean, really knew me. I didn't want to go to the program, but I couldn't cut myself off from our weekly sessions. Besides, he told me the program delivered about an 80 percent recovery rate. I was tired of living in a closet, and mostly I wanted my daughter back. So I put a great deal of thought into how I could get my body from here to there to attend those weekly group meetings.

I called the program's director and went through intake. That was the first step. The second was finding someone to take me to the meetings. The doctor told me not to rely on my parents for that help, so I called a friend I had made at college. She was a psychology major and was fascinated with what I was telling her. She said she'd take me to and from the meetings if she could sit in on them. I called the administrator, who gave his assent.

I started the program in September, and by November I could drive by myself to a small market a few blocks from home. I framed the receipt from that first store visit, for it represented a closet-free life. After I finished the program, the administrator asked if I wanted to work under supervision as a counselor in the program. Me? Why? He said I had done better than any other participant, and he thought I could help others recover. The only hitch was that I'd have to drive myself there and back home—alone.

I thought back to the day I'd gotten my butt into the psychiatrist's office, and I realized I had an inner strength, a courage hidden under all those layers of anxiety and panic. So I agreed to work in the program—or at least to take the risk and try. I worked with those groups for six years, and by 1987 I thought I had truly recovered. After all, I was banking, marketing, and running a home business.

Think again.

In the fall of that year, my aunt had a stroke. She had always been the deep roots in my life; she'd always loved and accepted me unconditionally, had never put me down. One day shortly after my aunt fell ill, while driving to a client's office, I felt the old force swell up within me. I darted home, ran into my apartment, locked the door, and headed for a closet. I see now, I thought. It doesn't go away. It waits in the bushes, in the shadows—ready to pounce.

I had enjoyed several years of comparative freedom, and I'd liked living closet-free. Sure, I only shopped in small neighborhood markets and went to the bank when I knew it wouldn't be busy. But I could also cross major intersections and wait for a red light to change without jumping out of my skin. This is nirvana, I thought, and now it's back to the closet. My daughter had moved back home, and I didn't want to lose her again, so I called a former colleague from the program to see if she would give me psychotherapy.

A few days later my father drove me to her office. This time I was able to coherently verbalize my feelings and symptoms. She said she'd take me on, but cautioned that I might have to journey to places I'd rather avoid. She also said she'd terminate me if I missed even one appointment, unless I was in surgery or dead, and that I would have to drive myself to her office. I agreed. The taste of freedom propelled me to.

She was right. In our sessions together I journeyed all the way back to my earliest memories. I visited and revisited family dynamics and those I had had with myself for forty-five years. I resisted. She pushed. I refused. She coerced. She had been where I was and knew how to handle me. I had been treated with kid gloves all my life, but I took on this task as an adult. I trusted the therapist and allowed her to lead me into the fire. She was right. I hadn't recovered in those six years since completing the program; I had accommodated. I made room for fear in various corners of my life, and I hid my anxiety and panic attacks, using them when they were needed. I used them to avoid life, to avoid responsibility for myself—to avoid myself.

Three and a half years after my first visit with this therapist, we both agreed I was "done." There remained a few things I had trouble doing, such as going to the dentist or to large supermarkets and driving on freeways by myself, but meeting men and dating? Well, that took about ten more years of self-searching and relationship resolution. Still, after "completing" myself with the therapist, I was working full-time in my home business, riding elevators to the fifth floor, raising my daughter, and even going out on an occasional date. I thought back to the girl who used to be me and wondered what had changed. What changed was the fact that holding onto anxiety no longer gave me a payoff, a hiding place. I deserved better than a closet, and I got something much, much better.

I kept in touch with the therapist, and one day she asked me if I wanted 100 percent recovery. I said yes. She told me about another program, called CHAANGE, that I could do on my own at home. The freedom I had acquired while in therapy was more than I ever expected to achieve; yet I still had baby-chick feathers. I wanted and needed 100 percent recovery. I wanted full-grown adult feathers, because I wanted to fly!

I started the CHAANGE program in January of 1990 and completed it in July—and I was flying. I returned to college, where I experienced only slight anxiety in the first week. I admit—I was waiting for it to jump out of the shadows at me. However, for weeks I experienced little to no anxiety, and by a few weeks later I suffered no discernible anxiety at all.

I decided to test the shadows. I went to a large supermarket. No anxiety. I drove on the freeway. No anxiety. A tooth broke, the pain was excruciating, and I went to the dentist for an emergency repair—alone. Normal anxiety. (I'd traveled a long and hard road to learn what was "normal" anxiety.) The dentist told me I was a delight to work on and that very few patients were as relaxed in the chair as I was that day.

That was in 1991. In 1994, I closed my home business and transferred to UCLA to complete my bachelor's degree. I figured if I could do a quarterly semester regimen—and at UCLA to boot—then I could do anything I wanted to do. I traveled to Virginia at Christmas in 1995 to visit my sister—alone. I negotiated the Atlanta airport to change planes—alone. I graduated UCLA in 1997, with my family gathered around me, and entered graduate school the following fall. The only problem I had was on the first day. I was walking from my car to my first graduate class when I felt the anxiety rising inside me. The tools I learned in the CHAANGE program jumped into gear, and within thirty seconds I realized that everyone is anxious on their first day of graduate school. I also realized that I deserved to be there. Two years later I began teaching English part-time at a community college while completing my studies. I experienced normal anxiety the first day, and none thereafter.

It's now 2001. I'll be the first person in my family to graduate with a master's degree this May, and I deserve it. I am flying with fully-grown, fluffy-white adult feathers that allow me to swoop and soar at my choosing. And I deserve them.

Today I taught my first college English class. I didn't bolt from the classroom, taking panic with me into the comforting recesses of the ladies' room or the nearest closet. I didn't scurry to my car, driving towards home at twenty miles per hour above the speed limit. What I did was fly!

I was first diagnosed with agoraphobia in 1981 at age thirty-nine. Since then, my recovery has led to my working as a counselor and administrator in an anxiety-recovery program, the publication in the United States and Canada of an article I wrote on agoraphobia, my running a home-based business, the completion of a B.A. in sociology at UCLA in 1997, and the attainment of an M.A. in English in 2001. I now teach English at a community college.

Commentary by Paul Foxman

Renee suffered from panic disorder with agoraphobia, triggered by the stress of college. At her lowest point she was a forty-something, housebound woman sitting for hours on the floor of a closet. Her remarkable recovery highlights some important issues and insights that deserve further discussion.

One issue for all agoraphobic individuals is resistance to change when there is a "payoff," as Renee calls it, to be gained from avoidance. As disabling as the condition can be, there is often a benefit—known as *secondary gain*—that can accompany agoraphobia. The most obvious benefit is the relief that comes from avoiding situations in which anxiety is anticipated. Beyond that, however, there may be more subtle payoffs, such as receiving attention, a lower stress level, and having an excuse for not dealing with unpleasant responsibilities (shopping, visiting relatives, making phone calls, etc.). One example was a woman I counseled whose agoraphobia resulted in dependence on her husband to drive her everywhere. I asked her, "Strange as this question may seem, is there anything you would lose if you recovered completely from anxiety?" After a moment of thought she answered, "Yes, I would spend much less time with my husband." Like this woman, you may need to address any payoffs from your anxiety disorder. This usually requires identifying other ways to obtain the same benefits without paying the price of anxiety symptoms.

Renee participated in two anxiety-treatment programs, both of which proved helpful. One of them was the CHAANGE program, the sixteen-week homework course described elsewhere in this book. The program was designed originally for homebound agoraphobia sufferers who could not travel to see a therapist. However, it is most effective when administered by a trained therapist, who can individualize the program for each participant, monitor progress, and be available to answer questions or address issues that may arise. In addition, a trained therapist can go beyond the program and focus on related matters, such as relationship issues, job stress, parenting, and other life concerns that contribute to or are affected by anxiety. Renee's therapist was available while she went through the homework program. For regions where no CHAANGE therapists are available locally, the organization provides a list of trained therapists who are willing to consult by telephone (see Resources).

The programs leading to Renee's recovery involved a structured, step-by-step procedure for overcoming anxiety. This feature is compatible with the "anxiety personality," whose traits include motivation, intelligence, perfectionism, and capacity to change if given the proper structure and directions. When we seek help, we are looking for concrete recommendations that will make a difference. On the other hand, we are likely to give up easily or become discouraged when results are not immediate. Therefore, a program that starts right away with specific instructions and skills to be practiced, such as learning to relax and breathe properly, is most likely to hold our interest and lead to success.

CHAPTER 27

SWEATY PALMS

by SHELLEY BUECHE

A seemingly innocuous question at the drive-through window: "Queso or shredded cheese?" That question sent me into an incoherent, sweating, seemingly semicatatonic state. Science fiction, you might ask? No. This was reality, the final stages of a full-blown panic attack.

Note the Greek origins of *agoraphobia*: "fear of the open marketplace." Translation: "scared to check your mailbox." My agoraphobia coincided with my first semester of college. I later endured postpartum panic attacks. For sufferers of agoraphobia, stress and major life changes, good and bad, can trigger a round of panic attacks. We typically begin to build safety nets, such as bringing a glass of water when traveling in a car (to ward off possible dehydration), carrying a car phone (to call a loved one who can perform CPR on a minute's notice), and even keeping a prescription of tranquilizers always on hand (you never know!). In addition, many sufferers arrive at a compromised level of awareness, whereby they learn to live with their anxiety by total avoidance of dreaded situations. This avoidance can grow from steering clear of the upper deck of a local freeway to ultimately shunning driving altogether.

My avoidance has been reduced by desensitization, that is, facing my fears directly. For most people, this means flying on a plane or handling a snake. But for me it meant walking around the block and checking my mail. Repeatedly facing your fears in this manner retrains the mind to think, "I can perform this action without (fill in the blank:

passing out? dying? having a heart attack?).” Just as a stroke patient may need to relearn to walk and talk, I needed to prove to myself that I could resume my daily activities without suffering any harmful consequences. Surrounding yourself with loved ones who truly understand what you are going through is a major help. When dining out with supportive persons, instead of my usual self-dialogue (“Oh, my God, what if I pass out? Who will call 911?”), I could instead think, “If I pass out, I know my husband will know what to do.” As silly as this sounds to most people, it works. By confronting your fears on a repeated basis, the anxiety diminishes.

To fully explain, recently I got a phone call from my mother informing me that her elderly dog was in distress. Hearing high-pitched wailing in the background triggered a panic attack in me. As we rallied around the dog, awaiting the mobile vet, I was overcome by stress. The only way I felt I could cope with the ensuing panic was by reminding myself that the vet was on her way, and while she was treating my mom’s dog, perhaps she could perform CPR on me should it become necessary! Looking back to that moment, I have to suppress a grin. The memory is not so distant, however, that I cannot immediately evoke the sweating and terror I felt during the situation. My mother’s dog had to be euthanized.

My history with panic attacks and agoraphobia remains ongoing. It started in 1977, when I became agoraphobic, then progressed to postpartum anxiety attacks in 1990 and 1992, and continues to the present. I now consider myself in a maintenance stage. I take antidepressants daily, which keeps my anxiety “in check.” However, during periods of extreme stress, I struggle to maintain my equilibrium. Rather than thinking of myself as “cured,” I think in terms of “maintenance.” As cliché as it sounds, I try to take each day as it comes.

I remind myself that everyone experiences fear. What distinguishes a panic attack is that the attack is irrational. Sometimes I am too hard on myself when I am experiencing real fear or anxiety. We all face trials and tribulations—the illness of a child or loved one, extreme weather conditions, or a close call in a vehicle. I have to remind myself that at times anxiety is a natural state and that I should not denounce myself for having these normal feelings.

Now, safety nets in place, I am happy to share my terrifying experiences in the hope that even a single reader might relate to my words and symptoms and seek help. This recognition is the first step toward managing stress in a healthy way.

> *Shelley Bueche is a freelance writer living in Austin, Texas. She is the mother of two elementary-aged sons and is married to a chemistry professor from Ireland. Shelley has occasional anxiety attacks during periods of extreme stress, but for the most part is able to conquer her fears.*

Commentary by Paul Foxman

Shelley distinguishes between an *anxiety disorder*, such as the panic, anxiety, and agoraphobia she experienced, and *normal anxiety*. Using gradual desensitization combined with medication, she made progress in reducing her symptoms, but she considers herself at a "maintenance" stage rather than "cured." Recognizing that anxiety is normal under certain conditions, Shelley is striving to reach that point in her recovery.

Anxiety recovery can be defined as having the knowledge, skills, and confidence to handle anxiety, whenever and wherever it may occur. You can realistically expect to reduce or eliminate your symptoms, including any avoidant behavior patterns you have developed to protect yourself from anxiety. But you are recovered only to the extent that you are no longer controlled by "fear of anxiety."

For example, one of my patients remarked after several months of therapy, "Dr. Foxman, I haven't had any anxiety now in about eight weeks, and I'm worried about it." In other words, in spite of her progress, she was afraid that she would relapse and not be able to handle the anxiety. I responded, "I think you are making great progress, but you remain fearful

about losing control. You need to test yourself and use your new knowledge and skills to handle any anxiety that might arise. You will be fully recovered *when you no longer think about anxiety."*

Anxiety recovery will not change one's basic personality or alter a biological sensitivity, although it will involve changes in the way an individual thinks, handles feelings, and acts. Therefore, someone with a history
of anxiety disorder will always be somewhat at risk for anxiety symptoms,
especially under stress. Nevertheless, with proper help and the right set
of concepts, skills, and attitudes, she or he can live a normal life free of
worry and anxiety.

CHAPTER 28

A GIFT OF HOPE

by XENIA MADISON, as told to Jenna Glatzer

I could sit here and rattle off my disorders all day. They run the gamut: OCD, body dysmorphic disorder (BDD), panic disorder, agoraphobia, attention-deficit disorder (ADD), depression, and generalized anxiety. What I've learned is that they're all just names and all just manifestations of the same thing.

My parents were heroin addicts. I was abandoned by my mother as a baby, and my grandparents found me and raised me. There were several custody battles and a lot of rage and confusion. I got lost in the shuffle. My mother was the "tragedy" in the family, and because her behaviors were so extreme, I don't think my grandparents even noticed what was happening to me. I dropped out of a Catholic academy after my junior year, despite the fact that I was a good student. Because I was bright, charismatic, and good with adults, like many other girls I was never diagnosed as having psychological and neurological conditions. I now realize that I had attention-deficit/hyperactivity disorder in addition to anxiety disorders even as a young child. My ADD made me feel "different" and misunderstood, which caused—guess what? Anxiety! I've learned that there is a very high comorbidity rate between ADD and anxiety disorders; since ADD also stems from imbalances in dopamine, serotonin, and other neurotransmitters, it can cause the same kinds of symptoms as anxiety.

On a deep level I carried a lot of fear about not being safe and cared for. OCD is characterized by that kind of doubt and uncertainty. My

OCD behaviors centered around my personal safety and fear of being harmed. Starting in my preteens I became hypervigilant to make sure nothing was awry. I kept a knife under my bed. I checked and rechecked the windows, the doors, the basement, the backseats of cars, everything. I became overobservant of the people around me. If I saw someone who I thought was sketchy, or a car out of place, I'd call the cops. I might see someone in the park and be convinced that he was a pedophile. Once I moved to my own apartment, if anything or anyone looked out of whack in the parking lot, I might drive around for forty-five minutes until I could feel safe walking into my home. I couldn't sleep when I was alone. I'd make lots of noise and rig escape routes in case someone broke in.

I also experienced mild panic symptoms and avoidant behavior in my preteen years, but they became severe only about seven or eight years ago—just before I married my husband, Jim. At that time I became agoraphobic for about two years. Jim would have to meet me at the car upon my return home from any destination.

Body dysmorphic disorder (BDD) is even more complex. I was obsessed with perfection in my appearance; I believed I had to be okay with my image to be safe in the world. I washed my hair and changed my clothes several times a day, and if my lipstick was bleeding I'd have to cancel appointments. If my purse wasn't hitting my back the right way, or if there was lint on my pants, that was enough to put me over the edge and make me go home. I'd have to leave the post office or drive off the road and go somewhere private to "fix" myself—apply more makeup, check the cowlick in the back of my hair, fix my collar.

You can imagine all the experiences I avoided! Ball games and other such situations with crowds were impossible because I was afraid I might be imperfect, and I couldn't let anyone see me that way. The most hurtful part was that I knew it didn't make any sense; I knew it was delusional, but I couldn't help it. I bought into the delusions hook, line, and sinker. It didn't help any that I got into the image business as a team manager for a large cosmetics company. That fed right into my obsessions.

I never knew what it was like to not feel exhausted all the time. I tried so hard to be perfect, and I wore myself out with my rituals. These were all attempts to become worthy. I kept wondering, "Why me?" Why was I so screwed up? I worked hard to pretend that I wasn't. I dressed for success but felt like an impostor. I felt everyone's pain, dealt with everyone's "stuff," and was hypersensitive to my family's dramas. There's a history of anxiety disorders on both sides of my family, and I tend to pick up on others' "vibes" and internalize everyone else's problems. Matters were made worse by my parents' drug problems and my being subjected to three court cases and a kidnapping before my mother's parents received custody of me at age seven.

When I was seventeen I sought therapy on my own and paid for it myself. I got heavily into drinking and experimented with drugs, and I tried to commit suicide at age nineteen. By my early twenties I was in big trouble with this undiagnosed anxiety. I knew something was wrong, and I needed outside sources to help me figure out what was happening. Even so, I found little relief until only a few years ago.

At twenty-nine, I couldn't hold it together any longer. I lived in terror, consumed by flaming OCD, BDD, and avoidant behaviors. I was ready for anything that might help me—at that point I didn't care *what*: brain surgery, medication, anything! I called my old therapist, went to specialists, got properly assessed, and started on medication for ADD and anxiety. I stepped back from my life. I cut my workload by about 75 percent and got rid of my calendar and my obligations. I retreated for about a year to figure out how to restructure my life.

The medications were lifesaving. Before, I had been "med-phobic" —typical for people with anxiety—and had been judgmental of people on medication. I remember thinking, "What's wrong with all these people on Prozac?" But I had come to a fragile breaking point where I was ready to do whatever it took to feel better. Amazingly, by about my fifth day on Zoloft, I noticed bliss and spontaneity, freedom from overthinking, and a sense of possibility—feelings I had never experienced in my life. Remembering that moment still makes me cry, and I remain so grateful to have learned that I no longer have to live in hell. Anxiety is a prison in which the sufferer is at the mercy of her or his brain chemicals. The medications helped to show me that I didn't have to wake up feeling consumed every day.

Before that turning point I had tried everything—breathing exercises, spiritual retreats, education, reading books and completing programs by Tony Robbins, taking baths, and lighting candles. It was all helpful, but adding these activities to my schedule was exhausting! My days were occupied with wellness rituals, yet they never relieved the consuming nature of my disorder. Now I have something to compare my earlier state to. Now that I know the difference, it gives me such pain to hear about people who are still suffering. I remember my own powerlessness and hopelessness, and it's a painful memory. I want to tell everyone that they can do it, afraid or not.

Besides finding the right medications and restructuring my life, being open and honest was also essential for my recovery. I had to face my family and say, "I'm messed up. I need help." Their outpouring of love was overwhelming. They were willing to do whatever I needed to help me get better, whether that was talking with me or taking the baby for a few hours. Their care and concern made me realize that I could have told them about my problems a long time ago!

And my husband, Jim, has been a tremendous help, too. If there ever was a perfect partner for an "anxiety head" like me, it's my husband. We've been together for ten years. In the beginning we partied a lot, but then we got sober together, and we matured together. He accommodated for my disorder by doing all the chores, errands, and other practical stuff. He took more than half the parenting responsibilities since early motherhood really pushed me over the edge. I couldn't even deal with myself; how was I going to take care of a baby? Jim is loyal, stable, dependable, and unconditionally loving. And through it all he managed to keep his integrity and avoid losing his sense of boundaries. He kept doing the things that were important to him, like sports, working out, and earning his master's degree, and he never broke promises to other people because of me.

I didn't realize how much he had put his life on hold until I started getting better. We were both angry at my past, and then I suddenly decided it was time to get out and live! I got selfish with my time when I finally had a day of freedom, so I'd hand him the baby and say, "Bye!" He also got selfish; he declared that he had put his life on hold long enough for me, and now it was his time. This was a growing phase. After lots of petty arguments, we realized we were both mad at the disorders, not at each other. We've grown much closer.

I attribute my recovery to the entire path I've been through. As painful as it all was, I'm grateful and wouldn't change a thing, because all of the highs and lows—the anger, hurt, peace, sadness, rest, and relaxation—all of that was necessary to get me where I am now. I am benefiting in every imaginable way from those years of torture.

The singular thing that separates me from people who are still suffering is acceptance. The medications played an important role, but my attitude was the most important piece of recovery. Everything changed for me when I decided to accept the fact that I'm crippled and I'm doing it crippled. That means I give myself permission to have a breakdown. I give myself permission to shut down for a few days when I need to, flake out on calling people back, be angry, or do whatever else I need to do. I didn't give myself those permissions before, because I didn't accept this disorder in myself. Now I know I have choices, and I don't need to do anything to "fix" myself. I can just be where I am today, and my happiness doesn't have to be contingent on anything. I set myself up for success because instead of simply declaring, "I kicked this," I can accept that if it ever comes back I'll be that much more prepared to deal with it.

I now work as a life-empowerment coach, and I specialize in helping adults with OCD and ADD. I knew that my purpose in life would be to help others, but the messenger had to understand the message before passing it on. Now, every day, I am there to let other people know that they don't have to live in hell any longer. I know I was tortured so I could give this gift to others—to help them accept the painful parts of life, restructure, and live again.

Anxiety has been a huge gift in my life. It's there to make us wake up, get grounded, and accept ourselves. It's there to remind us that it's time to honor ourselves, right here and right now.

> *I live on the Central Coast of California with my husband and daughter. I have been clean and sober for ten years and have been consulting and helping people ever since then. As a life coach/empowerment strategist, I help people help themselves and embrace and live their potential. In March 2002, I began an ADHD women's support group in San Luis Obispo County. I'm the founder and coach of ADD Outlook, which offers fresh approaches for brighter ADHD futures, and I'm a member of the International Coach Federation. My practice is transglobal; I work by telephone session and do some cybercoaching. I offer an array of program options that can fit the needs of just about anyone. For information about my telecoaching, call (805) 550-8330. For information about my support group, call (866) 426-8611. You can also e-mail me at addoutlook@msn.com.*

Commentary by Paul Foxman

Xenia suffered from a wide range of anxiety disorders and other conditions, such as body dysmorphic disorder (BDD), depression, and attention-deficit disorder (ADD), some of which can be linked to her unstable and traumatic childhood. Fortunately, Xenia received a "gift of hope" and achieved a remarkable recovery. What seems to have turned the tide for her was medication treatment.

ADD is characterized by impulsivity, inattention, and distractibility and is usually evident beginning in childhood. In some cases, hyperactivity (high energy; restless behavior pattern) is also involved. The cause of ADD is unclear, but many professionals consider it to be a genetic, neurological disorder. Others point to food additives and other chemicals as the cause of the disorder. Whatever the cause, ADD makes it difficult for many people to function successfully in school and in their relationships. In many cases the academic and social consequences of the condition contribute to anxiety. Fortunately, medication is often highly effective; the most common drugs used are stimulants (e.g., Dexedrine and Ritalin), which have a paradoxically calming, focusing effect on ADD.

Xenia also dealt with an unusual problem known as body dysmorphic disorder. This disorder involves distortions in a person's perception of his or her own body. For example, in many cases people see themselves as large or overweight when objective standards would contradict such perceptions. When the distorted body image involves size, attempts to lose weight by dieting and compulsive exercise may become excessive or out of control. In other cases, preoccupation with an imagined defect in one's appearance becomes excessive and causes distress in social, occupational, or other important areas of functioning. To alleviate BDD, individual psychotherapy, group therapy, and body-image work can be effective. This may include feedback from others as to physical appearance, work on self-esteem and self-acceptance (see the commentary following Chapter 13), and consciously altering cognitive patterns (e.g., changing such tendencies as perfectionism and unreasonable expectations).

When Xenia reached her breaking point at the age of twenty-nine, she started taking Zoloft, a new-generation SSRI (selective serotonin-reuptake inhibitor) drug approved for anxiety. After just five days, she noticed an unfamiliar but positive feeling that she describes as "bliss and spontaneity, [and] freedom from overthinking." In spite of her fear and judgmental attitude towards drugs, Zoloft not only controlled her symptoms, but also it gave her a new perspective on life.

One of the benefits of medication for anxiety is a reduction in symptoms that enables the sufferer to learn new skills and to benefit from other forms of help. When a person can sleep at night, concentrate, and free up some energy, she or he is better equipped to follow through with other recovery activities discussed throughout these stories and commentaries. Indeed, Xenia explored many self-help paths and participated in seminars, workshops, and recovery meetings, all of which contributed to her hard-earned serenity.

CHAPTER 29

FROM NORMALITY TO THE BRINK OF SUICIDE

by HELENA WOJTCZAK

In my early twenties I was a strong and fit young woman with a responsible job in London. Then I began to gain weight and to suffer panic attacks. Doctors treated the two problems as unrelated.

For the first few years the panic attacks occurred only occasionally and randomly. I'd be in a supermarket or theatre and suddenly a huge wave of terror would engulf me and I'd have to rush outside. Knowing they could strike at any moment kept me in a constant state of tension. After an attack in an aircraft in 1983, I ceased flying. Doctors said it was a psychiatric condition. Their only cure was medication, which I repeatedly declined. I was sent to a psychiatrist.

When I told them about my weight increase, doctors insisted that I overate and advised a high-carbohydrate, low-fat diet. This made me heavier. In my thirties I took up an aerobic sport, badminton, which I played for two hours almost every day for eighteen months. Still, my weight increased.

I've relocated several times over seventeen years, so I've been treated by twelve medical experts, under whose care my panic attacks became progressively worse and more frequent. Meanwhile, I also got fatter until I weighed double my "correct" weight.

In my mid-thirties new symptoms arose. Between daily panic attacks I felt emotionally unstable, scared of the world, anxious, and unable to cope with the smallest problem. I felt strange sensations in my whole body, as though I were riding a roller coaster. There was always something wrong with me; every day I'd feel weepy, angry, irritable, exhausted, nervous, anxious, and depressed. Every moment was a struggle to feel and act normal at work and in my social life, despite how I felt inside. Every visit to the doctor resulted in his or her offering— and my declining—drugs.

Starting in mid-1998, I endured panic attacks every day, everywhere and anywhere, and I almost became agoraphobic. I tried herbal and homeopathic substances, specifically Bach Rescue Remedy and aconite. These quelled the panic attacks temporarily, but an hour later another would terrorize me. I told my doctor about these effects, hoping the information would help him treat my condition. He just said they were "sugar pills" (the irony of this will be seen later). He insisted I needed drugs; I refused, so he sent me to a psychiatrist, who prescribed the same drugs.

By the spring of 2000, my life was a nightmare. I was preoccupied twenty-four/seven with managing the panic attacks (now happening every hour or two, day and night), the horrendous mood swings, indigestion, memory loss, irritability, loss of concentration, blurred vision, and roller-coaster emotions. I had overwhelming cravings for sweet things. I'd wake every night around 2:00 A.M., shaking uncontrollably from head to toe, my body cold and my head very hot, feeling frightened and agitated. I swigged from a bottle of sweet wine I kept by my bed. The panic ebbed away, only to return with a vengeance an hour later. I was bewildered and terrified.

I tried desperately to hold on to my position as a training administrator and struggled to keep my illness a secret, but that became impossible. I was dismissed in April 2000. I became convinced that it would not be long before I would have to enter a mental hospital and lose everything I had.

Some panic attacks paralyzed one side of my face and gave me blurred vision and severe migraines. During one of these I rushed to a doctor's office, terribly agitated and distressed. She said it was "just" a panic attack. Twice I called an ambulance in the middle of the night, because I appeared to be having a heart attack. The doctors found nothing wrong with me.

By June 2000 my life was no longer worth living. I knew I had to submit to medication. A doctor I had never seen before prescribed paroxetine without question; I was in and out of the consulting room in two minutes. I took the first one at noon and became uncontrollably agitated for twelve hours. After sleeping from 2:00 A.M. to 5:00 A.M., I awoke, floating in a dreamlike state. I sat and wept, feeling suicidal. I phoned the Samaritans, a suicide-crisis hotline. One of the things I discussed with the counselor was a friend's suggestion that I see a certain kinesiologist. Since two therapists specializing in complementary treatment had failed to cure me, I had repeatedly declined my friend's suggestion. But the Samaritan urged me to see the kinesiologist, just in case she had something new to say. I decided to listen.

For my first appointment with the kinesiologist my brain was still dopey from the paroxetine, so my partner had to accompany me. As I lay on the couch the kinesiologist held my wrist for a few seconds, then laid her hands on my stomach. Then she announced that I was hypoglycemic.

I was mystified, so she explained that my pancreas malfunctioned, producing too much insulin in response to sugar, white flour, white rice, and caffeine. An overproduction of insulin drives the blood-glucose level down very fast; then adrenaline surges, causing feelings of intense panic. Since the brain cannot store glucose it is the first organ to malfunction, resulting in mental confusion, blurred vision, and an inability to concentrate. My pancreas malfunctioned because it had been damaged by overgrowth of an intestinal yeast called *candida*. This overgrowth was caused by antibiotics, which kill the beneficial bacteria that normally keep candida under control. She said I must have taken some recently. I had—just four months before.

She told me to keep to an anticandida diet for a few weeks, then to a hypoglycemic diet. Above all, I was to eat no sugar. My immediate reaction was that she was talking nonsense. How could food be the cause of such horrendous nervous and mental symptoms? It was far too simple to be true. However, after talking it through with my partner, a devotee of the kinesiologist, I decided to try the suggested diet.

As soon as I got home I began to surf the Net, where I found many sites, support groups, and diets for the hypoglycemic. When I saw the list of symptoms associated with hypoglycemia, I became very angry. I had told no fewer than twelve doctors that I suffered these symptoms, yet none of them had diagnosed hypoglycemia. My belief in doctors was shattered.

The more I researched, the more everything began to make sense. One of my doctors had dismissed aconite as "mere sugar pills." Yes, homeopathic pills are made of sucrose; that's why they worked. They temporarily raised my blood sugar. And it wasn't the alcohol in the sweet wine that quelled my panic, but the sugar. And Bach Rescue Remedy contains . . . brandy! I realized that my body craved chocolate and sodas because it was instinctively leading me to sugar, which could raise my blood glucose. The trouble is:

1. eating sugar swiftly raises the blood-glucose level, so you feel good again, *but*

2. eating sugar also stimulates the pancreas to overproduce insulin

3. insulin drives down the blood glucose

4. a plummet in blood glucose causes panic attacks (and sugar cravings)

5. eating sugar swiftly raises the blood glucose, starting the cycle all over again

For years, I'd been on a kind of sugar-induced internal roller-coaster ride.

So I tried the diet. As soon as I eliminated caffeine, sugar, white flour, and white rice, the panic attacks disappeared. I went though a period of near disbelief: Yes, it really *was* that simple. I proved by experiment that sugar both caused and quelled all my panic attacks. In a few weeks, all the other symptoms decreased and disappeared. When I proved to myself that I was *not* mentally ill, I wept tears of relief and happiness.

The kinesiologist told me I needed to convalesce; my internal organs had undergone terrible stress for many years. I researched many websites and read several books about hypoglycemia. Everything I read confirmed what the kinesiologist had said. Furthermore, I learned that my being overweight was caused by my inability to metabolize carbohydrates over many years, which caused me to store them as fat. This was the first link I'd read between panic attacks and being overweight.

The dietary advice given by doctors and dieticians had made my condition worse. Their lists of foods to eat included breakfast cereals, baked beans, low-fat butter substitutes, and white breads, all of which contain sugar. My doctor denied that the condition existed. When asked to explain why my panic symptoms disappeared after I eliminated certain foods, she simply said she was glad I was "feeling a bit better." She denied giving me antibiotics. Later, her colleague admitted she had forgotten to record prescribing them. (If you want the names of these doctors, e-mail me.)

I looked back over my life. The quirks I had attributed to personality were in fact symptoms of low or unstable blood glucose. For example, I described myself as "not a morning person"; upon waking I was grouchy, sensitive, and lethargic. I always needed several cups of strong tea (i.e., a caffeine and sugar fix) to rejoin the human race. In the course of a day, for no apparent reason, I'd swing from bad-tempered and/or depressed to lighthearted, boisterous, and vivacious, so I labeled myself "moody." Once I had stabilized my blood glucose, I had to get to know myself all over again. This midlife psychological challenge was almost traumatic.

After a few weeks I visited places where I'd always suffered panic attacks, but none came. I flew to Holland—a forty-five-minute flight. Then I flew to the other side of the planet for the holiday of a lifetime.

I could barely believe that just six months before I'd had panic attacks on the local bus!

I became vigilant about sugar. It is slipped into the most extraordinary products: prepackaged ham, low-fat hummus, and smoked salmon. Safeway puts it on seasoned raw chicken. By sticking to the diet, I've healed my pancreas so that only processed cane sugar (sucrose) is still on the "banned" list. I eat chocolate made with fructose and can tolerate the small amounts of dextrose added to processed foods.

My medical records indicate that I suffered from a psychiatric illness for seventeen years. My doctor won't amend them. I was shortlisted for a job recently, but was rejected after the employer read my records.

On the plus side, I have not had a panic attack for eighteen months. My life is totally different. I have now returned to the "old me" that I used to know—extroverted, brave, strong, confident, levelheaded, calm, and very sane! I have started my own business working from home, and every June I send a thank-you card to the kinesiologist for saving my life.

Helena was born in 1958 and grew up in London. She holds a B.Sc. Honours degree in psychology and social science. She is single and lives in Sussex. Contact her at eastsussex.lady@virgin.net

Commentary by Paul Foxman

Helena suffered from weight problems and disabling panic attacks for seventeen years and apparently consulted a dozen doctors who saw no connection between the two symptoms. In her case one of the fundamentals of health—the role of diet and nutrition—was overlooked as a basis for anxiety.

The connection between diet and anxiety is so important that I devote an entire chapter to the topic in my book, *Dancing with Fear*. I point out that many aspects of diet can produce anxiety symptoms. For example, our body's blood-sugar level fluctuates according to what, how, and when we eat. Sharp rises in blood sugar, resulting from eating simple carbohydrates (white bread as well as sugared candy, cakes, and cookies), are associated with increases in adrenaline—the "anxiety hormone." Low blood sugar, resulting from insulin production in response to large quantities of simple carbohydrates, can produce a host of symptoms—blurry vision, mental confusion, weakness, dizziness, headaches, irritability, and others—that mimic panic and anxiety. The same symptoms can also result from an inconsistent eating schedule.

Furthermore, frequent fluctuations in blood sugar can damage the pancreas, the insulin-producing gland. In Helena's case, this led to an inability to properly handle carbohydrates, which her body resorted to storing as fat. For this reason she gained weight in spite of weight-loss diets and exercise.

A number of other eating behaviors, particularly those associated with attempts to lose weight, can cause similar damage. These include skipping meals, binge eating, weight-loss diets, and dependence on comfort foods (usually high in fat or sugar) to cope with unpleasant emotions.

I am tempted to suggest an anxiety recovery diet. However, each of us is physically and emotionally unique, and even our individual nutritional needs vary from day to day in response to stress, climate, activity level, and other factors. Therefore, I avoid rigid rules and formulas in making dietary recommendations. Instead, here is a sampling of dietary guidelines:

- Eat on a regular schedule
- Eat small meals four to six times a day to maintain even blood sugar
- Drink an adequate supply of fresh water on a regular basis
- Be attuned to your hunger level and eat accordingly
- Eat primarily whole, minimally processed foods with the most nutritional value
- Avoid caffeine; seek alternatives to coffee (such as herbal teas and grain-based brews)

- Avoid sugar; learn to use fruit for sweets
- Use the USDA pyramid chart as a nutritional guideline
- Learn the creative art of cooking, and develop some favorite healthful dishes
- Read, learn, and expand your awareness of nutrition (see Resources)
- Love your body and develop an intimate familiarity with it
- Engage in regular exercise, which aids digestion and food assimilation
- Discover sources of emotional nourishment other than food
- Consult a dietician for guidance if necessary

C H A P T E R   3 0

THE LONG WAY BACK TO ME

by PATTY MIRANDA

There I was, minding my own business, when it hit. One minute I was laughing and living, and the next I was thrown into the icy grip of fear. Not fear like, "I haven't got a thing to wear." Not fear like, "Did I leave the iron on?" Fear like, "I'm dying." Heart pounding. Chest tightening. Can't breathe. Throat closing. Those last two—the breath thing and the throat thing—they were my undoing. They were the symptoms my panic seemed to exploit above all the rest. "What the hell happened? One minute ago I could breathe," I'd think. "I could smile. I could think clearly." I had a good life. A husband and two small, adorable children. We went to hockey games together. We played soccer in the yard. We went for long walks. We lived. Panic erased all of that. Its main mission is to render you helpless. Its main goal is eventually, after repeated attacks, to render you hopeless. I know that now. I didn't know that then.

My first bout with panic disorder included a visit to the emergency room, visits to a psychiatrist, and finally, in an all-out war with the demon, a stay in the hospital. I can't recall one moment of peace from fear. My life as I knew it simply disappeared, replaced by a horrifying new reality. Just the thought of leaving the house would set off a massive attack. My days were spent paralyzed by panic on the outside and screaming at the top of my lungs on the inside. I vigilantly fought sleep, for I was sure that I would never wake up again.

I became convinced that every time I tried to swallow I stood a very good chance of choking to death. I was convinced that I was always one breath away from suffocating. I was put on meds. No change. The meds were increased. Unfortunately this particular medication had a bad effect on me and merely fed my panic. By the time I was put in the hospital I had stopped eating altogether and was only taking in sips of water. I didn't know that my symptoms were quite common among panic sufferers. I didn't know that I wasn't alone. I didn't know that I had an actual illness. I thought I was crazy and that I was going to spend what little time I had left in the hospital. Alone. Scared.

The worst pain of all was seeing the faces of my family members when they visited. I started to see some of their helplessness turn into hopelessness. Who could blame them? What had I done in the past few months that even resembled an attempt to help myself get better? That was it. Either I could lie in the hospital bed and die, or I could fight back. Since the dying part seemed to be taking a long time and was quite painful for everyone, I decided to try and find my way back to me. I had two children to raise, and although my life had stopped with the first panic attack, their lives were only beginning. Time for a plan.

Part of my plan was to start acting normal, even though I felt, quite literally, like a fish out of water. Since one day at a time was way too hard, I started with one bite at a time. If I could take one bite of food at each meal, I knew that eventually I could take two, then three, and so on. It worked. I was healed. After a few short weeks, no meds, no doctors, I was cured! No—better than cured, I was so normal that I was convinced that nothing had ever been wrong with me. It had all been a nightmarish mixture of bad medicine and bad doctors. I got back to living and doing and being! Phew! It was all behind me. Until....

Three totally panic-free years later it hit again. It started with the eating. That damn throat-closing thing. The panic followed fast and furious. Things quickly spun out of control. Intensifying the fear was the thought that I might not escape it this time. I couldn't excuse it all away. There was something wrong with me. I couldn't eat. I couldn't sleep. I couldn't leave the house. Fear consumed me. Panic ruled once more. It owned me.

After a few months of trying my hardest to will it away, I got my butt in gear and got in to see a psychologist. On the very first visit he explained panic disorder. On the very first visit he explained the importance of breathing. See, most of us have forgotten how to breathe right, or never really did it right to begin with. By the end of that first visit, I had mastered big stomach-raising breaths. The choking thing— gone. I had my work cut out for me, but knowing that I wasn't alone, knowing that there was a name for the feelings I was having, knowing what it was all about—that was a huge step towards healing. About the same time that I began feeling more confident and more relaxed, we lost our health insurance. So therapy came to a halt. But I was okay. Finally it was all behind me. Well, not exactly.

There I was, another glorious, panic-free three years later...well, you know the rest. You see, the last time, I had learned *what* it was all about, but I hadn't gotten to the part where I learned *how* to deal with it. I hadn't learned coping skills, beyond breathing. Then I became allergic to bee stings. Now, this fact in and of itself did not bring out the panic. However, I was given a bee-sting kit and was told by the doctor that I should "only use it if you get stung and have trouble breathing, or if your throat starts closing up."

What? I swear, if the doctor had told me to watch out for my arm falling off, I would have been fine. I would have gone home a happy woman. Okay, maybe not happy, but certainly not the quivering mess that I became after those words. The scenario played in my mind on an endless film reel. Yeah, I get stung, and trust me, whether or not I'm having a full-blown allergic reaction, it's going to feel like I can't breathe and like my throat is closing up. I was consumed by this thought. I was convinced that I could never stay calm enough to judge if I was having a reaction or if I was having a panic attack.

Ah, the vicious cycle on which panic thrives. You panic, you experience fear, you fear experiencing panic again, and the circle continues.

As long as I stayed inside the house I was free from total panic attacks. When I was outside, exposed to the threat of the stinging beasts, I was a terrified, hyperventilating mess. I live in the mid-Atlantic region, so I only had to worry about going outside from around March to, oh, about November. That still left three good, panic-free months. I could live with that, right? After one miserable spring and summer, locked in the house out of fear, and with the next spring fast approaching, I knew I couldn't live with that.

I saw a shrink. I was put on an antidepressant. Then I was lucky enough to find a therapist who not only specialized in anxiety disorders, but who had been there and done that: a clinical social worker who was a recovered panic sufferer. This was the key. She got me outside, and she talked me through the panic. She helped me to go from calm to terrified and back to calm. She helped me see that I was already surviving panic. Every time I walked outside, every time I saw a bee and didn't run or freak out, I took a little more power away from the panic. I was that strong without even knowing it. We worked on building the strength and defeating the panic. Through exposure, and through her wonderful insights, I was able to get off of the medication and to live the life that panic had tried so hard to interrupt.

Now it's been well over eight years since my last panic attack. I've learned a few things along the way. Not one treatment will work for everyone. In the end, what worked for me was the combination of becoming educated about this disorder and its effects on me, and finding a caring, skillful therapist who truly knew what I was feeling. If you think you've tried everything to get better, yet you're still suffering, trust me on this one: There's always one more thing to be tried. Don't—I repeat—*don't* ever stop trying. You're worth the effort. We're all worth the effort. Get educated. Drop any guilt, embarrassment, or shame that you may be feeling. Panic disorder is an equal opportunity imposer. It is not a sign of weakness. It is not a sign of insanity. It is a normal human reaction that in some of us has gotten kicked into overdrive. It is manageable. It can be conquered.

I still face situations that push my panic button. The difference is that now I know my enemy. I know, inside out, how panic works on me. I have learned the coping skills necessary to diffuse it. Each time panic returned to me, I knew a little more about how to deal with it, and I knew a little more about myself. Eventually I learned to have more faith in the power of me than I had in the power of panic.

> *I am an optioned screenwriter living in Maryland with my husband, two sons, and one very lovable, very round tabby named Sophie. My hobbies include beekeeping and sword swallowing. (Just kidding.) Is pestering Hollywood producers considered a hobby?*

Commentary by Paul Foxman

Patty's anxiety followed an episodic course with disabling symptoms followed by long periods of normal life. She sought professional help at each episode, including medication, hospitalization, and psychotherapy. It was a frustrating "long way back" for her because each treatment was incomplete. I believe Patty could have been spared years of suffering had she received a more comprehensive therapy experience in the early stages of her anxiety disorder.

Several key steps were instrumental in Patty's recovery, but one deserves special attention. One of her therapists was a psychologist who educated her about panic disorder and emphasized the importance of breathing. Unfortunately, just as Patty was feeling more confident and relaxed, she lost her health insurance and terminated therapy. Nonetheless, what she learned with this therapist kept her going for three "glorious, panic-free" years. Patty does not give us details about the breathing skills she learned in therapy, so I will fill in with some pertinent information about this essential anxiety-control skill.

Breathing is often taken for granted and considered a simple, automatic function that cannot be controlled. However, many people fail to breathe properly, and as a result they suffer from a loss of health, vitality, and alertness. Natural, deep breathing actually regulates other bodily systems, such as the cardiovascular, digestive, and neuromuscular systems. Therefore, by learning how to breathe naturally you can relax and counteract anxiety.

Try evaluating your breathing pattern with two simple exercises. For the first, place one hand on your chest and the other hand on your diaphragm (just above your stomach). As you breathe, notice whether both areas expand and contract, or whether one—or both—holds still. In natural breathing, the full participation of lower and upper lungs is involved. The second exercise is to make a continuous "ahh" sound in your normal voice while timing yourself with a second hand on a watch or clock. You should be able to maintain the sound for at least twenty seconds.

To improve your breathing, try these basic breathing exercises:

1. While standing, lean back, raise your arms, breathe in, and hold your breath while stretching up and back. Then straighten up, exhale, and breathe deeply several times. This stretches the chest, abdominal, and back muscles, which permits the lungs to expand and breathe more deeply.

2. In a sitting position, make a continuous "ahh" sound in your normal voice as you exhale. Practice regularly, and try to extend the length of time you can sustain the sound.

3. Relax in a sitting position, and make a groaning sound while exhaling. On the following inhalation, try to make the same sound. It may be difficult at first, but you can do it with practice. Feel the air being sucked into your lungs for fuller breathing.

4. Lie down on your back with a soft pillow under your head. Cover your eyes with a piece of cloth, and begin breathing slowly and deeply. Let your mind travel slowly through your body from head to toes, and breathe relaxation into each muscle. Concentrate on maintaining an even flow of breath, forming a new habit of deep, slow breathing.

CHAPTER 31

My Knight

by ROBERTA BREHM

My story is a little different—I don't have an anxiety disorder, but my husband, Gary, does. We live in Leader, a small town in Saskatchewan, Canada, where Gary is a self-employed farmer. We have been together for twelve years, and married for eight. For as long as he can remember, Gary has struggled with anxiety. For years, he had general anxiety, then extreme mood swings and anger, and, eventually, full-blown panic attacks. However, he thought what he felt was normal, so he didn't seek help until February 2000, when things got really bad.

During his attacks Gary would become rigid and sweat, and would endure extreme bodily temperature changes, fluctuating between hot flashes and coldness, feelings of visual unreality, and pain in his chest from a racing heart.

He went to a general practitioner to ask for a prescription for sleeping pills. The doctor also prescribed Paxil, which proved to be a double-edged sword. Gary had very serious problems taking the drug. He felt "dead," as though he had no emotions. He also couldn't sleep at all, lost his sex drive, and endured major panic attacks while taking it, so he stopped after a few days. However, his short time on the drug seemed to trigger an ugly string of events. He suffered mild attacks for about a month, so I convinced him to see another doctor. This one recommended that my husband see a professional therapist, but Gary refused.

He continued having panic attacks, which he thought were still aftereffects of the Paxil. However, the attacks grew worse and worse, and finally his sister, who has also suffered from anxiety, told him about Xanax. The doctor prescribed the drug for him, and it worked for a while, but then came even bigger attacks.

These attacks were so terrible that they stopped Gary from leaving the house altogether. In July he endured four days of complete hell; he was convinced that he was going to meet his maker. He had to stop working, something he hadn't let himself do before. Gary pushed me away, which confused me. I grew angry as his panic attacks worsened, and I became so scared for him that I almost began having anxiety attacks of my own! I would awaken two or three times a night to check on him, just like a mother who has to phone home from work every few hours to check on her baby.

Our marriage was not strained during these times, because I always knew that the children and I were the bright spot in his life. However, the frustration we both felt about his condition put a strain on each of us. There has always been terrific commitment in our relationship, and this ordeal tested it. We have two sons (ages four and seven), and the older one knew that something was wrong. He was very worried for his dad.

Gary finally consented to allow me to take him to a small city emergency room about one hundred miles away, as long as I promised that I wouldn't let them take away his sleeping pills. He thought he would die without them. I agreed and followed through with the promise. I drove 120 miles an hour; I realized once we reached the hospital that I had wet myself from fright. The ER doctor immediately diagnosed Gary with panic disorder, as our family doctor had already done. The ER doctor wanted Gary to see a therapist, and Gary finally agreed.

Due to the severity of Gary's condition, the psychiatrist agreed to stay late the following afternoon to see him. We stayed overnight in a hotel, which Gary doesn't remember; he was in the middle of having a nervous breakdown. The next afternoon we went to the psychiatrist, who determined that Gary had severe panic disorder and prescribed Rivotril.

Gary was scared and skeptical of the new drug, so he took only a very small piece of one tablet. He felt better immediately. Now, this is a man who hadn't eaten in six weeks, figuring that food was the cause of his attacks. He sent me straight to McDonald's for two Big Macs. He ate them and had no attacks before settling down for a very restful sleep.

It is now a year later. Gary has not suffered another attack, and for the first time in his life he goes out comfortably. Last year our oldest son played hockey, and Gary could not even go watch him without first drinking alcohol. Now he's an excellent hockey dad. We could never before go out for an evening, and now we often go to restaurants where we spend hours just talking. And just last week our son was out of school, so the whole family went away for a week-long vacation. We even went to a dinner theatre. My husband is a changed man! He used to self-medicate with alcohol, and now he doesn't even have the urge. He found better tools to help him deal with anxiety. One of the things that has helped Gary is the program called Emotional Freedom Techniques (EFT), an acupressure treatment designed for a person to do on his own at home (for more information, visit the website at www.emofree.com).

My family has been very supportive and understanding; they thank God Gary got help before he did something terrible to himself. Gary's own family now realizes that quite a few of them also have anxiety disorders. Our relationship has never been stronger, because we have found freedom. I am outgoing and enjoy social functions, holidays, sports, dances, and camping. Now Gary can join me comfortably.

To the other caretakers and family members of people with anxiety disorders, I want to say, "Be patient." You can't force anyone to get help, but you can stand by your loved one and be there to help when they do decide to get help. Never give up looking until you find the right doctor and until your loved one finds the right medications. Read as much as you can about this disease. It robs a person of his or her life, but don't let it take everything! The sword to slay the dragon is out there; keep searching. Help is available. For supporters, there are lots of speed bumps before the road gets smooth, but stick with your loved ones no matter what the dragon tells them to say to you. The final result is worth it. I'm so proud today to be able to say that my knight has slain the dragon.

> *I am twenty-eight years old, and I work six days a week at the post office. I am active in a group called Anxiety Disorders—The Caregivers, which offers a mailing list for support people of individuals with panic and anxiety disorders. You can sign up at http://groups.yahoo.com/group/ACSL.*

Commentary by Paul Foxman

This is one of the book's few anxiety stories about men, and it touches on some uniquely male issues, such as the resistance many men feel towards seeking psychological help. Some men will be more likely to accept help from a male therapist with whom they can identify. In my practice, for example, I have a higher than average percentage of male patients, probably because I have gone public (in my book, lectures, and television appearances) about my own anxiety story. On the other hand, some men will turn to women when they need emotional understanding and support. When such preferences exist, they should be taken into account, but the choice should be based more on the competence and experience—rather than the gender—of the mental-health professional.

Are there any special considerations in counseling men with anxiety? Generally speaking, men have fewer skills than women for expressing their feelings, and this may be important to address in therapy. For example, men often lack the "emotional vocabulary" for naming their feelings. This is usually the result of inexperience, so men must acquire a new language for feelings. In my book, *Dancing with Fear*, I include a list of approximately forty feelings and encourage readers to use these words to name and recognize their feelings on a daily basis.

I also use male metaphors for communicating with men about stress and anxiety. For example, I equate the impact of chronic stress to the damage caused by running a car constantly at five thousand RPMs. Wear and tear on the body is similar to burning out an engine from enthusiastic or irresponsible use; the "preventive-maintenance routine" involves regular stress-reduction practices. I also emphasize the need for monitoring the body for symptoms of stress or anxiety, the way one would read automobile gauges that provide feedback on engine conditions and performance.

Some men are willing to view anxiety as a medical condition for which a prescription drug is a reasonable and appropriate solution. Roberta's husband, Gary, for example, seemed to accept the use of sleeping pills as prescribed by his *medical doctor*, but he did not agree to see a *psychiatrist* until he was completely out of control. The medical approach is likely to provide some relief, and it could open the door to the idea that there are other techniques, such as meditation or relaxation practice, for achieving the same results.

CONCLUSION

by JENNA GLATZER

So, there you have it. Thirty-one remarkable success stories—plus commentary from a psychologist who has conquered an anxiety disorder himself—for a grand total of thirty-two people who have beaten their anxiety dragons. I hope you have identified with these stories, and I hope they have inspired you. I want you to become the next success story. Please know that the people in this book aren't superhuman—they are people just like you who have gone through the same battle you're fighting, and they've won. And so can you.

I want you to close this book with three thoughts in mind: You are not crazy, you are not alone, and there is hope. The key to recovery is inside of you. You are strong enough to win this fight, and you deserve to live a full, wonderful life.

Let anxiety teach you to treat yourself well—to talk to yourself in positive terms, to celebrate your successes, and to comfort yourself when things aren't going so well. Let it be your "wake-up call" to spend more time exercising, getting in touch with your spirituality, eating well, sleeping well, and working on your self-esteem.

When I put together this book, it was my hope that every reader who would pick it up would feel like they'd just made thirty-two new friends. Each of us wrote our stories with the deep desire to help you realize that you don't have to live a life ruled by anxiety anymore. We're all on your side, and we want you to join us in the "conqueror's circle."

Please do whatever it takes to get well. Even when you think you've tried everything, keep turning over those stones and finding something else to try. Know that you're worth the effort. Know that you have at least thirty-two people who are praying for you and thinking about you.

You can visit us on the Internet at www.absolutewrite.com/ anxiety.htm, or contact me at jenna@absolutewrite.com.

Wishing you endless happiness,

Jenna

BIBLIOGRAPHY

Airola, Paavo. *Hypoglycemia: A Better Approach*. Phoenix, AZ: Health Plus Publications, 1984.

Bailey, Covert. *Fit or Fat?* Boston: Houghton Mifflin, 1978.

Ballentine, Rudolph M. *Diet and Nutrition: A Holistic Approach*. Honesdale, PA: Himalayan Institute Press, 1982.

Beck, Aaron T. *Cognitive Therapy and the Emotional Disorders*. New York: New American Library, 1979.

Benson, Herbert, with William Proctor. *Beyond the Relaxation Response: How to Harness the Healing Power of Your Personal Beliefs*. New York: Time Books, 1984.

Benson, Herbert, with Mary Stark. *Timeless Healing: The Power and Biology of Belief*. New York: Fireside, 1997.

Bloomfield, Harold H. *Healing Anxiety with Herbs*. New York: HarperCollins, 1998.

Borysenko, Joan. *Minding the Body, Mending the Mind*. Reading, MA: Addison-Wesley, 1987.

Bourne, Edmund J. *The Anxiety and Phobia Workbook*. Oakland, CA: New Harbinger, 1990.

Branden, Nathaniel. *The Psychology of Self-Esteem*, 32nd Edition. New York: John Wiley & Sons, 2000.

Burns, David D. *Feeling Good: The New Mood Therapy*. New York: William Morrow & Co., 1980.

Dossey, Larry. *Healing Words: The Power of Prayer and the Practice of Medicine*. San Francisco: HarperCollins, 1993.

Dufty, William F. *Sugar Blues*. New York: Warner Books, 1975.

Fox, Bronwyn. *Power over Panic: Freedom from Panic/Anxiety Related Disorders*. New York: Alpha Books, 2001.

Foxman, Paul. *Dancing with Fear: Overcoming Anxiety in a World of Stress and Uncertainty*. Northvale, NJ: Jason Aronson, Inc., 1999.

Gawain, Shakti. *Creative Visualization*. Novato, CA: New World Library, 1995.

LeShan, Lawrence. *How to Meditate*. New York: Little Brown & Co., 1999.

Lidell, Lucy. *The Sivananda Companion to Yoga*. New York: Simon and Schuster, 1983.

McKay, Matthew, and Patrick Fanning. *Self-Esteem: A Proven Program of Cognitive Techniques for Assessing, Improving, and Maintaining Your Self-Esteem*, 3rd Edition. Oakland, CA: New Harbinger, 2000.

Moyers, Bill. *Healing and the Mind*. New York: Main Street Books, 1995.

Ponichtera, Brenda J. *Quick and Healthy Recipes and Ideas*. The Dalles, OR: ScaleDown, 1991.

Robertson, Laurel, Carol Flinders, and Brian Ruppenthal. *Laurel's Kitchen: A Handbook for Vegetarian Cookery and Nutrition*. Berkeley, CA: Ten Speed Press, 1986.

Rodale, J. *The Complete Book of Food and Nutrition*. Emmaus, PA: Rodale, 1971.

Schwartz, Jeffrey M., with Beverly Beyette. *Brain Lock: Free Yourself from Obsessive-Compulsive Behavior*. New York: ReganBooks, 1996.

Seagrave, Ann, and Faison Covington. *Free from Fears*. New York: Pocket Books/Simon and Schuster, 1987. (Out of print but available from CHAANGE, listed in Resources, under "Self-Help Programs.")

Weekes, Claire. "Simple, Effective Treatment of Agoraphobia." *American Journal of Psychotherapy*, 23(3): 357–369.

Weekes, Claire. *Hope and Help for Your Nerves*. New York: Signet, 1978.

Weekes, Claire. *Peace from Nervous Suffering*. New York: Signet, 1978.

Wurtman, Judith J. *Managing Your Mind and Mood Through Food*. New York: HarperCollins, 1988.

RESOURCES

Organizations

Anxiety Disorders Association of America

11900 Parklawn Dr., Ste. 100
Rockville MD 20852
(301) 231-9350
Website: www.adaa.org

This organization maintains a list of psychiatrists, psychologists, social workers, and "layperson specialists" (usually people who have recovered from anxiety disorders) who specialize in research and in treating clients with anxiety disorders. There's a wealth of information on its website; you can find self-help groups, books and tapes, studies, and more.

Obsessive-Compulsive Foundation, Inc.

337 Notch Hill Rd.
North Branford CT 06471
(203) 351-2190
Website: www.ocfoundation.org

A not-for-profit organization of over ten thousand people with OCD and their families and friends. The foundation maintains referral lists of mental-health professionals specializing in OCD, support groups, message boards, and more. Members receive a newsletter six times a year, as well as educational booklets.

TERRAP

(800) 9-PHOBIA (974-6242)

A popular organization and method for treating panic and phobias. (The organization's name is short for "territorial apprehension.") The structured program includes cognitive-behavioral therapy, in vivo desensitization (practicing coping techniques in real-life situations with the help of a therapist), education, and support in group or individual sessions.

Alliance for People with Social Phobia

SPNewsletter

PO Box 58281

Cincinnati OH 45258-0281

Website: www.spnewsletter.com

Free newsletter (six issues per year) for people with social phobias. The organization also hosts activity groups and support groups, and works to increase community awareness about social phobias.

National Institute of Mental Health (NIMH)

6001 Executive Blvd., Rm. 8184 MSC 9663

Bethesda MD 20892-9663

(888) 8-ANXIETY (826-9438)

Website: www.nimh.nih.gov/anxiety/anxiety/index.htm

The website and brochures produced by this federal agency (part of the National Institutes of Health) include facts about anxiety disorders, treatments, and resources to find help.

Freedom from Fear

308 Seaview Ave.

Staten Island NY 10305

(718) 351-1717

Website: freedomfromfear.com

Offers free anxiety and depression screenings and consultations. The website provides links to studies, referrals, news, and a message board. Members receive a newsletter about mental-health treatment, an invitation to an international pen-pal network, and access to seminars.

Self-Help Programs

CHAANGE (Center for Help for Anxiety/Agoraphobia through New Growth Experiences)

128 Country Club Dr.

Chula Vista CA 91911

(800) 276-7800

Website: www.chaange.com

As discussed throughout the book, this program aims for total recovery. Call for a free information kit. A state-by-state list of CHAANGE-trained therapists is included, along with a brochure and introductory cassette tape.

Midwest Center for Stress and Anxiety

106 N. Church St.

PO Box 205

Oak Harbor OH 43449

(800) 511-6896

Fax: (419) 898-0669

Website: www.stresscenter.com

Home of Lucinda Bassett's fifteen-week self-help course, Attacking Anxiety and Depression.

Anxieties.com

Website: www.anxieties.com

Free online self-help guides for panic disorder, OCD, fear of flying, social anxiety, PTSD, and more. Also includes links to order books and tapes.

Anxiety Busters

Free anxiety help-line: (215) 635-4700

Website: www.anxietybusters.com

Open 10:00 A.M. to 10:00 P.M. EST seven days a week to help callers with anxiety-related troubles. Also offers a ten-week audiotape program to combat anxiety disorders.

Overcoming Social Anxiety: Step By Step

(602) 230-7316

Website: www.socialanxietyinstitute.org/audioseries.html

A program of twenty audiotapes using cognitive-behavioral therapy (CBT) to help people overcome social anxiety.

Websites

Tapir

www.algy.com/anxiety/index.html

This site is a grassroots effort to help people with anxiety disorders. I highly, highly recommend it. It contains tons of information, but, more importantly, it includes features to allow people with anxiety disorders and caretakers to connect with other people in similar situations. There are pen-pal lists, personal-story pages, message boards, and more. It is one of the oldest and most popular resources on the Internet for people with anxiety disorders.

Mental Help Net

www.mentalhelp.net

Includes sections discussing symptoms, treatments, organizations, online resources, and research about specific mental-health issues, including anxiety disorders. A big, comprehensive website; not to be missed!

Anxiety Self-Help

www.anxietyselfhelp.com

This website, run by a contributor to this book, offers a whole range of treatment ideas, including meditations, herbal remedies, traditional medicines, affirmations, and books.

About.com's Mental Health Website

www.mentalhealth.about.com/health/mentalhealth/mbody.htm

Up-to-date information about a variety of anxiety disorders. The site features articles, forums, a chat room, links to great resources, and a free newsletter.

International Emetophobia Society

www.emetophobia.org

A website meant to educate and desensitize people with a fear of vomiting. Includes a message board, a chat room, illustrations, newsletter—and don't miss the "strange activities" list.

Anxiety Disorders—The Caregiver

www.pacificcoast.net/~kstrong

Support for support people! This website is meant for caregivers, family, and friends of people with anxiety disorders. Plenty of information, community, and resources.

Social Anxiety Australia

www.socialanxiety.com.au

Informational website, support groups, and message board for people in Australia with social anxiety disorder.

Social Phobia Net

www.socialphobianet.com

Run by an individual with social anxiety, this website includes discussion boards, a chat room, and accounts of other people's experiences.

Veritas Programming

www.sover.net/~schwcof/about2.html

Free or low-cost booklets and other publications about anxiety disorders, particularly post-traumatic stress disorder (PTSD).

Panic and Anxiety Hub

www.paems.com.au

There's a lot to read here, including articles, techniques for self-help, research and studies, a bookstore to browse through, and more. Also offers one-on-one support (paid) via e-mail and a chat room.

PubMed

www.ncbi.nlm.nih.gov/PubMed

Free, searchable database of medications and medical research.

Peer Support Network

www.anxietytofreedom.com

Run by Kim Phelan, this website offers message boards, a newsletter, affirmations, a support list, and resources for people with anxiety disorders.

Araneum Nostrum

http://araneum.mudservices.com

A cyber support group for people with anxiety disorders and their caretakers and loved ones. Includes a twenty-four-hour cyber "talker," similar to a chat room, but with more capabilities and room for imagination (visitors can perform actions, show emotions, and walk from room to room).

Index

THE PLEASURE PRESCRIPTION: To Love, to Work, to Play — Life in the Balance *by* Paul Pearsall, Ph.D. ***New York Times* Bestseller!**

This bestselling book is a prescription for stressed-out lives. Dr. Pearsall maintains that contentment, wellness, and long life can be found by devoting time to family, helping others, and slowing down to savor life's pleasures.

Pearsall's unique approach draws from Polynesian wisdom and his own 25 years of psychological and medical research. For readers looking for a way of life that promotes healthy values and living, *The Pleasure Prescription* provides answers.

288 pages ... Paperback $13.95 ... Hardcover $23.95

CREATING EXTRAORDINARY JOY: A Guide to Authenticity, Connection, and Self-Transformation *by* Chris Alexander

Creating Extraordinary Joy takes us on a journey of personal discovery in which we become alive to who we are, where we are in life, and what we value highly. It also helps us connect to the authenticity and true purpose of others in a condition called "synergy," where the joining of spirit and emotion between two people creates something greater than both.

Using inspirational teachings, images from nature, simple but powerful exercises, and real-life examples, Chris Alexander describes the ten steps of life mastery. Each step yields a life lesson that takes us toward the goals of deepening our passion, opening to abundance, and giving and receiving love. This inspirational guide is more than a book; it is a path to our best self.

288 pages ... Paperback $16.95 ... Hardcover $26.95

LOVING YOUR PARTNER WITHOUT LOSING YOUR SELF
by Martha Beveridge, MSSW

This book explains how to maintain your sense of self in a relationship. Beveridge, an experienced therapist, shows why romantic relationships often deteriorate from intense love into day-to-day struggles that tear couples apart, and gives practical and unique strategies for transforming these struggles into deeper intimacy. These include:

— getting past the ABCs (Attacking, Blaming, Criticizing)
— recognizing the symptoms of poor boundaries (clinging, jealousy, acting single, running away)
— dealing with the smokescreen issues: time, money, sex

256 pages ... Paperback $14.95 ... Hardcover $24.95

ORDER FORM

NAME

ADDRESS

CITY/STATE   ZIP/POSTCODE

PHONE   COUNTRY (outside of U.S.)

TITLE	QTY	PRICE	TOTAL
Conquering Panic & Anxiety... *(paper)*		@ $15.95	
Conquering Panic & Anxiety... *(cloth)*		@ $27.95	

Prices subject to change without notice

Please list other titles below:

		@ $	
		@ $	
		@ $	
		@ $	
		@ $	
		@ $	
		@ $	

Check here to receive our book catalog ❑   FREE

Shipping Costs

By Priority Mail: first book $4.50, each additional book $1.00
By UPS and to Canada: first book $5.50, each additional book $1.50
For rush orders and other countries call us at (510) 865-5282

TOTAL _____
Less discount @_____%   (_____)
TOTAL COST OF BOOKS _____
Calif. residents add sales tax _____
Shipping & handling _____
TOTAL ENCLOSED _____

Please pay in U.S. funds only

❑ Check ❑ Money Order ❑ Visa ❑ MasterCard ❑ Discover

Card # _____ Exp. date _____

Signature _____

Complete and mail to:
Hunter House Inc., Publishers
PO Box 2914, Alameda CA 94501-0914
Website: www.hunterhouse.com
Orders: (800) 266-5592 or email: ordering@hunterhouse.com
Phone (510) 865-5282 Fax (510) 865-4295

CPA 9/2002